ECONOMIC
SOPHISMS

ECONOMIC SOPHISMS

by

FREDERIC BASTIAT

Translated from the French
and Edited by
ARTHUR GODDARD

Introduction by
HENRY HAZLITT

The Foundation for Economic Education, Inc.
Irvington-on-Hudson, New York

Economic Sophisms

The Foundation for Economic Education, Inc.
30 South Broadway
Irvington-on-Hudson, NY 10533
(914) 591-7230

Publisher's Cataloging in Publication
(Prepared by Quality Books Inc.)

Bastiat, Frederic, 1801–1850.
  [Sophisms economiques. English]
  Economic sophisms / Frederic Bastiat
  p. cm.
  Previously published: Princeton, N.J., Van Nostrand, 1964.
  ISBN 0-910614-14-8

  1. Free trade. I. Title

HF1721.B37 1996   382'.71
                         QBI95-20678

Library of Congress Catalog Card Number: 95-83126

First edition, 1964
Second printing, 1968
Third printing, 1975
Fourth printing, 1991
Fifth printing, 1996

Manufactured in the United States of America

About the Author

Frederic Bastiat (1801–1850) was a French economist, statesman, and author. He was the leader of the free-trade movement in France from its inception in 1840 until his untimely death in 1850. The first 45 years of his life were spent in preparation for five tremendously productive years writing in favor of freedom. Bastiat was the founder of the weekly newspaper *Le Libre Échange*, a contributor to numerous periodicals, and the author of sundry pamphlets and speeches dealing with the pressing issues of his day. Most of his writing was done in the years directly before and after the Revolution of 1848—a time when France was rapidly embracing socialism. As a deputy in the Legislative Assembly, Bastiat fought valiantly for the private property order, but unfortunately the majority of his colleagues chose to ignore him. Frederic Bastiat remains one of the great champions of freedom whose writings retain their relevance as we continue to confront the old adversary.

Preface to the
English-Language Edition

Ever since the advent of representative government placed the ultimate power to direct the administration of public affairs in the hands of the people, the primary instrument by which the few have managed to plunder the many has been the sophistry that persuades the victims that they are being robbed for their own benefit. The public has been despoiled of a great part of its wealth and has been induced to give up more and more of its freedom of choice because it is unable to detect the error in the delusive sophisms by which protectionist demagogues, national socialists, and proponents of government planning exploit its gullibility and its ignorance of economics.

It was with the aim of exposing the most influential and widespread of these economic fallacies that Bastiat began, in 1844, to contribute to the *Journal des économistes* the brilliant succession of essays that comprise the present volume. The first series appeared in book form in 1845; and the second series, three years later. Increasingly in the years that have elapsed since their first publication, these essays have come to be recognized as among the most cogent and persuasive refutations of the major fallacies of protectionism—fallacies that are still with us today and that will continue to crop up as long as the public remains uninstructed: "The introduction of machinery means fewer jobs"; "Protective tariffs keep domestic wages high"; "We need laws to equalize the conditions of production"; "Imports must be restricted to restore the balance of trade"; "High prices mean a high standard of living"; "There are no economic laws or absolute principles"; "We need colonies to provide markets for the products of our industry"; "Free trade places us at the mercy of our enemies in case of war"; etc., etc. The great lesson which all these essays teach, in one form or another, is the necessity of always looking at economic questions from the point of view of the consumer, rather than that of the producer.

What gives this work its unique quality and places it among the classics of economic literature is not only the logical rigor with which each fallacy is demolished, but the highly original and striking way in which the author uses wit, irony, satire, dialogue, and apologue to reduce erroneous ideas to patent absurdity, as, for example, in his famous and often separately translated petition of the candlemakers for protection against the competition of the sun.

In preparing the present translation, I have had the opportunity of consulting, and have occasionally availed myself of the wording, of an earlier, unpublished version, as well as of some explanatory notes, produced by a different translator, to whom I should have been glad to give here the credit due him had he not stipulated that his name not be mentioned. The present version is based on a careful comparison with the French texts—*Œuvres complètes*, ed. by P. Paillotet (Paris: Guillaumin et Cie., 1854–64), vols. IV and V, and *Mélanges d'économie politique* (Brussels: Meline, Cans, et Cie., 1851), I, 1–232. I have sought to make the wording and style of this translation conform, so far as possible, to the terminology used in the two other works of Bastiat, *Selected Essays on Political Economy* and *Economic Harmonies,* also newly translated for this series, and to the usage customary in books on economics written in the English language. At the same time, every effort has been made to assist the reader to understand the topical and other allusions of the French text by the addition of translator's notes, wherever it has been at all possible to provide them. So labeled, these have been enclosed in brackets and placed, for convenience, at the bottom of the pages where the items to which they make reference appear. The notes of the French editor, likewise enclosed in brackets, appear at the back of the book, where they are labeled merely "Editor," together with Bastiat's own notes, which stand without brackets or label. Where the French editor has indicated a cross reference to an essay included in the volume of selected essays being published in this series, or to a chapter or passage in *Economic Harmonies,* the original reference to the French edition has been replaced by one directing the reader to the English translation.

ARTHUR GODDARD

Introduction

Frédéric Bastiat was born at Bayonne, France, on June 29, 1801. His father was a wholesale merchant, but Frédéric was orphaned at the age of nine and was brought up by his grandfather and his aunt.

He seems to have had a good, though not an extraordinary education, which included languages, music, and literature. He began the study of political economy at nineteen and read principally Adam Smith and Jean-Baptiste Say.

Bastiat's early life, however, was not primarily that of a scholar. At the age of seventeen he went to work in his uncle's counting-house and spent about six years there. Then he inherited his grandfather's farm at Mugron and became a farmer. He was locally active politically, becoming a *juge de paix* in 1831 and a member of the *conseil général* of the Landes in 1832.

Bastiat lived in a revolutionary period. He was fourteen when Napoleon was defeated at Waterloo and exiled to St. Helena. He lived through the Revolution of 1830. But what first inspired his pamphleteering activity was his interest in the work of Cobden and the English Anti-Corn-Law League against protection. In 1844 he rose to immediate prominence with the publication of his article on "The Influence of French and English Tariffs on the Future of the Two Peoples" in the *Journal des économistes*.

Then began the outpouring of a brilliant series of articles, pamphlets, and books that did not cease till his premature death in 1850. There came first of all the first series of *Sophismes économiques,* then the various essays and the second series of *Sophismes,* and finally, in the last year of his life, the *Harmonies économiques.*

But the list of Bastiat's writings in this short span of six years

does not begin to measure his activities. He was one of the chief
organizers of the first French Free Trade Association at Bordeaux;
he became secretary of a similar organization formed in Paris; he
collected funds, edited a weekly journal, addressed meetings, gave
lecture courses—in brief, he poured out his limited energies un-
sparingly in all directions. He contracted a lung infection. He
could breathe and nourish himself only with difficulty. Finally, too
late, his ill-health forced him to Italy, and he died at Rome, at the
age of forty-nine, on Christmas Eve, 1850.

It is ironic that the work which Bastiat considered his master-
piece, the *Harmonies économiques* that cost him so much to write,
did far more to hurt his posthumous reputation than to help it. It
has even become a fashion for some economists to write about
Bastiat patronizingly or derisively. This fashion reaches a high
point in an almost contemptuous one-page notice of Bastiat in the
late Joseph A. Schumpeter's *History of Economic Analysis.* "It is
simply the case," writes the latter, "of the bather who enjoys himself in the shallows and then goes beyond his depth and drowns.
. . . I do not hold that Bastiat was a bad theorist. I hold that he
was no theorist."*

It is not my purpose here to discuss the theories of the *Economic
Harmonies.* That is done very competently by Dean Russell in the
Introduction to the new translation of the *Harmonies* published
simultaneously with this new translation of the *Sophisms.* But
there is a germ of truth in Schumpeter's comment, and we can
acknowledge this candidly and still see the much greater truth
about Bastiat that Schumpeter missed. It is true that Bastiat, even
in the *Sophisms,* made no great original contribution to abstract
economic theory. His analysis of errors rested in the main on the
theory he had acquired from Smith, Say, and Ricardo. The short-
comings of this theory often made his exposures of fallacies less
cogent and convincing than they otherwise might have been. The
discerning reader of the *Sophisms* will notice, for example, that
Bastiat never shook off the classic cost-of-production theory of
value, or even the labor theory of value, though his total argument
is often inconsistent with these theories. But, then, no other

* (New York: Oxford University Press, 1954), p. 500.

economist of Bastiat's time (with the exception of the neglected German, von Thünen) had yet discovered marginal or subjective value theory. That was not to be expounded until some twenty years after Bastiat's death.

Schumpeter's judgment of Bastiat is not only ungenerous but unintelligent, and for the same reason that it is unintelligent to deride an apple tree for not bearing bananas. Bastiat was not primarily an original economic theorist. What he was, beyond all other men, was an economic pamphleteer, the greatest exposer of economic fallacies, the most powerful champion of free trade on the European Continent. Even Schumpeter (almost in a slip of the pen) concedes that if Bastiat had not written the *Economic Harmonies,* "his name might have gone down to posterity as the most brilliant economic journalist who ever lived." What the "might have" is doing here I do not know. It has so gone down.

And this is no mean achievement, nothing to be treated patronizingly. Economics is pre-eminently a practical science. It does no good for its fundamental principles to be discovered unless they are applied, and they will not be applied unless they are widely understood. In spite of the hundreds of economists who have pointed out the advantages of free markets and free trade, the persistence of protectionist illusions has kept protectionist and price-fixing policies alive and flourishing even today in most countries of the world. But anyone who has ever read and understood Bastiat must be immune to the protectionist disease, or the illusions of the Welfare State, except in a very attenuated form. Bastiat killed protectionism and socialism with ridicule.

His chief method of argument was the method of exaggeration. He was the master of the *reductio ad absurdum.* Someone suggests that the proposed new railroad from Paris to Madrid should have a break at Bordeaux. The argument is that if goods and passengers are forced to stop at that city, it will be profitable for boatmen, porters, hotelkeepers and others there. Good, says Bastiat. But then why not break it also at Angoulême, Poitiers, Tours, Orléans, and, in fact, at all intermediate points? The more breaks there are, the greater the amount paid for storage, porters, extra cartage. We could have a railroad consisting of nothing but such gaps—a *negative railroad!*

Are there various other proposals to discourage efficiency, in order to create more jobs? Good, says Bastiat. Let's petition the king to forbid people from using their right hands, or maybe even have them chopped off. Then it will require more than twice as many people, and twice as many jobs, to get the same work done (assuming consumption is the same).

But Bastiat's supreme jest was the petition of the candlemakers and their allied industries for protection against the unfair competition of the sun. The Chamber of Deputies is asked to pass a law requiring the closing of all windows, dormers, skylights, outside shutters, inside shutters, and all openings, holes, chinks, and fissures by which the light of the sun can enter houses. The blessings that will result from this, in an increased business for the candlemakers and their associates, are then all solemnly itemized, and the argument conducted according to the recognized principles of all protectionist arguments.

The petition of the candlemakers is devastating. It is a flash of pure genius, a *reductio ad absurdum* that can never be exceeded, sufficient in itself to assure Bastiat immortal fame among economists.

But Bastiat had more than scintillating wit and felicity of expression. His logic, too, was powerful. Once he had grasped and explained a principle, he could put the argument in so many lights and forms as to leave no one an excuse for missing or evading it. Again and again he shows the fallacies that grow out of exclusive concern with the problems of individual producers. He keeps pointing out that consumption is the end of all economic activity, and production merely the means, and that the sacrifice of the consumer's interest to that of the producer is "the sacrifice of the end to the means."

If at least some of us see some of these truths more clearly today, we owe a large part of our clear-sightedness to Frédéric Bastiat. He was one of the earliest economists to attack the fallacies not only of protection but of socialism. He was answering socialist fallacies, in fact, long before most of his contemporaries or successors thought them even worthy of attention. I have not said much here about his refutations of socialist arguments, because these refutations occur rather in the *Essays* and in the *Harmonies* than in the *Sophisms;* but they constitute a very important part of his contribution.

Bastiat is accused of being a propagandist and a pleader, and he was. It was unfortunate that for so long he stood alone, while other "orthodox" economists refrained from criticizing socialism or defending capitalism for fear of losing their reputations for "scientific impartiality," and so left the field entirely to the socialist and communist agitators who were less timorous in this respect.

We could use more Bastiats today. We have, in fact, desperate need of them. But we have, thank Heaven, Bastiat himself, in a new translation; and the reader of these pages will not only still find them, as Cobden did, "as amusing as a novel," but astonishingly modern, for the sophisms he answers are still making their appearance, in the same form and almost in the same words, in nearly every issue of today's newspapers.

HENRY HAZLITT

Table of Contents

First Series

Author's Introduction to the French Edition

> In political economy, there
> is much to learn and little
> to do.—Bentham.*

I have attempted, in this brief volume,[1] to refute some of the arguments that are raised against the introduction of free trade.

I am not engaging here in controversy with the protectionists. Rather, I am trying to instill a principle into the minds of sincere men who hesitate to take a stand on the issue because they are in doubt.

I am not one of those who say that the advocates of protectionism are motivated by self-interest. Instead, I believe that the opposition to free trade rests upon errors, or, if you prefer, upon *half-truths*. The mistrust of free trade is quite sincere. Otherwise there would not be so many people who express fear of it.

I am, perhaps, aiming too high, but—I confess—I should like this brief work to become, as it were, the *handbook* of those who are called upon to judge between the two principles. Unless one has a long-standing familiarity with the doctrines of free trade, his ideas are continually being colored by the sophisms of protectionism in one form or another. To clear his mind of them, he must each time go through a lengthy process of analysis; and

---

* [Jeremy Bentham (1748–1832), influential English philosopher and jurist. His *Book of Fallacies* probably suggested to Bastiat the title of the present work.— TRANSLATOR.]

not everyone has the time to undertake this task, legislators least of all. That is why I have tried to furnish such an analysis ready-made.

But, it may be asked, are the benefits of freedom so well hidden that they are evident only to professional economists?

Yes, we must admit that our opponents in this argument have a marked advantage over us. They need only a few words to set forth a half-truth; whereas, in order to show that it is a half-truth, we have to resort to long and arid dissertations.

This situation is due to the nature of things. Protection concentrates at a single point the good that it does, while the harm that it inflicts is diffused over a wide area. The good is apparent to the outer eye; the harm reveals itself only to the inner eye of the mind.[2] In the case of free trade, it is just the reverse.

The same is true of almost all economic questions.

You may say, "Here is a machine that has put thirty workmen out on the street."

Or, "Here is a spendthrift whose behavior encourages every branch of industry."

Or, again, "The conquest of Algiers has doubled the trade of Marseilles."

Or, finally, "Government expenditures provide a living for a hundred thousand families."

Everyone will understand you, for your propositions are lucid, simple, and self-evident. You may go further, and deduce the following principles from them:

Machinery is an evil.

Extravagance, conquests, and heavy taxes are all good.

And your theory will be all the more widely accepted because you will be able to support it with undeniable facts.

But, for our part, we cannot limit ourselves to the consideration of a single cause and its immediate effect. We know that this effect itself becomes in its turn a cause. In order to pass judgment on a measure, we must, then, trace it through the whole chain of its effects to its final result. In other words, we are reduced, quite frankly, to *an appeal to reason.*

But at once we find ourselves assailed by the familiar clamor:

You are theorists, metaphysicians, ideologists,* utopians, and doctrinaires; and all the prejudices of the public are roused against us.

What, then, are we to do? We must invoke the patience and good will of the reader, and, if we can, present our conclusions in so clear a light that truth and error show themselves plainly; so that once and for all the victory will go to either protectionism or free trade.

In this connection I have an important observation to make.

Some excerpts from this brief volume have appeared in the *Journal des économistes.*

In an otherwise favorable criticism that the Vicomte de Romanet† published (cf. the *Moniteur industriel,‡* May 15 and 18, 1845), he alleges that I am asking for the *abolition of tariffs*. M. de Romanet is mistaken. What I am asking for is the abolition of the protectionist system. We do not refuse to pay taxes to the government; but, if it were possible, we should like to dissuade the governed from taxing one another. Napoleon once said: "The tariff should be, not an instrument of taxation, but a means of protecting industry." We maintain the contrary, and say: "The tariff should not be an instrument of reciprocal robbery in the hands of the workers, but it can be a mechanism for taxation as good as any other." We are so far—or, to involve only myself in this struggle, I am so far—from asking for the abolition of tariffs, that I view them as a key element of our future financial stability. I believe them capable of producing immense revenues for the treasury; and, to speak plainly, in view of the slowness with which sound economic doctrines are spreading as compared to the rapidity with which government expenditures are increasing, I rely more upon the needs of the

* [The ideologists referred to here and at this time were the followers of Étienne Bonnot de Condillac (1715–1780), who was concerned mainly with psychology but also wrote about politics and economics. Napoleon used the word "ideologist" as a derisory denotation for visionary and impractical thinkers, and Bastiat is using it in the same sense.—TRANSLATOR.]

† [Auguste, Vicomte de Romanet, author of *Rapport fait au Comité central pour la défense du travail national* (1843), publicist, and protectionist.—TRANSLATOR.]

‡ [Newspaper of the Committee for the Defense of Domestic Industry, a protectionist organization founded by P. A. H. Mimerel de Roubaix. See *infra*, p. 12.—TRANSLATOR.]

treasury than upon the power of an enlightened public opinion for achieving commercial reform.

"But, after all," I may be asked, "what are your conclusions?"

I have no need to reach conclusions. I am only combatting sophisms; that is all.

"But," people may insist, "it is not enough to tear down; you must offer something constructive." I, for my part, think that to tear down an error is to build up the truth that stands opposed to it.

Beyond that, I have no reluctance to state what my wishes are. I should like to have public opinion persuaded to approve a tariff law framed in something like these terms:

> The following *ad valorem* rates shall be imposed:
> Goods of prime necessity 5%
> Goods of secondary necessity 10%
> Luxury goods .... 15% or 20%

No doubt these distinctions belong to a domain of ideas entirely foreign to political economy properly so called, and I am far from thinking them to be as useful and as just as people commonly suppose them to be. However, that is not my subject here.

1

Abundance and Scarcity

Which is preferable for man and for society, abundance or scarcity?

"What!" people may exclaim. "How can there be any question about it? Has anyone ever suggested, or is it possible to maintain, that scarcity is the basis of man's well-being?"

Yes, this has been suggested; yes, this has been maintained and is maintained every day, and I do not hesitate to say that the *theory of scarcity* is by far the most popular of all theories. It is the burden of conversations, newspaper articles, books, and political speeches; and, strange as it may seem, it is certain that political economy will not have completed its task and performed its practical function until it has popularized and established as indisputable this very simple proposition: "Wealth consists in an abundance of commodities."

Do we not hear it said every day: "Foreigners are going to flood us with their products"? Thus, people fear abundance.

Has not M. de Saint-Cricq* said: "There is overproduction"? Thus, he was afraid of abundance.

Do not the workers wreck machines? Thus, they are afraid of overproduction, or—in other words—of abundance.

Has not M. Bugeaud† uttered these words: "Let bread be dear,

* [Pierre Laurent Barthélemy, Comte de Saint-Cricq, member of the Chamber of Deputies, Minister of Commerce from January 4, 1828 to August 8, 1829, and later a Peer of France.—TRANSLATOR.]

† [T. R. Bugeaud de la Piconnerie (1784–1849), known chiefly as a military leader. He was also a member of the Chamber of Deputies, was interested in agriculture, and endorsed protectionist principles.—TRANSLATOR.]

7

and the farmer will be rich"? Now, bread can be dear only because it is scarce. Thus, M. Bugeaud was extolling scarcity.

Has not M. d'Argout* based his argument against the sugar industry on its very productivity? Has he not said again and again: "The sugar beet has no future, and its cultivation cannot be extended, because just a few hectares of sugar beets in each department† would be enough to supply all the consumers in France"? Thus, as he sees things, good consists in barrenness and scarcity; and evil, in fertility and abundance.

Do not *La Presse, Le Commerce,* and the majority of the daily newspapers publish one or more articles every morning to prove to the Chambers‡ and to the government that it is sound policy to legislate higher prices for everything through manipulation of the tariff? Do not the Chambers and the government every day comply with this injunction from the press? But tariffs raise the prices of things only because they reduce their *supply* in the market! Thus, the newspapers, the Chambers, and the government put the theory of scarcity into practice, and I was right to say that this theory is by far the most popular of all theories.

How does it happen that in the eyes of workers, of publicists, and of statesmen, abundance seems dangerous and scarcity advantageous? I propose to trace this illusion to its source.

We observe that a man acquires wealth in proportion as he puts his labor to better account, that is to say, as *he sells at a higher price.* He sells at a higher price in proportion to the shortage, the scarcity, of the type of commodity produced by his labor. We conclude from this that, at least so far as he is concerned, scarcity enriches him. Applying this mode of reasoning successively to all workers, we deduce from it the *theory of scarcity.* Thereupon we proceed to put the theory into practice, and, in order to favor all producers, we artificially raise prices and cause a scarcity of all

---

* [Antoine Maurice Appolinaire, Comte d'Argout (1782–1858), administrator and fiscal specialist, Governor of the Bank of France.—TRANSLATOR.]

† [A hectare is 2.471 acres. A department is the largest administrative subdivision of France, averaging about 3,000 square miles.—TRANSLATOR.]

‡ [The legislature of France, comprising the Chamber of Peers and the Chamber of Deputies.—TRANSLATOR.]

goods by restrictive and protectionist measures, the elimination of machinery, and other analogous means.

The same holds true of abundance. We observe that, when a product is plentiful, it sells at a low price; thus, the producer earns less. If all the producers are in this plight, they are all poverty-stricken; hence, it is abundance that ruins society. And, as every person holding a theory seeks to put it into practice, one sees in many countries the laws of man warring against the abundance of things.

This sophism, phrased as a generalization, would perhaps make little impression; but, when applied to a particular set of facts—to this or that industry or to a given class of producers—it is extremely specious, and this is easily explained. It constitutes a syllogism which, although not *false,* is *incomplete.* Now, what is *true* in a syllogism is always and necessarily present to the mind. But what is *incomplete* is a negative quantity, a missing element that it is quite possible and even very easy not to take into account.

Man produces in order to consume. He is at once both producer and consumer. The argument that I have just set forth considers him only from the first of these points of view. From the second, the argument would lead to an opposite conclusion. Could we not say, in fact:

The consumer becomes richer in proportion as he *buys* everything more cheaply; he buys things more cheaply in proportion as they are abundant; hence, abundance enriches him; and this argument, extended to all consumers, would lead to the *theory of abundance!*

It is an imperfect understanding of the concept of *exchange* that produces these illusions. If we analyze the nature of our self-interest, we realize clearly that it is double. As sellers, we are interested in *high prices,* and, consequently, in scarcity; as buyers, we are interested in *low prices,* or, what amounts to the same thing, in an abundance of goods. We cannot, then, base our argument on one or the other of these two aspects of self-interest without determining beforehand which of the two coincides with and is identifiable with the general and permanent interest of the human race.

If man were a solitary animal, if he worked solely for himself, if he consumed directly the fruits of his labor—in short, *if he did not engage in exchange*—the theory of scarcity could never have been introduced into the world. It would be all too evident, in that case, that abundance would be advantageous for him, whatever its source, whether he owed it to his industriousness, to the ingenious tools and powerful machines that he had invented, to the fertility of the soil, to the liberality of Nature, or even to a mysterious *invasion* of goods that the tide had carried from abroad and left on the shore. No solitary man would ever conclude that, in order to make sure that his own labor had something to occupy it, he should break the tools that save him labor, neutralize the fertility of the soil, or return to the sea the goods it may have brought him. He would easily understand that labor is not an end in itself, but a means, and that it would be absurd to reject the end for fear of doing injury to the means. He would understand, too, that if he devotes two hours of the day to providing for his needs, any circumstance (machinery, the fertility of the soil, a gratuitous gift, no matter what) that saves him an hour of this labor, so long as the product is as great, puts that hour at his disposal, and that he can devote it to improving his well-being. He would understand, in short, that a *saving in labor* is nothing else than *progress*.

But *exchange* hampers our view of so simple a truth. In society, with the division of labor that it entails, the production and the consumption of an object are not performed by the same individual. Each person comes to regard his labor no longer as a means, but as an end. Exchange creates, in relation to each object, two interests, that of its producer and that of its consumer; and these two interests are always directly opposed to each other.

It is essential to analyze them and to study their nature.

Take the case of any producer. In what does his immediate self-interest consist? It consists in two things: (1) that the smallest possible number of persons engage in the same kind of labor as he; and (2) that the greatest possible number of persons be in quest of the product of his labor. Political economy expresses this more succinctly in these terms: that the supply be very limited, and the demand very extensive; in still other terms: limited competition, and unlimited market.

In what does the immediate self-interest of the consumer consist? That the supply of the product he wants be extensive, and the demand limited.

Since these two interests are mutually incompatible, one of them must necessarily coincide with the social or general interest, and the other must be hostile to it.

But which one should legislation favor, as being the expression of the public weal—if, indeed, it should favor either one of them?

To know this, it suffices to discover what would happen if the secret desires of men were fulfilled.

In so far as we are producers, it must be admitted, each of us has hopes that are antisocial. Are we vineyardists? We should be little displeased if all the vines in the world save ours were blighted by frost: *this is the theory of scarcity*. Are we the owners of ironworks? We want no other iron to be on the market but our own, whatever may be the public need for it, precisely because this need, keenly felt and incompletely satisfied, brings us a high price: *this too is the theory of scarcity*. Are we farmers? We say, with M. Bugeaud: Let bread be costly, that is to say, scarce, and the farmers will prosper: *this is still the theory of scarcity*.

Are we physicians? We cannot blind ourselves to the fact that certain physical improvements, such as better public sanitation, the development of such moral virtues as moderation and temperance, the progress of knowledge to the point at which everyone can take care of his own health, and the discovery of certain simple, easily applied remedies, would be just so many deadly blows struck at our profession. In so far as we are physicians, our secret wishes are antisocial. I do not mean to say that physicians actually give expression to such wishes. I like to believe that they would welcome with joy the discovery of a universal cure; but it would not be as physicians, but as men and as Christians that they would yield to such an impulse: by a laudable act of self-abnegation, they would take the point of view of the consumer. But in so far as the physician practices a profession, in so far as he owes to that profession his well-being, his prestige, and even the means of supporting his

family, it is impossible for his desires—or, if you will, his interests—
not to be antisocial.

Do we make cotton textiles? We wish to sell them at the price
that is most advantageous *for us*. We should heartily approve the
proscription of all rival manufacturers; and though we do not dare
to express this wish publicly or to seek its full realization with any
likelihood of success, we nevertheless attain it to a certain extent
by roundabout means: for example, by excluding foreign textiles,
so as to diminish the *supply,* and thereby to produce, by the use
of force and to our profit, a *scarcity* of clothing.

In the same way, we could make a survey of all industries, and
we should always find that producers, as such, have antisocial attitudes. "The merchant," says Montaigne,* "prospers only by the
extravagance of youth; the farmer, by the high cost of grain; the
architect, by the decay of houses; officers of justice, by men's law-
suits and quarrels. Even the ministers of religion owe the honor
and practice of their high calling to our death and our vices. No
physician takes pleasure in the good health of even his friends; no
soldier, in the peace of his country; and so it goes for the rest."

It follows that, if the secret wishes of each producer were realized, the world would speedily retrogress toward barbarism. The
sail would take the place of steam, the oar would replace the sail,
and it in turn would have to yield to the wagon, the latter to the
mule, and the mule to the packman. Wool would ban cotton,
cotton would ban wool, and so on, until the scarcity of all things
made man himself disappear from the face of the earth.

Suppose for a moment that legislative power and executive authority were put at the disposal of the Mimerel Committee,† and
that each of the members of that association had the right to introduce and enact a favorite law. Is it very hard to imagine what sort
of industrial code the public would be subjected to?

If we now turn to consider the immediate self-interest of the
consumer, we shall find that it is in perfect harmony with the

---

* [Michel de Montaigne (1533–1592), famed humanistic essayist of the Renaissance.
—Translator.]

† [A businessmen's association headed by P. A. H. Mimerel de Roubaix (1786–1871),
a textile manufacturer.—Translator.]

general interest, i.e., with what the well-being of mankind requires.
When the buyer goes to the market, he wants to find it abundantly
supplied. He wants the seasons to be propitious for all the crops;
more and more wonderful inventions to bring a greater number of
products and satisfactions within his reach; time and labor to be
saved; distances to be wiped out; the spirit of peace and justice to
permit lessening the burden of taxes; and tariff walls of every sort
to fall. In all these respects, the immediate self-interest of the
consumer follows a line parallel to that of the public interest. He
may extend his secret wishes to fantastic or absurd lengths; yet
they will not cease to be in conformity with the interests of his
fellow man. He may wish that food and shelter, roof and hearth,
education and morality, security and peace, strength and health,
all be his without effort, without toil, and without limit, like the
dust of the roads, the water of the stream, the air that surrounds
us, and the sunlight that bathes us; and yet the realization of these
wishes would in no way conflict with the good of society.

Perhaps people will say that, if these wishes were granted, the
producer's labor would be more and more limited, and finally
would cease for want of anything to occupy it. But why? Because, in
this extreme hypothetical case, all imaginable wants and desires
would be fully satisfied. Man, like the Almighty, would create all
things by a simple act of volition. Will someone tell me what
reason there would be, on this hypothesis, to deplore the end of
industrial production?

I referred just now to an imaginary legislative assembly composed of businessmen, in which each member would have the
power to enact a law expressing his *secret wish* in his capacity as a
producer; and I said that the laws emanating from such an assembly would create a system of monopoly and put into practice the
theory of scarcity.

In the same way, a Chamber of Deputies in which each member
considered solely his immediate self-interest as a consumer would
end by creating a system of free trade, repealing all restrictive laws,
and removing all man-made commercial barriers—in short, by
putting into practice the theory of abundance.

Hence, it follows that to consult solely the immediate self-interest of the producer is to have regard for an antisocial interest; whereas to consider as fundamental solely the immediate self-interest of the consumer is to take the general interest as the foundation of social policy.

Allow me to emphasize this point, at the risk of repeating myself.

There is a fundamental antagonism between the seller and the buyer.[1]

The former wants the goods on the market to be *scarce,* in short supply, and expensive.

The latter wants them *abundant,* in plentiful supply, and cheap.

Our laws, which should at least be neutral, take the side of the seller against the buyer, of the producer against the consumer, of high prices against low prices,[2] of scarcity against abundance.

They operate, if not intentionally, at least logically, on the assumption that *a nation is rich when it is lacking in everything.*

For they say it is the producer who must be favored, by being assured a good market for his product. To achieve this end, it is necessary to raise its price; to raise its price, it is necessary to limit the supply; and to limit the supply is to create scarcity.

Just suppose that, at the present moment, when these laws are in full force, a complete inventory were taken, not in terms of monetary value, but in terms of weight, size, volume, and quantity, of all the objects existing in France that are capable of satisfying the wants and tastes of its people—meat, cloth, fuel, wheat, colonial products, etc.

Suppose further that the following day all barriers to the importation of foreign goods into France were removed.

Finally, suppose that, in order to determine the consequences of this reform, a second inventory is taken three months later.

Is it not true that there will be in France more wheat, livestock, cloth, linen, iron, coal, sugar, etc., at the time of the second inventory than at the time of the first?

This is so true that our protective tariffs have no other goal than to prevent us from importing all these things, to limit their supply, to forestall a decline in their prices, and to prevent their abundance.

Now, are we to believe that the people are better fed under the laws that prevail at present, because there is *less* bread, meat, and sugar in the country? Are they better clad, because there is *less* linen and woolen cloth? Are their houses better heated, because there is *less* coal? Is their labor made easier, because there is *less* iron and copper, or because there are *fewer* tools and machines?

But, you say, if foreigners *flood* us with their products, they will carry off our money!

Well, what difference does that make? Men are not fed on cash, they do not clothe themselves with gold, nor do they heat their houses with silver. What difference does it make whether there is more or less money in the country, if there is more bread in the cupboard, more meat in the larder, more clothing in the wardrobe, and more wood in the woodshed?

Restrictive laws always present us with the same dilemma.

Either we admit that they produce scarcity, or we do not admit it.

If we do admit it, we thereby confess that they inflict upon the people all the harm that they can do. If we do not admit it, then we deny that they limit the supply of goods and raise their prices, and consequently we deny that they favor the producer.

Such laws are either injurious or ineffective. They cannot be useful.[3]

2

Obstacle and Cause

To regard the obstacle as the cause—to mistake scarcity for abundance—is to be guilty of the same sophism in another guise. It deserves to be studied in all its forms.

Man in the primitive state is destitute of everything.

Between his destitution and the satisfaction of his wants there is a multitude of *obstacles*, which it is the goal of labor to surmount. It is curious to inquire how and why these very obstacles to his well-being have come to be mistaken for its cause.

Suppose I need to travel to a point a hundred leagues away. But between the point of departure and my destination are mountains, rivers, swamps, impenetrable forests, and highwaymen—in short, *obstacles*; and, to surmount these obstacles, I must exert myself vigorously, or—what comes to the same thing—others must exert themselves on my behalf and charge me for doing so. Is it not clear that under these circumstances I should have been better off if these obstacles did not exist in the first place?

To go through the long journey of life from the cradle to the grave, man must ingest a vast quantity of food, protect himself from the inclemency of the weather, and guard against or cure himself of a host of diseases. Hunger, thirst, sickness, heat, and cold are just so many obstacles strewn along his path. In a state of isolation he would have to overcome all of them by hunting, fishing, farming, spinning, weaving, and building; and it is clear that it would be better for him if these obstacles were fewer in number, and better still if they did not exist at all. In society, he does not personally attack each of these obstacles, but others do so for him;

16

and he in turn removes one of the obstacles confronting his fellow men.

It is also clear that, all things considered, it would be better for all mankind, or for society, if obstacles were as easy to overcome and as infrequent as possible.

But if one scrutinizes social phenomena in detail and the attitudes of men as they have been modified by exchange, one soon sees how men have come to confuse wants with wealth and obstacle with cause.

The division of labor, which results from the opportunity to engage in exchange, makes it possible for each man, instead of struggling on his own behalf to overcome all the obstacles that stand in his way, to struggle against only *one,* not solely on his own account, but for the benefit of his fellow men, who in turn perform the same service for him.

Now, the result is that each man sees the immediate cause of his prosperity in the obstacle that he makes it his business to struggle against for the benefit of others. The larger the obstacle, the more important and more intensely felt it is, then the more his fellow men are disposed to pay him for having overcome it, that is, the readier they are to remove on his behalf the obstacles that stand in his way.

A physician, for instance, does not occupy himself with baking his own bread, making his own instruments, or weaving or tailoring his own clothes. Others do these things for him, and, in return, he treats the diseases that afflict his patients. The more frequent, severe, and numerous these diseases are, the more willing people are—indeed, the more they are obliged—to work for his personal benefit. From his point of view, illness—which is a general obstacle to human well-being—is a cause of his individual well-being. All producers, with respect to their particular field of operation, reason in the same manner. The shipowner derives his profits from the obstacle called *distance;* the farmer, from that called *hunger;* the textile manufacturer, from that called *cold;* the teacher lives on *ignorance;* the jeweler, on *vanity;* the lawyer, on *greed;* the notary, on possible *bad faith,* just as the physician lives on the *illnesses* of mankind. It is therefore quite true that each profession has an immediate interest in the continuation, even the extension, of the particular obstacle that is the object of its efforts.

Seeing this, theorists attempt to found a system on the basis of these attitudes on the part of individuals and declare that need is wealth, that labor is wealth, and that the obstacle to well-being is well-being itself. To multiply obstacles is, in their eyes, to encourage industry.

Then the statesmen take over. They hold the power of the government in their hands; and what is more natural than to put it to use in increasing and spreading obstacles, since this is the same as increasing and spreading wealth? They say, for example: "If we prevent iron from coming from the places where it is abundant, we create in our own country an obstacle to obtaining it. This obstacle, when it is felt acutely, will induce people to pay in order to get rid of it. A certain number of our fellow citizens will devote themselves to struggling against it, and this obstacle will make their fortune. The greater it is, that is, the scarcer, the more inaccessible, the more difficult to transport, the more remote from the blast furnaces the ore is, the more manpower all the branches of this industry will employ. Hence, let us bar foreign iron ore; let us create the obstacle, so as to create the need for labor to struggle against it."

The same reasoning leads to the proscription of machinery.

Here, let us say, are some men who need to store their wine. This is an obstacle; and here are some other men whose job it is to remove the obstacle by making tuns. It is fortunate, then, that the obstacle exists, since it provides employment for a part of the domestic labor force and enriches a certain number of our fellow citizens. But then an ingenious machine is invented that fells the oak, squares it, divides it into staves, assembles them, and transforms them into wine-barrels. The obstacle is greatly diminished, and with it the affluence of coopers. Let us pass a law that will preserve both of them. Let us outlaw the machine.

To get at the root of this sophism, one need only remind oneself that human labor is not an *end*, but a *means. It never remains unemployed.* If it removes one obstacle, it turns to another; and mankind is rid of two obstacles by the same amount of labor that used to be needed to remove only one. If the labor of coopers ever becomes useless, it will turn in another direction. But with what, people ask, would it be paid? With exactly what pays for it today; for when a certain amount of labor becomes available as a result of the removal of an obstacle, a corresponding quantity of goods also becomes available for the remuneration of labor. To maintain that the time will ever come when human labor will lack employment, it would be necessary to prove that mankind will cease to encounter obstacles. But in that case labor would not be simply impossible; it would be superfluous. We should no longer have anything to do, for we should be omnipotent; and we should only have to pronounce a *fiat* to have all our needs and all our desires satisfied.[1]

3

Effort and Result

We have just seen that there are obstacles between our wants and their satisfaction. We succeed in eliminating these obstacles or in lessening them by employing our productive capacities to overcome them. Thus, it may be said, in a very general way, that industry is an effort followed by a result.

But what constitutes the measure of our well-being, that is, of our wealth? Is it the result of the effort? Or is it the effort itself? There is always a ratio between the effort applied and the result obtained. Does progress consist in the relative increase in the first or in the second term of this ratio?

Both theses have had their defenders, and political economists are divided in their opinions about them.

According to the first thesis, wealth is the result of labor. It increases proportionately to the increase in the *ratio of result to effort*. Absolute perfection, whose archetype is God, consists in the widest possible distance between the two terms, that is, a situation in which no effort at all yields infinite results.

The second contends that effort itself constitutes and measures wealth. To progress is to increase the *ratio of effort to result*. Its ideal may be represented by the toil of Sisyphus—at once barren and eternal.*1

Naturally, the proponents of the first doctrine welcome everything that tends to diminish exertion and to increase output: the

* [Sisyphus, in Greek mythology, is the symbol of human futility. For his crimes on earth he was condemned to spend eternity in the underworld rolling a heavy stone to the top of a mountain only to have it roll back to its starting place.—TRANS-LATOR.]

powerful machines that add to the strength of man; exchange, which permits him to get a better share of the natural resources that are distributed in varying amounts on the face of the earth; intelligence, which makes discoveries; experience, which confirms hypotheses; competition, which stimulates production; etc.

Just as logically, the proponents of the second doctrine welcome everything that has the effect of increasing exertion and of diminishing output: privileges, monopolies, restrictions, interdictions, the suppression of machinery, infertility, etc.

It is well to note that the *universal practice* of mankind is always guided by the principle on which the first doctrine is founded. No one has ever seen, and no one ever will see, any person who works, whether he be farmer, manufacturer, merchant, artisan, soldier, writer, or scholar, who does not devote all the powers of his mind to working better, more quickly, and more economically —in short, *to doing more with less.*

The opposite doctrine is the stock in trade of theorists, legislators, journalists, statesmen, and cabinet ministers—men, in brief, whose role in this world is to conduct experiments on the body of society.

Yet it is notable that, with respect to their personal concerns, they act on the same principle as everyone else; that is, they seek to obtain from their labor the greatest possible quantity of useful results.

People will perhaps think I am exaggerating, and that there are no real *Sisyphists.*

If this means that in practice no one carries the principle to its logical extreme, I willingly agree. This is always the case when one starts from a false premise. It soon leads to such absurd and injurious consequences that one is obliged to stop short. That is why it is never the practice of industry to permit *Sisyphism;* the penalty would follow the mistake too closely not to expose it. But in the realm of speculation, such as theorists and statesmen engage in, one can cling to a false principle for a long time before being made aware of its falsity by its complex practical consequences, especially in areas with which one is unfamiliar; and when these finally do reveal their origin, one adopts the opposite principle, thereby contradicting oneself, and seeks justification in that incomparably absurd modern axiom: In political economy there are no absolute principles.

Let us see, then, whether the two conflicting principles that I have just described do not prevail, by turns, the one in the practice of industry, the other in industrial legislation.

I have already repeated a saying of M. Bugeaud; but M. Bugeaud is actually two persons, a farmer and a legislator.

As a farmer, M. Bugeaud directs all his efforts toward the twofold end of saving labor and of obtaining bread cheaply. When he prefers a good plow to a poor one; when he improves his pastures; when, in order to turn over his soil, he substitutes as far as possible the action of the wind for that of the harrow or the hoe; when he summons to his aid all the processes whose power and efficacy science and experience have shown him; he has and can have only one goal: *to diminish the ratio of effort to result*. Indeed, we have no other way of judging the skill of the farmer and the extent of the improvement effected by his operations than to measure what they have subtracted from the effort and added to the result; and, as all the farmers in the world act in accordance with this principle, one can say that all men strive, undoubtedly to their advantage, to obtain bread and all other commodities more cheaply— that is, to lessen the effort needed to have a given quantity at their disposal.

This indisputable tendency of mankind, once its existence is verified, should suffice, it would seem, to make the correct principle clear to the legislator and show him in what way he ought to help industry (in so far as it is within his province to do so); for it would be absurd to say that the laws of man should run counter to the laws of Providence.

However, M. Bugeaud, the legislator, has been heard to exclaim: "I understand nothing of the theory of cheapness; I should prefer to see bread more expensive and work more abundant." And, in consequence, the deputy from the Dordogne votes for legislative measures whose effect is to hinder trade, precisely because trade procures for us indirectly what direct production can furnish us only at a higher cost.

Now, it is quite evident that the principle of M. Bugeaud, the legislator, is diametrically opposed to that of M. Bugeaud, the farmer. To be consistent, either he would have to vote against every restrictive measure, or he would have to put into practice on his own farm the principle that he proclaims from the rostrum. He would, in the latter case, have to sow his seed in the most barren field, for in that way he would succeed in *working a great deal in order to obtain little result.* He would have to eschew the use of the plow, since tilling the soil by hand would satisfy his twofold desire for dearer bread and more abundant toil.

The avowed object and acknowledged effect of restrictive measures is to increase the amount of labor necessary for a given result.

Another of its avowed objects and acknowledged effects is to raise prices, which means nothing more nor less than a scarcity of goods. Thus, carried to its extreme, the policy of restriction is pure *Sisyphism,* as we have defined it: *infinite labor, without any result.*

Baron Charles Dupin,* said to be the torch of learning among the peerage in the science of economics, accuses the railroads of *injuring navigation;* and it is certainly natural for a swifter conveyance to lessen the use of a comparatively less efficient one. But railroads can harm shipping only by taking away its business; they can take away its business only by doing the job of transportation more cheaply; and they can transport goods more cheaply only *by lowering the ratio of the effort applied to the result obtained,* since this is precisely what constitutes low cost. Thus, when Baron Dupin deplores this diminution in the labor employed to obtain a given result, he is following the doctrine of *Sisyphism.* Logically, since he prefers the ship to the train, he ought to prefer the wagon to the ship, the packsaddle to the wagon, and the basket to every other known means of transport, for it is the one that demands the most labor for the least result.

"Labor constitutes the wealth of a nation," was the saying of M. de Saint-Cricq, the Minister of Commerce who has imposed so many fetters on commerce. It should not be supposed that this was

---

* [Baron P. C. F. Dupin (1784–1873), an engineer, mathematician, statistician, and economist; member of the Chamber of Peers and Minister of the Navy.—TRANSLATOR.]

merely an elliptical proposition meaning: "The results of labor constitute the wealth of a nation." No, this economist definitely meant to say that the *intensity* of labor is the measure of wealth; and the proof is that, step by step, from one restriction to another (and always with the best of intentions), he managed to get France to double the amount of labor expended in order to provide itself, for example, with the same quantity of iron. In England iron then cost eight francs; in France it cost sixteen. Assuming that one day of labor costs one franc, it is clear that France could, by way of exchange, obtain for itself a quintal* of iron for eight days' labor. Thanks to the restrictive measures of M. de Saint-Cricq, France came to need sixteen days' labor in order to obtain a quintal of iron by direct production. Twice the labor to satisfy an identical need, hence twice the wealth; hence too, wealth is measured, not by the result, but by the intensity, of labor. Is this not *Sisyphism* in its purest form?

And so that there might be no mistaking his meaning, His Excellency has taken the trouble to explain his ideas more fully; and just as he has called the intensity of labor *wealth,* so he can be heard calling the abundance of the results of labor, or of things suitable for satisfying our wants, *poverty.* "Everywhere," he says, "machinery has replaced manual labor; everywhere there is over-production; everywhere the balance between productive capacity and consumer purchasing power has been upset." It is clear, according to M. de Saint-Cricq, that if France was in a critical situation, it was because it was producing too much; its labor was too intelligent, too fruitful. We were too well fed, too well clothed, too well provided with all things; production became too rapid and outran our demands. It was necessary to put an end to this calamitous situation, and for that purpose to compel us, by restrictive measures, to work more so as to produce less.

I have also cited the opinion of another Minister of Commerce, M. d'Argout. It deserves our attention for a moment. In an effort to strike a blow at the sugar-beet industry, he said:

* [A quintal varies greatly from place to place; in this context it is probably the metric measure of 100 kilograms or 220.46 pounds.—TRANSLATOR.]

Doubtless the cultivation of the sugar beet is useful, but *its usefulness is limited*. Its potentialities fall far short of the gigantic developments that people are fond of predicting for it. To be convinced of this, one need only note that its cultivation will of necessity be confined to the limits set by the demands of the consumers. Double, triple if you will, the present consumption of sugar in France; *you will still find that a very small portion of the land will be enough to satisfy the needs of the consumers.* [Now, there's a remarkable complaint!] Do you desire proof of this? How many hectares were planted in sugar beets in 1828? A total of 3,130, or 1/10,540 of the arable land. How many are there today, when native sugar supplies one-third of our consumption? A total of 16,700 hectares, or 1/1,978 of the arable land, or forty-five centiares per commune.* Even if we assume that native sugar were to supply the whole of our consumption, we should still have only 48,000 hectares cultivated in sugar beets, or 1/689 of the arable land.[2]

There are two elements to be noted in this quotation: the facts and the doctrine. The facts tend to establish that it takes little land, capital, and manual labor to produce a great deal of sugar, and that every commune in France would provide itself with an abundant supply by devoting one hectare of its area to cultivating the sugar beet. The doctrine consists in regarding this circumstance as harmful, and in seeing in the very efficiency and productiveness of the new industry a *limit to its usefulness*.

I am not going to set myself up here as the defender of the sugar beet, nor do I mean to pass judgment on the strange facts advanced by M. d'Argout;[3] but it is worth while to examine the doctrine of a statesman to whom France for a long time entrusted the fate of its agriculture and its commerce.

I said at the beginning that there is a variable ratio between the intensity of labor and its result; that absolute imperfection consists in an infinite effort without any result; absolute perfection, in

* [The centiare is 1/10,000 of the hectare, one square meter, or 1.196 square yards. The commune is the smallest administrative unit in France, averaging less than ten square miles. The error may be Argout's, Bastiat's, or the publisher's, but *centiare* here should read *are* (1/100 of a hectare): with about 35,000 communes in France, there would be about 0.45 hectare, or forty-five ares, per commune in sugar beets. —TRANSLATOR.]

an unlimited result without any effort; and perfectibility, in the progressive diminution of effort by comparison with the result.

But M. d'Argout teaches us that what we view as life is actually death, and that the importance of an industry is in direct proportion to its unproductiveness. What is to be expected, for example, from the cultivation of the sugar beet? Do you not see that 48,000 hectares of land, with capital and labor in proportion, would be enough to supply all France with sugar? Hence, this is an industry *with a limited usefulness*—limited, of course, with respect to the labor it demands, for, according to the former Minister of Commerce, demanding a large quantity of labor is the only manner in which an industry can be useful. This usefulness would be still more limited if, thanks to the fertility of the soil or the vigor of the sugar beet, we were to harvest from 24,000 hectares what we can now obtain from only 48,000. Oh, how much better if it only took twenty times, one hundred times, the land, capital, and labor *to achieve the same result!* We might build some hopes on the new industry, and it would be worthy of the full protection of the state, for it would offer a vast field for our domestic labor force. But to produce much with little! That sets a bad example, and it is time for the law to set things to rights.

But what holds true for sugar cannot be false in regard to bread. If, therefore, the *usefulness* of an industry is to be judged, not by the number of needs that it is capable of satisfying with a definite amount of labor, but, on the contrary, by the increase in labor that it demands in order to satisfy a given quantity of needs, what we should wish for, clearly, is that each hectare of land produce little wheat, and that each kernel of wheat contain little sustenance —in other words, that our land should be unfruitful; for then the amount of land, capital, and labor that would be required to feed the people would be comparatively much greater; one could even say that job opportunities would be in direct proportion to this unfruitfulness. The prayers of Messrs. Bugeaud, Saint-Cricq, Dupin, and d'Argout would be answered: bread would be expensive; work, abundant; and France, rich, at least in the sense that these gentlemen give to the word.

What we should desire still more is that human intelligence

should be enfeebled or extinguished; for, so long as it survives, it ceaselessly endeavors to increase the *ratio of the end to the means and of the product to the effort.* It is in this, and in this alone, that intelligence consists.

Thus, *Sisyphism* has been the doctrine of all those who have been entrusted with the fate of our country's industry. It would not be fair to reproach them for that. This principle guides our cabinet ministers only because it prevails among our legislators; it prevails among our legislators only because they are representative of the electorate; and the electorate is imbued with it only because public opinion is saturated with it.

I feel it my duty to repeat here that I am not accusing such men as Messrs. Bugeaud, Dupin, Saint-Cricq, or d'Argout, of being *Sisyphists* absolutely and under all circumstances. They are certainly not so in their private business activities; certainly each one of them obtains for himself, *by way of exchange,* what it would cost him much more to procure for himself *by direct production.* But I do say that they are *Sisyphists* when they keep the country from doing the same thing.[4]

4

Equalizing the Conditions of Production

It has been said . . . . but, in order to avoid being charged with putting sophisms into the mouths of the protectionists, I prefer to let one of their most vigorous champions speak for them.

We believe that our protective tariffs should simply represent the difference between the net cost of a commodity that we produce and the net cost of a similar commodity produced in a foreign country. . . . . A protective tariff computed on this basis merely assures free competition; . . . . free competition exists only where there is equality in the costs and conditions of production. In the case of a horse race, the weight that each of the horses is to carry is ascertained, and conditions are equalized; otherwise, the horses would no longer be competitors. In the case of commerce, if one of the sellers can bring his goods to market more cheaply than the others, he ceases to be a competitor and becomes a monopolist. . . . . If you abolish this protection, which represents the difference in net costs, the foreigner will invade your market and acquire a monopoly.[1]

Each person ought to wish, for his own sake as well as for the sake of his fellow citizens, that the production of the country be protected against foreign competition, *whenever a foreigner can furnish goods at a lower price.*[2]

This argument recurs time and again in the writings of the protectionist school. I propose to examine it carefully, and to this end I solicit the reader's attention and patience. I shall concern myself first with the inequalities that stem from the nature of things, and then with those that are derived from various taxes.

Here as elsewhere we find the advocates of protectionism taking the point of view of the producers; whereas we defend the cause of the unfortunate consumers, whom they absolutely refuse to take into consideration. The protectionists compare the field of industry to a *race track*. But at the race track, the race is at once *means* and *end*. The public takes no interest in the contest aside from the contest itself. When you spur your horses on with the single *end* of learning which is the fastest runner, I agree that you should equalize their weights. But if your *end* were getting an important and urgent piece of news to the winning post, would it be consistent for you to put obstacles in the way of the horse that had the best chance of getting there first? Yet that is what you protectionists do with respect to industry. You forget its desired result, which is man's *well-being;* by dint of begging the question, you disregard this result and even go so far as to sacrifice it.

But since we cannot persuade our opponents to accept our point of view, let us adopt theirs, and examine the question in relation to production.

I shall try to establish:

(1) That to equalize the conditions of production is to attack exchange at its very foundations.

(2) That it is not true that job opportunities within a country may be choked off by the competition of more favored countries.

(3) That, even if this were true, protective tariffs do not equalize the conditions of production.

(4) That free trade equalizes these conditions as much as they can be equalized.

(5) Finally, that it is the least favored countries that gain the most from exchange.

1. To equalize the conditions of production is not only to obstruct exchange to some extent but also to attack exchange at its very foundations; for exchange is based precisely on the diversity, or, if you prefer, on the inequalities of fertility, skill, climate, and temperature, that you are seeking to eliminate. If Guienne sends wines

to Brittany, and if Brittany sends wheat to Guienne,* it is because
these two provinces offer different conditions for production. Is
international trade conducted on a different basis? Moreover, to
attack the inequalities in conditions that give rise to exchange and
that account for it is in effect to attack exchange itself. If the protectionists had the power to give legal effect to their convictions,
they would reduce all men to the snail's life of utter isolation. A
rigorously logical analysis would show, besides, that there is not
one of their sophisms that would not lead to ruin and annihilation.

2. It is not true, *in practice,* that inequality in the conditions of
production between two similar industries necessarily involves
the failure of the less favored one. At the race track, if one of the
horses wins the prize, the other loses it; but when two horses work
to produce something useful, each will produce an amount in
proportion to his strength; and although the stronger will render
the greater service, it does not follow that the weaker will render
none at all. Wheat is grown in all the departments of France, although there are among them enormous differences in fertility;
and if by chance there is one department in which no wheat is
grown, it is because it would not pay to grow wheat even for consumption there. By analogy it is clear that under the system of
free trade, despite comparable differences, wheat would be grown
in every kingdom in Europe; and if there were one that decided
to discontinue the cultivation of wheat, it would do so because it
had found, *in its interest,* a better use for its land, its capital, and
its manpower. And why does not the fertility of one department
nullify the efforts of the farmer in a neighboring, less favored department? Because economic phenomena have a flexibility, an
elasticity, and, so to speak, *capacities for achieving equalization*
that appear to have altogether escaped the notice of the protectionist school. The protectionists accuse us of being doctrinaire;
but they are the ones that are doctrinaire in the highest degree, for
they build the whole edifice of their doctrine on the basis of a
single fact rather than on an aggregation of facts. In the example
cited above, the differences in the value of various pieces of land

* [Two geographical provinces of France, Guienne being in the southwestern part
of the country and Brittany in the northwestern part.—TRANSLATOR.]

are what compensate for the differences in their fertility. Your land produces three times as much as mine. Yes, but it cost you ten times as much, so that I can still compete with you. There is the whole secret. And observe that superiority in some respects leads to inferiority in others. It is precisely because your land is more fertile that it is more expensive, so that it is not *accidentally*, but *necessarily*, that an equilibrium is established or tends to be established; and it cannot be denied that the system of free trade is the one that most favors this tendency.

I have taken as my example a branch of agriculture, but I could just as well have cited a branch of industry. There are tailors at Quimper;* but this does not prevent there being tailors in Paris, although the latter pay much more for rent, furnishings, workers, and food. But they also have a much different clientele, and this fact suffices not only to redress the balance but even to tip it to their side.

Thus, when one speaks of equalizing the conditions of production, one should at least ascertain whether free trade does not do what one seeks to accomplish by arbitrary control.

This natural equalizing tendency of economic phenomena is so important to the discussion and at the same time so well suited to fill us with admiration at the providential wisdom that presides over the regulation of a society based on equal rights that I ask leave to dwell on it for a moment.

The protectionists are wont to say: "Such and such a nation has an advantage over us because its people can obtain coal, iron, machinery, and capital cheaply; we cannot compete with them."

I shall later examine some of the further implications of this proposition. For the present, I shall confine myself to the problem of ascertaining whether a superiority in one respect and an inferiority in another do not, in the end, counterbalance each other and thereby tend to reach a true equilibrium.

Suppose there are two countries, A and B. A has all sorts of

* [A city of about 20,000 inhabitants in Brittany, possessing great beauty of location and considerable historical and architectural significance. However, probably because of its distance from Paris, it has often been the target of jokes in about the same vein as those directed at the fictitious "Dogpatch" in the United States.—TRANSLATOR.]

advantages over B. From this you infer that industry will be concentrated in A, and that B is powerless to make anything. A, you say, sells much more than it buys; B buys much more than it sells. I could dispute this, but I shall adopt your position.

On this hypothesis, labor is in great demand in A, and soon its wages rise.

Iron, coal, land, food, and capital are all in great demand in A, and soon their prices rise.

Meanwhile labor, iron, coal, land, food, and capital all go begging in B, and soon all wages and prices fall there.

Nor is this all. Since A is selling all the time and B is buying all the time, money passes from B to A. It abounds in A and is scarce in B.

But an abundance of money means that it costs a great deal to buy anything. Thus, in A, to the *really high cost of living* that stems from a very active demand is added a *nominally high cost of living* resulting from the overabundance of precious metals.

A scarcity of money means that little is needed for each purchase. Thus, in B a *nominally low cost of living* comes to be combined with a *really low cost of living*.

In these circumstances, industry will have all sorts of motives— motives, if I may say so, intensified to the highest degree—for deserting A and going to establish itself in B.

Or, to return to reality, let us say that industry would not have awaited this moment, for abrupt relocations are repugnant to its nature; from the very outset, in the absence of restrictions, it would have been gradually dividing and distributing itself between A and B according to the laws of supply and demand, that is to say, according to the laws of justice and utility.

And when I say that, if it were possible for industry to concentrate in one area, this very fact would give rise to an irresistible tendency toward decentralization, I am indulging in no idle hypothesis.

Let us listen to what was said by a manufacturer in addressing the Manchester Chamber of Commerce (I omit the figures with which he supported his argument):

Once we exported textiles; then this exportation gave place to that of yarn, which is the raw material of textiles; subsequently, to that of machines, which produce the yarn; later, to that of capital, with which we build our machines; and finally, to that of our workers and our industrial skill, which are the source of our capital. All these resources have gone, one after another, to serve where they found it most advantageous to do so—wherever the cost of living is lower and life is simpler —and so today, in Prussia, in Austria, in Saxony, in Switzerland, and in Italy, we see vast industries supported by English capital, manned by English workers, and managed by English engineers.

You see clearly that Nature, or rather Providence, which is more ingenious, more intelligent, and more discerning than your narrow and rigid theory supposes, has not permitted the existence of that concentration of labor, that monopoly of all advantages, which you argued was a positive and irremediable fact. Providence has seen to it, by means as simple as they are unfailing, that there should be simultaneous dispersion, diffusion, interdependence, and progress. All these are tendencies that your restrictive laws paralyze as much as they can; for such measures tend in their turn, by isolating communities, to perpetuate and intensify the differences in their respective conditions of production, to prevent their equalization, to bar their commingling, to neutralize countervailing forces, and to immobilize nations in their respective positions of superiority or inferiority.

3. In the third place, to say that a protective tariff equalizes the conditions of production is to give currency to an error by a faulty mode of expression. It is not true that an import duty equalizes the conditions of production. These are the same after the tax as they were before. At worst, all that such a duty equalizes are the *conditions of sale*. It may be said perhaps that I am playing on words, but I reply by making the same charge against my opponents. If they cannot prove that production and sale are synonymous, I am justified in charging them, if not with playing on words, at least with confusing them.

Permit me to illustrate what I mean by an example:

Let us assume that some Parisian speculators decide to devote themselves to the production of oranges. They know that oranges from Portugal can be sold in Paris for ten centimes; they, on the other hand, because of the seedling-flats and greenhouses they will need and the cold weather that will often thwart their efforts, cannot ask less than a franc* if they are to make any profit at all. They demand that Portuguese oranges be subject to a tariff of ninety centimes. By means of this customs duty, they say, the *conditions of production* will be equalized; and the Chamber, yielding as always to this kind of reasoning, imposes a duty of ninety centimes on foreign oranges.

Now, I maintain that despite this tariff the *conditions of production* are in no way changed. The law has taken away none of the heat from the sun at Lisbon, nor has it rendered the frosts at Paris less frequent or less bitter. The ripening of oranges will continue to be *natural* on the banks of the Tagus† and *artificial* on the banks of the Seine; that is, growing oranges will require a great deal more human labor in one country than in the other. All that will be equalized are the *conditions of sale:* the Portuguese will have to sell us their oranges for one franc, ninety centimes of which will go to pay the tariff. This will evidently be paid by the French consumer. And see how absurd the result will be. On each Portuguese orange consumed, the country will lose nothing; for the ninety centimes extra charged the consumer will be paid into the treasury. Money will change hands, but it will not be lost. However, on each French orange consumed, ninety centimes, or nearly that much, will be lost; for the buyer will certainly lose it, and the seller just as certainly will not gain it, since, on this hypothesis, he will have received for the orange no more than its net cost. I leave it to the protectionists to draw the conclusion.

4. If I have insisted on this distinction between the conditions of production and the conditions of sale, a distinction that the protectionists will doubtless find paradoxical, it is because I am about to use it as the basis for inflicting on them yet another, even

* [There are 100 centimes in a franc.—TRANSLATOR.]

† [The principal river of Portugal, on whose estuary Lisbon is situated.—TRANSLATOR.]

stranger paradox: Do you want to really equalize the *conditions of production?* Then permit free trade.

"Oh!" they will say; "this is really too much. You are carrying your joke too far!" Very well! If only to satisfy their curiosity, I ask the protectionists to follow my argument to its conclusion. It will not be long. I revert to the example I have been using.

If we assume, for the moment, that the average daily income of each Frenchman is one franc, it will follow incontestably that to produce *directly* one orange in France will take one day's work or its equivalent; whereas to produce the exchange-value of a Portuguese orange will take only one-tenth of that day's labor, which means nothing else than that at Lisbon the sun accomplishes what at Paris can be performed only by human labor. Now, is it not evident that, if I can produce an orange, or—what comes to the same thing—enough to buy it, with one-tenth of a day's labor, the conditions of that production are for me exactly the same as those for the Portuguese producer himself, save for the transportation to Paris, the cost of which must be charged to me? Hence, it is clear that free trade equalizes the conditions of production, whether it is direct or indirect, as far as they can be equalized, because it does away with all differences save one that is inevitable, that of transportation.

Moreover, free trade also equalizes the conditions of enjoyment, of satisfaction—in short, of consumption. People seem never to take this aspect of the matter into consideration; yet it is the crux of the whole discussion, since, after all, consumption is the ultimate goal of all our productive efforts. Under a system of free trade, we should enjoy the benefits of the Portuguese sun just as Portugal itself does; and the inhabitants of Le Havre would have just as much access to the advantages that Nature conferred upon Newcastle in the form of mineral resources, and under the same conditions, as the people of London do.

5. As the protectionists can see, I find myself in a paradoxical humor and am now disposed to go even farther. I contend, and I quite sincerely believe, that if two countries have unequal conditions of production, *the one of the two that is the less favored by Nature has the more to gain from free trade.* In order to prove

this, I shall have to depart somewhat from the customary form of a work of this kind. I shall do so, nevertheless, first because the foregoing thesis expresses my whole point, and then because this digression will provide me with the opportunity to expound an economic law of the highest importance. Indeed, I think that when this law is properly understood, all those sects that in our day have been seeking in the land of fantasy the economic harmony that they have been unable to discover in Nature will be led to take a more scientific view of things. I refer to the law of consumption, which the majority of economists should perhaps be reproached for having too much neglected.

Consumption is the end, the final cause, of all economic phenomena, and it is consequently in consumption that their ultimate and definitive justification is to be found.

Nothing, whether favorable or unfavorable, has effects that touch only the producer. The advantages that Nature and society lavish upon him, as well as the disadvantages that they inflict upon him, slip away from him, so to speak, and tend insensibly to be absorbed and dissolved into the community, that is, the mass of the consumers. This is an admirable law both in its cause and in its effects; and he who succeeded in explaining it fully would, I think, have the right to say: "I have not passed through this life without paying my debt to society."

Every circumstance that favors the work of production brings pleasure to the producer, for the *immediate effect* is that he can render more services to the community and ask a greater remuneration from it. Every circumstance that hampers production brings pain to the producer, for the *immediate effect* is to limit his services and consequently his remuneration. Precisely because the *immediate* benefits or hardships from fortunate or unfortunate circumstances are necessarily felt first by the producer, he is irresistibly impelled to seek the former and to avoid the latter.

In the same way, when a worker succeeds in improving his skill, he reaps the *immediate* benefit of the improvement. This is necessary to convince him to work intelligently; and it is just, for it is only fair that an effort crowned with success should bring its reward with it.

But I assert that these good and bad consequences, although permanent in themselves, do not permanently remain with the producer. Otherwise, the inequalities existing among men would become ceaselessly and progressively greater, and that is why these benefits and hardships quickly become part of the general destiny of mankind.

How does this process take place? I shall explain it by means of a few examples.

Let us go back to the thirteenth century. The men who then practiced the art of copying received for the service they performed a *remuneration determined by the average rate of wages.* Among these copyists, there was one who sought and discovered the means of multiplying rapidly copies of the same work. He invented printing.*

At first, one man became rich, while many others were being impoverished. However marvelous this discovery was, one might, at first sight, have hesitated to decide whether it was harmful or beneficial. Apparently it was introducing into the world, as I have said, an element of limitless inequality. Gutenberg profited by his invention and employed his profits to extend its use indefinitely, until he had ruined all the copyists. As for the public, the consumers, they gained little, for Gutenberg was careful to lower the price of his books only just enough to undersell his rivals.

But God had the wisdom to introduce harmony not only into the movement of the spheres but also into the internal machinery of society. Hence, the economic advantages of this invention did not remain the exclusive possession of one individual, but instead became for all eternity the common inheritance of all mankind.

In time, the process became known. Gutenberg was no longer the only printer; others imitated him. Their profits at first were considerable. They were compensated very well for being in the vanguard of the imitators, and this extra compensation was neces-

---

* [Johann Gutenberg (1398?–1468), a citizen of Mainz, Germany, who is generally credited (perhaps erroneously) with having invented the technique of printing with movable type, was not a copyist, and may very well have not profited from his printing enterprises. Bastiat's knowledge of Gutenberg may have come in part from the various forged documents about Gutenberg current and accepted in Europe in the early 1800's.—TRANSLATOR.]

sary to attract them and to induce them to contribute to the great, approaching, final result. They earned a great deal, but they earned less than the inventor, for *competition* was beginning to operate. The price of books kept falling lower and lower, and the profits of imitators kept diminishing as the invention became less novel, that is, as imitation became less deserving of especial reward. Soon the new industry reached its normal state: the remuneration of printers no longer was exceptionally large, and, like that of scribes in earlier days, it was determined only *by the average rate of wages.* Thus, production itself became once more the measure of compensation. Yet the invention nonetheless constituted an advance; the saving of time, of labor, of effort to produce a given result, for a fixed number of copies, had nonetheless been realized. But how was this saving manifested? In the cheapness of books. And to whose profit? To the profit of the consumer, of society, of mankind. Printers, who henceforth had no exceptional merit, no longer received an exceptional remuneration. As men, as consumers, they doubtless shared in the advantages that the invention had conferred upon the community. But that was all. In so far as they were printers, in so far as they were producers, they had returned to the conditions that were customary for all the producers in the country. Society paid them for their labor, and not for the usefulness of the invention. That had become the common and freely available heritage of all mankind.

I confess that the wisdom and the beauty of these laws evoke my admiration and respect. In them I see Saint-Simonianism: *To each according to his capacity; to each capacity according to its production.** In them I see communism, that is to say, the tendency of goods to become the *common* heritage of men; but a Saint-Simonianism, a communism, regulated by infinite foresight, and in no way abandoned to the frailty, the passions, and the tyranny of men.

* [Saint-Simonianism was the name applied to the doctrines and program of Claude Henri de Rouvroy, Comte de Saint-Simon (1772–1837), historically the founder of French socialism, who urged the establishment of an industrial state administered according to "scientific" principles. His works were influential in his time and for many years after.—TRANSLATOR.]

What I have said of printing can be said of all the tools of production, from the nail and the hammer to the locomotive and the electric telegraph. Society possesses all of them in having an abundance of consumers' goods; and *it possesses them as gratuitous gifts,* since their effect is to reduce the price of commodities; and all that part of the price that has been eliminated as a result of the contribution of inventions to production clearly makes the product to that extent *free of charge.* All that remains to be paid for is current human labor; and it is paid without regard to the result of the invention, at any rate when the invention has gone through the inevitable cycle that I have just described. We may take the saw as an example. I summon a workman to my house, he comes with a saw, I pay him two francs a day, and he makes twenty-five boards for me. If the saw had not been invented, he would perhaps not have finished one board; yet I would have paid him no less for the day. The *utility* produced by the saw is thus a gratuitous gift I receive from Nature; or rather, it is a portion of the inheritance that I have received, *in common* with my fellow men, from the wisdom of our ancestors. The same is true of agricultural implements. I have two workmen in my field. One works with a plow, the other with a spade. The results of their work are quite different, but their daily wage is the same; for the remuneration is proportionate, not to the utility produced, but to the effort, the labor, demanded.

I entreat the reader's patience and beg him to believe that I have not lost sight of free trade. I hope he will be good enough to remember the conclusion I have reached: *Remuneration is proportionate, not to the utility that the producer offers on the market, but to his labor.*[3]

So far I have taken my examples from among human inventions. I should like now to deal with advantages conferred by Nature.

Every product results from the collaboration of Nature and man. But the portion of utility that Nature contributes is always free of charge. It is only the portion of utility due to human labor that becomes the object of exchange, and consequently of remuneration. The latter doubtless varies greatly in proportion to the intensity of the labor, its skill, its promptitude, its timeliness, the demand for it, the momentary absence of competition, etc., etc. But it is nonetheless true, in principle, that the contribution of the laws of Nature, though involved in all production, counts for nothing in the price of the product.

We do not pay for the air we breathe, although it is so useful to us that we could not live two minutes without it. Nevertheless we do not pay for it, because Nature furnishes it to us without the need of any human labor. But if we want to separate from it one of the gases of which it is composed—for example, in order to conduct an experiment—we have to make an effort, or, if we have someone else make the effort for us, we must give him the equivalent effort embodied in some other product. From this it is evident that exchange is concerned with exertion, effort, labor. It is not really the oxygen that I am paying for, since it is everywhere at my disposal, but the labor needed for isolating it, labor that I have been spared and that I must pay for. Will it be said that there is something else to pay for—supplies, materials, equipment? But it is still the labor connected with these things that I am paying for. The price of the coal used represents the labor needed to extract and transport it.

We do not pay for the light of the sun, because it is a gratuitous gift of Nature. But we do pay for that of gas, of tallow, of oil, and of wax, because in these cases there is some human labor to be remunerated; and note that the remuneration is proportioned so closely to the labor, and not to the utility, that one of these illuminants, although casting a much more intense light than another, may still cost less simply because the same quantity of human labor produces more of it.

If, when the water carrier comes to supply my house, I paid him in proportion to the *absolute utility* of water, my whole fortune would not be enough. But I pay him in proportion to the pains he has taken. If he demanded more money, others would do this work for me, and, ultimately, in case of need, I should do it myself. The real object of our bargain is not the water, but rather the labor performed to obtain the water. This point is so important and the conclusions that I am going to draw from it throw so much light on the question of the freedom of international trade that I believe I ought to elucidate it with some additional examples.

The nutritive substance in potatoes does not cost us very much, because we can obtain many potatoes with little labor. We pay more for wheat because Nature demands a greater amount of human labor for its production. It is evident that, if Nature did for the latter what it does for the former, the prices of both would tend to become equal. However, the producer of wheat cannot go on forever earning much more than the producer of potatoes. The law of supply and demand stands in the way.

If, by a happy miracle, the fertility of all arable land happened to increase, the consumer and not the farmer would reap the advantage of this phenomenon, for it would result in abundance and therefore in low food prices. Since each hectoliter* of wheat would involve less labor, the farmer could exchange the wheat only for some other product that involved a lesser quantity of labor. If, on the contrary, the fertility of the soil should suddenly diminish, the share of Nature in production would be less, and that of labor more, so that the cost of the product would be higher. Thus, I was right in saying that every economic phenomenon in the long run diffuses its effects among the consumers, i.e., all mankind. So long as you have not followed its consequences that far, so long as you stop at the *immediate* effects, those that concern only one man or one class of men *as producers,* you are not an economist; any more than you are a doctor if, instead of following the effects of a potion through the entire organism, you confine yourself to observing how it affects the palate or the throat.

The tropical regions are very well suited to the production of sugar and of coffee. This means that Nature does the larger portion of the work and leaves little to be done by human labor. But, then, who reaps the advantage of this liberality on the part of Nature? It is not these regions, for competition allows them to receive remuneration only for the labor expended; instead, it is mankind, for the result of this liberality is termed *cheapness,* and cheapness benefits everyone.

---

* [A metric unit of volume equaling 2.838 bushels.—TRANSLATOR.]

In a temperate zone where coal and iron ore are at the surface, one need only stoop down to get them. At first, I readily agree, it is the inhabitants of the favored region who will profit from this lucky circumstance. But soon, as competition develops, the price of coal and iron ore will continue to fall until the gift of Nature is available free of charge to everyone, and human labor alone is remunerated in accordance with the average rate of wages.

Thus, as a result of the operation of the law of supply and demand, the gifts of Nature, like improvements in the processes of production, are—or continually tend to become—the common and gratuitous heritage of the consumers, the masses, mankind in general. Hence, the countries that do not possess these advantages have everything to gain by exchanging with those that do possess them, for exchange involves the *products of labor,* without regard to the utilities contributed to these products by Nature; clearly, the most favored countries are those that have combined with their labor the greatest number of these *natural utilities* in making a given product. Their products, which represent less labor, are less well remunerated; in other words, they are *cheaper,* and if all the gifts of Nature result in *lower costs,* evidently it is not the producing country, but rather the consuming country, that reaps the benefit.

Hence, we see how absurd it is for a consuming country to reject a product precisely because it is cheap. This is like saying: "I do not want anything that Nature gives me. You can make a product and sell it to me for only half as much of my labor as I should have to expend to make it for myself. You can do this because in your country Nature has done half the work. Very well! I, for my part, refuse to buy the product, and I shall wait until your climate, by becoming more inclement, forces you to demand twice as much labor on my part; then I can deal with you *on an equal footing.*"

A is a favored country; B is a country ill-treated by Nature. I hold that exchange is advantageous for both of them, but especially for B; because what are exchanged in commercial transactions are not *utilities,* but *values.* Now, A includes *a greater amount of utility in the same value,* since the utility of the product includes the contributions of both Nature and human labor, whereas its value corresponds only to the contribution of labor. Therefore, the bargain is entirely to the advantage of B. By paying the producer in A simply for his labor, B receives into the bargain more natural utility than it gives.

We are now in a position to formulate the general rule.

Exchange involves the bartering of *values;* and since competition makes value the equivalent of labor, exchange involves the bartering of equal quantities of labor. What Nature has contributed to the products in the exchange is given by both parties to the transaction *free of charge and into the bargain,* whence it follows necessarily that exchange carried on with the countries most favored by Nature is the most advantageous.

The theory whose outlines I have attempted to sketch in this chapter still stands in need of a great deal of development. I have considered it only in its bearing on the subject of free trade. But perhaps the attentive reader may have perceived in it the fertile seed that is destined, when it matures, to eradicate not only protectionism, but, along with it, Fourierism,* Saint-Simonianism, communism, and all those schools of thought that aim at excluding the law of *supply and demand* from the governance of the world. From the point of view of the producer, competition doubtless often clashes with our *immediate* self-interest; but, if one considers the general aim of all labor, i.e., universal well-being—in a word, if one adopts the point of view of the consumer—one will find that competition plays the same role in the moral world as equilibrium does in the physical world. It is the basis of true communism, of true socialism, and of that equality of wealth and position so much desired in our day; and if so many sincere publicists and well-intentioned reformers demand *arbitrary controls,* it is because they do not understand *free exchange.*[4]

---

* [Fourierism was the term applied to the doctrines and program of F. C. M. Fourier (1772–1837), a French socialist who urged the reconstruction of society on the basis of large groups of about 1,600 persons, called "phalanges," each occupying a common building, or "phalanstery." His ideas were very influential at home and abroad; Brook Farm, Massachusetts, was an experimental society based on Fourierism.—Translator.]

5

Our Products Are Burdened
with Taxes

This is the same sophism. People demand that a tariff be levied on a foreign product in order to neutralize the effects of a domestic tax imposed upon the same product when it is made in France. The issue here is the same as the one we have just considered, namely, that of equalizing the conditions of production. We have little more to say on the subject. The domestic tax is an artificial obstacle that has exactly the same result as a natural obstacle, which is to force a rise in the price. If the price rises to the point at which there is a greater loss in making the product ourselves than in importing it from abroad by producing its exchange-value, then *leave things as they are.* In his own self-interest, the individual will know well enough to choose the lesser evil. I could, in fact, refer the reader to the preceding demonstration; but the sophism that I have to combat here reappears so often in the petitions of grievances and the requests—I might almost say, demands—of the protectionist school that it deserves a special discussion.

If we are talking about one of those exceptional taxes that are imposed on certain products, I readily grant that it is equitable to impose the same tax on the foreign product. For example, it would be absurd to free foreign salt from the salt tax, but not because France would lose anything from the economic point of view; for the contrary is true. Whatever one may say, principles are immutable; and France would gain by removing the tax, just as it will

44

always gain by removing any obstacle, whether natural or artificial. But in this case the obstacle has been erected for a fiscal purpose. This purpose must be achieved; and if foreign salt were sold on our market duty-free, the treasury would lose hundreds of millions of francs which it would have to raise by means of some other tax. There would be an evident inconsistency in creating an obstacle in order to avoid achieving one's purpose. It would have been better, in that case, to have had recourse at the very outset to this other tax and not to have taxed French salt. These, then, are the only circumstances in which I admit the propriety of a customs duty, *not protective,* but revenue-producing, on a foreign commodity.

But it is fallacious to argue that a country, simply because it has a heavier tax burden than its neighbor, should protect itself by tariffs against the competition of its rival, and this is the sophism I propose to attack.

I have said several times that I mean to limit myself to purely theoretical considerations and to expose, as far as possible, the sources of the protectionists' errors. If I were engaging in polemics, I should ask them: "Why do you direct your tariffs principally against England and Belgium, the most heavily taxed countries in the world? Am I not justified in viewing your argument as nothing but a pretext?" But I am not one of those who believe that one is a protectionist solely from motives of self-interest and not by conviction as well. Protectionism is too popular for its adherents to be regarded as insincere. If the majority of people had faith in free trade, we should have free trade. It is doubtless motives of self-interest that have been responsible for the imposition of our tariffs, but only after having produced sincere conviction. "The will," says Pascal,* "is one of the principal organs of belief." But the belief is no less real for having its roots in the will and in the secret promptings of selfishness.

Let us revert to the sophism based on the premise of the domestic tax burden.

* [Blaise Pascal (1623–1662), great French ascetic, religious philosopher and writer, and geometer; his best-known work, the *Pensées,* comprises fragments of his incomplete planned defense of the Christian religion.—TRANSLATOR.]

The state can put its taxes to either a good or a bad use. It puts them to a good use when it performs services for the public equivalent to the value it receives from the public. It puts them to a bad use when it squanders its revenues without giving the public anything in return.

In the first case, it is a sophism to say that the taxes render the conditions of production in the country that pays them less favorable than the conditions of production in a country that is free of such taxes. We pay twenty millions for courts and police forces, it is true; but we do get courts and police forces, with the security that they provide us and the time that they save us; and it is hardly likely that production is either safer or brisker among those nations, if there are any, in which each man takes the law into his own hands. We pay several hundred millions for highways, bridges, harbors, and railroads; granted. But we have these railroads, these harbors, these bridges, and these highways; and unless we made a mistake in building them, it cannot be said that they render us inferior to nations that are not, it is true, burdened with the taxes needed to support a public works program, but that, at the same time, have no public works. And this explains why, while we blame our domestic taxes for our industrial inferiority, we direct our tariffs precisely against those countries that are themselves the most tax-ridden. The fact is that taxes, when properly used, have bettered rather than worsened the *conditions of production* in these countries. Thus, we must again conclude that protectionist sophisms not only deviate from the truth, but are contrary to it, are, in fact, at the opposite pole from it.[1]

As for domestic taxes that produce little revenue, abolish them if you can; but surely the strangest imaginable method of neutralizing their effects is to supplement taxes levied for public purposes with taxes levied for the profit of individuals. A fine way, indeed, to correct the situation! The state has taxed us too much, you say. Well, all the more reason for not taxing one another besides!

A protective tariff is a tax directed against foreign goods, but that falls, let us never forget, on the domestic consumer. Now, the consumer is the taxpayer. And is it not ridiculous to tell him: "Since your taxes are heavy, we shall raise the price of everything you buy; since the state takes a part of your income, we shall hand over another part of it to a monopolist"?

But let us delve further into this sophism, which is so much in vogue among our legislators, although it is quite extraordinary that the very people who defend unproductive taxes (for that is what they are assumed to be on our present hypothesis) are the ones who attribute to them our alleged industrial inferiority in order to justify other taxes and restrictions as compensatory devices.

It seems clear to me that neither the essence nor the consequences of protectionism would in any way be altered if it took the form of a direct tax levied by the state and distributed as subsidies to privileged industries by way of indemnification.

Let us assume that, while foreign iron cannot be sold on our market for less than eight francs, French iron cannot be sold for less than twelve.

On this hypothesis, the government has two ways of assuring the French producer a domestic market.

The first is to impose a customs duty of five francs on foreign iron. It is clear that this would definitely bar the iron from the French market, since it could no longer be sold for less than thirteen francs, that is, eight francs net price and five francs for the tax, and that at this price it would be driven from the market by French iron, which we assumed to be only twelve francs. In this case the buyer, the consumer, would bear all the costs of protection.

On the other hand, the state might levy a tax of five francs on the public and give the proceeds as a subsidy to the ironmaster. The protective effect would be the same. In this case too, foreign iron would be excluded from the French market; for our ironmaster would sell his product at seven francs, which with the five-franc subsidy would give him a remunerative return of twelve francs. But with domestic iron available for seven francs, the foreigner could not sell his at eight.

Between these two systems I can see only one difference. Their principle is the same; their effect is the same: but in one case the protection is paid only by certain individuals; in the other, by everyone.

I frankly confess my preference for the second system. It seems to me more just, more economical, and more honest: more just, because if society wants to pay bounties to certain of its members, everybody should contribute to them; more economical, because it will save much of the cost of collection and will eliminate many restrictions; finally, more honest, because the public would then see clearly the nature of the operation and realize what it is being made to do.

But if the protectionist system had taken this form, it would be really laughable to hear people say: "We pay heavy taxes for the army, the navy, the courts, public works, the public schools, the national debt, etc.; they amount to more than a billion francs. That is why it would be good for the state to take still another billion from us, for the relief of those poor ironmasters, those poor stockholders of the Anzin Company,* those unfortunate owners of woodlands, those useful codfishers."

One has only to examine matters closely to be convinced that this is what the sophism I am combatting amounts to. Do what you will, gentlemen; you cannot *give money* to some without taking it away from others. If you absolutely insist on draining the taxpayer dry, well and good; but at least do not treat him like a fool. Do not tell him: "I am taking this money from you to repay you for what I have already taken from you."

It would be an endless task to attempt to criticize everything that is false in this sophism. I shall confine myself to three points.

You argue that, since France is overburdened with taxes, it is necessary to protect this or that industry. But we have to pay these taxes in any case, whether or not there is protection. If, then, the spokesman of a particular industry argues: "We share in the payment of taxes; they raise our costs of production, and we demand that a protective tariff be levied so as to raise correspondingly the selling price of our product," what does such a demand amount to but that the burden of the tax be shifted onto the rest of the community? The object of the demand is to recover, by raising the

* [The Anzin Company was a remarkable business organization, already close to a century old in Bastiat's day, based on huge coal-mining operations in northeastern France.—TRANSLATOR.]

price of the product, the amount of the tax paid by the industry. Now, since the total revenue from all taxes must always flow into the treasury, and since the public has to assume the burden of the rise in price, it pays not only its own share of the tax but that of this industry as well. But, you say, everyone will be protected. In the first place, that is impossible; and even if it were possible, where would be the relief? I shall pay for you, and you will pay for me; but the tax will have to be paid nonetheless.

Thus, you are the victims of an illusion. You pay taxes in order to have an army, a navy, a church,* public schools, courts, highways, etc., and yet you want to free first one industry, then a second, then a third, from its share of taxes, in every case by distributing the burden among the public. But you do nothing but create endless complications, with no result except these complications themselves. If you could show me that a rise in prices that is due to protection falls on foreigners, I might see some plausibility in your argument. But if, before the enactment of the proposed law, the French public was paying the tax, and if, after the law is enacted, it will pay the customs duty as well as the tax, I really cannot see what will be gained by the law.

But I go even further: I maintain that, the heavier our taxes on domestic products, the more quickly must we open our harbors and our frontiers to the goods of foreign countries less heavily taxed than we. And why? To shift to them a larger part of our tax burden. Is it not an incontestable axiom of political economy that taxes ultimately fall upon the consumer? Thus, the more our foreign trade expands, the more foreign consumers will reimburse us for the taxes embodied in the products we sell them; whereas we should have to make them, in this respect, a lesser repayment, since, according to our hypothesis, their products are less heavily taxed than ours.

Finally, with respect to these heavy taxes that you are using as a justification for the protectionist system, have you ever asked yourself whether it is not the system itself that produces them? I do wish

---

* [The Catholic Church in France was a state church, financed by taxes levied on the whole public.—TRANSLATOR.]

someone would tell me what would be the use of large standing armies and powerful navies if trade were free. . . . . But that is the concern of the politicians.

> And let us not confuse, by probing too deeply,
>   Their affairs with ours.*2

6

The Balance of Trade

Our opponents have adopted a tactic that puts us in a most embarrassing position. When we expound our doctrine, they accept it in the most respectful manner possible. When we attack their principles, they abandon them with the best grace in the world. They ask only that our doctrine, which they accept as true, be relegated to books, and that their principles, which they admit to be faulty, constitute the rule in the realm of practical affairs. Grant them the management of tariffs, and they will leave to you the domain of theory.

"Surely," said M. Gaulthier de Rumilly* on a recent occasion, "none of us wants to revive the old theories of the balance of trade." Very well; but, M. Gaulthier, it is not enough just to give error a passing slap on the wrist; you must also avoid arguing, immediately afterward and for two whole hours, as if that error were truth.

Let me speak of M. Lestiboudois.† Here we have a man who reasons consistently and argues logically. There is nothing in his conclusions that is not to be found in his premises; he does not demand to do in practice anything that he does not justify in theory. Whether the principle that he takes as his initial premise is true may be open to question, but at least he does base his reasoning on a principle. He believes and loudly proclaims that if France gives ten in order to receive fifteen, it loses five; and it is quite plain that he would draft laws accordingly.

"The important thing," he says,

* [L. M. C. H. Gaulthier de Rumilly (1792–1884), a Deputy and an authority on tariffs, railroads, and trade.—TRANSLATOR.]
† [G. T. Lestiboudois (1797–1876), a Deputy and a doctor.—TRANSLATOR.]

51

is that the amount of our imports keeps on increasing all the time and exceeds the amount of our exports, which is to say that every year France buys more foreign products and sells fewer domestic products. The figures prove it. What do we see? In 1842, imports exceeded exports by 200 millions. These facts seem to me to prove, in the clearest way, that domestic industry *is not sufficiently protected*, that we depend for our supplies on foreign industry, and that the competition of our rivals is crushing our own industry. The present law seems to me to recognize the fact that it is not true, as economists have declared, that when we buy, we necessarily sell a corresponding quantity of merchandise. It is evident that we can buy, not with our customary products, not with our income, not with the fruits of current labor, but with our capital, with products that have been accumulated by saving, with those that are needed for production—that is to say, we can consume and dissipate the proceeds of previous savings, we can impoverish and ruin ourselves, and entirely use up our national capital. *This is exactly what we are doing. Every year we give away 200 million francs to foreigners.*

Here, at least, is a man who makes his views clear. There is no hypocrisy in this language. The principle of the balance of trade is openly avowed. France imports 200 millions more than it exports. Thus, France loses 200 millions yearly. And what is the remedy? To restrict imports. The conclusion is unexceptionable.

It is therefore M. Lestiboudois who will have to bear the brunt of our attack; for how can one argue with M. Gaulthier? If you say to him, "The principle of the balance of trade is false," he will reply to you, "That is just what I said from the start." If you tell him, "But the principle of the balance of trade is true," he will tell you, "That is what I have established in my conclusion."

The economist school will doubtless censure me for arguing with M. Lestiboudois. They will say that combatting the principle of the balance of trade is like tilting at windmills.

But we must be careful, for the principle of the balance of trade is not as old, sick, or dead as M. Gaulthier would have us believe; for the whole Chamber, including M. Gaulthier himself, has espoused, in its votes, the theory of M. Lestiboudois.

However, in order not to weary the reader, I shall not probe very deeply into this theory. I shall content myself with submitting it to the test of facts.

We are constantly being told that our free-trade principles are valid only in theory. But, tell me, gentlemen, do you think that the account books of businessmen are valid in practice? It seems to me that if there is anything in the world that has the authority of practice when the question concerns profits and losses, it is commercial accounting. Are we to suppose that all the businessmen in the world have been in agreement for centuries to keep their books in such a way that they would show profits as losses and losses as profits? Instead, I should prefer to believe that M. Lestiboudois is a poor economist.

Now, after one of my friends, a businessman, had carried out two transactions that had had very different results, I was curious to compare the accounting methods of the bank with those of the customhouse, as interpreted by M. Lestiboudois, with the approval of our six hundred lawmakers.

M. T. despatched a ship from Le Havre to the United States, with a cargo of French goods, chiefly those known as *specialties of Parisian fashion,* totaling 200,000 francs. This was the amount declared at the customhouse. When the cargo arrived at New Orleans, it had to pay a shipping charge of ten per cent and a tariff of thirty per cent, which brought the total to 280,000 francs. It was sold at a profit of twenty per cent, or 40,000 francs, for a total price of 320,000 francs, which the consignee converted into cotton. This cotton had to pay ten per cent more, for transportation, insurance, commissions, etc.; so that, when the new cargo arrived at Le Havre, its cost amounted to 352,000 francs, and that was the figure entered into the accounts of the customhouse. Finally, M. T. again realized, on this return trip, twenty per cent profit, or 70,400 francs; in other words, the cotton sold for 422,400 francs.

If M. Lestiboudois requires it, I shall send him some figures taken from the books of M. T. There he will see, *in the credit column* of the profit-and-loss account—that is to say, as profit—two entries, one for 40,000 francs and the other for 70,400 francs; and

M. T. is fully satisfied that in this respect his accounting is not in error.

And yet, what do the figures in the account books of the custom-house tell M. Lestiboudois regarding this transaction? They tell him that France has exported 200,000 francs, and that it has imported 352,000 francs; whence the honorable deputy concludes *"that it has consumed and dissipated the proceeds of previous savings, that it has impoverished and is on the way to ruining itself, that it has given away 152,000 francs of its capital to foreigners."*

Some time afterward, M. T. despatched another ship with a similar cargo, worth 200,000 francs, of products of our domestic industry. But the unfortunate vessel sank while leaving the harbor, and there was nothing else for M. T. to do but to inscribe in his books two brief entries phrased thus:

Sundry goods due to X: 200,000 francs for the purchase of various commodities carried by ship N.

Profits and losses due to sundry goods: 200,000 francs *for ultimate total loss* of the cargo.

Meanwhile, the customhouse on its part was entering 200,000 francs into its *export* ledger; and as it will never have anything to enter into the opposite *import* ledger on this account, it follows that M. Lestiboudois and the Chamber will view this shipwreck *as a clear net profit* of 200,000 francs for France.

There is still a further conclusion to be drawn from all this, namely, that, according to the theory of the balance of trade, France has a quite simple means of doubling her capital at any moment. It suffices merely to pass its products through the customhouse, and then throw them into the sea. In that case the exports will equal the amount of her capital; imports will be nonexistent and even impossible, and we shall gain all that the ocean has swallowed up.

"You're just joking," the protectionists will say. "We couldn't possibly have been saying anything so absurd." Indeed you have, and, what is more, you are acting upon these absurd ideas and imposing them on your fellow citizens, at least as far as you can.

The truth is that we should reverse the principle of the balance of trade and calculate the national profit from foreign trade in terms of the excess of imports over exports. This excess, minus expenses, constitutes the real profit. But this theory, which is the correct one, leads directly to the principle of free trade. I present this theory to you, gentlemen, just as I do all the others that have been the subjects of the preceding chapters. Exaggerate it as much as you wish; it has nothing to fear from that test. Assume, if it amuses you, that foreigners flood our shores with all kinds of useful goods, without asking anything from us; even if our imports are *infinite* and our exports *nothing,* I defy you to prove to me that we should be the poorer for it.[1]

7

A Petition

From the Manufacturers of Candles, Tapers, Lanterns, Candlesticks, Street Lamps, Snuffers, and Extinguishers, and from the Producers of Tallow, Oil, Resin, Alcohol, and Generally of Everything Connected with Lighting.

To the Honorable Members of the Chamber of Deputies.

Gentlemen:

You are on the right track. You reject abstract theories and have little regard for abundance and low prices. You concern yourselves mainly with the fate of the producer. You wish to free him from foreign competition, that is, to reserve the *domestic market* for *domestic industry*.

We come to offer you a wonderful opportunity for applying your—what shall we call it? Your theory? No, nothing is more deceptive than theory. Your doctrine? Your system? Your principle? But you dislike doctrines, you have a horror of systems, and, as for principles, you deny that there are any in political economy; therefore we shall call it your practice—your practice without theory and without principle.

We are suffering from the ruinous competition of a foreign rival who apparently works under conditions so far superior to our own for the production of light that he is *flooding* the *domestic market* with it at an incredibly low price; for the moment he appears, our sales cease, all the consumers turn to him, and a branch of French industry whose ramifications are innumerable is all at once reduced to complete stagnation. This rival, which is none other than the sun, is waging war on us so mercilessly that we suspect he is being stirred up against us by perfidious Albion (excellent diplomacy nowadays!), particularly because he has for that haughty island a respect that he does not show for us.*

We ask you to be so good as to pass a law requiring the closing of all windows, dormers, skylights, inside and outside shutters, curtains, casements, bull's-eyes, deadlights, and blinds—in short, all openings, holes, chinks, and fissures through which the light of the sun is wont to enter houses, to the detriment of the fair industries with which, we are proud to say, we have endowed the country, a country that cannot, without betraying ingratitude, abandon us today to so unequal a combat.

Be good enough, honorable deputies, to take our request seriously, and do not reject it without at least hearing the reasons that we have to advance in its support.

First, if you shut off as much as possible all access to natural light, and thereby create a need for artificial light, what industry in France will not ultimately be encouraged?

If France consumes more tallow, there will have to be more cattle and sheep, and, consequently, we shall see an increase in cleared fields, meat, wool, leather, and especially manure, the basis of all agricultural wealth.

If France consumes more oil, we shall see an expansion in the cultivation of the poppy, the olive, and rapeseed. These rich yet soil-exhausting plants will come at just the right time to enable us to put to profitable use the increased fertility that the breeding of cattle will impart to the land.

Our moors will be covered with resinous trees. Numerous swarms of bees will gather from our mountains the perfumed treasures that today waste their fragrance, like the flowers from which they emanate. Thus, there is not one branch of agriculture that would not undergo a great expansion.

The same holds true of shipping. Thousands of vessels will engage in whaling, and in a short time we shall have a fleet capable

* ["Perfidious Albion" is England, along with a typically French jibe at the English fog, which keeps the sun from interfering with artificial light in England as much as it does in France. During the 1840's, Franco-English relations were occasionally very tense.—TRANSLATOR.]

of upholding the honor of France and of gratifying the patriotic aspirations of the undersigned petitioners, chandlers, etc.

But what shall we say of the *specialties of Parisian manufacture?* Henceforth you will behold gilding, bronze, and crystal in candlesticks, in lamps, in chandeliers, in candelabra sparkling in spacious emporia compared with which those of today are but stalls.

There is no needy resin-collector on the heights of his sand dunes, no poor miner in the depths of his black pit, who will not receive higher wages and enjoy increased prosperity.

It needs but a little reflection, gentlemen, to be convinced that there is perhaps not one Frenchman, from the wealthy stockholder of the Anzin Company to the humblest vendor of matches, whose condition would not be improved by the success of our petition.

We anticipate your objections, gentlemen; but there is not a single one of them that you have not picked up from the musty old books of the advocates of free trade. We defy you to utter a word against us that will not instantly rebound against yourselves and the principle that guides your entire policy.

Will you tell us that, though we may gain by this protection, France will not gain at all, because the consumer will bear the expense?

We have our answer ready:

You no longer have the right to invoke the interests of the consumer. You have sacrificed him whenever you have found his interests opposed to those of the producer. You have done so in order *to encourage industry and to increase employment.* For the same reason you ought to do so this time too.

Indeed, you yourselves have anticipated this objection. When told that the consumer has a stake in the free entry of iron, coal, sesame, wheat, and textiles, "Yes," you reply, "but the producer has a stake in their exclusion." Very well! Surely if consumers have a stake in the admission of natural light, producers have a stake in its interdiction.

"But," you may still say, "the producer and the consumer are one and the same person. If the manufacturer profits by protection, he will make the farmer prosperous. Contrariwise, if agriculture is prosperous, it will open markets for manufactured goods." Very well! If you grant us a monopoly over the production of lighting during the day, first of all we shall buy large amounts of tallow, charcoal, oil, resin, wax, alcohol, silver, iron, bronze, and crystal, to supply our industry; and, moreover, we and our numerous suppliers, having become rich, will consume a great deal and spread prosperity into all areas of domestic industry.

Will you say that the light of the sun is a gratuitous gift of Nature, and that to reject such gifts would be to reject wealth itself under the pretext of encouraging the means of acquiring it?

But if you take this position, you strike a mortal blow at your own policy; remember that up to now you have always excluded foreign goods *because* and *in proportion as* they approximate gratuitous gifts. You have only *half* as good a reason for complying with the demands of other monopolists as you have for granting our petition, which is in *complete* accord with your established policy; and to reject our demands precisely because they are *better founded* than anyone else's would be tantamount to accepting the equation: $+\times=+-$; in other words, it would be to heap *absurdity* upon *absurdity*.

Labor and Nature collaborate in varying proportions, depending upon the country and the climate, in the production of a commodity. The part that Nature contributes is always free of charge; it is the part contributed by human labor that constitutes value and is paid for.

If an orange from Lisbon sells for half the price of an orange from Paris, it is because the natural heat of the sun, which is, of course, free of charge, does for the former what the latter owes to artificial heating, which necessarily has to be paid for in the market.

Thus, when an orange reaches us from Portugal, one can say that it is given to us half free of charge, or, in other words, at *half price* as compared with those from Paris.

Now, it is precisely on the basis of its being *semigratuitous* (pardon the word) that you maintain it should be barred. You ask: "How can French labor withstand the competition of foreign labor when the former has to do all the work, whereas the latter has to do only half, the sun taking care of the rest?" But if the fact that a product is *half* free of charge leads you to exclude it from competition, how can its being *totally* free of charge induce you to admit it into competition? Either you are not consistent, or you should, after excluding what is half free of charge as harmful to our domestic industry, exclude what is totally gratuitous with all the more reason and with twice the zeal.

To take another example: When a product—coal, iron, wheat, or textiles—comes to us from abroad, and when we can acquire it for less labor than if we produced it ourselves, the difference is a *gratuitous gift* that is conferred upon us. The size of this gift is proportionate to the extent of this difference. It is a quarter, a half, or three-quarters of the value of the product if the foreigner asks of us only three-quarters, one-half, or one-quarter as high a price. It is as complete as it can be when the donor, like the sun in providing us with light, asks nothing from us. The question, and we pose it formally, is whether what you desire for France is the benefit of consumption free of charge or the alleged advantages of onerous production. Make your choice, but be logical; for as long as you ban, as you do, foreign coal, iron, wheat, and textiles, *in proportion* as their price approaches *zero,* how inconsistent it would be to admit the light of the sun, whose price is zero all day long!

8

Differential Tariffs

An impoverished farmer of the Gironde* had lovingly tended a vine slip. After much fatigue and toil he finally had the good fortune to harvest enough grapes from it to make a cask of wine, and he forgot that each drop of this precious nectar had cost his brow a drop of sweat. "I shall sell it," he told his wife, "and with the price I shall buy enough material to enable you to furnish a trousseau for our daughter."

The honest peasant took his cask of wine to the nearest town, and there he met a Belgian and an Englishman. The Belgian said to him: "Give me your cask of wine, and I will give you fifteen parcels of yarn in exchange."

The Englishman said: "Give me your wine, and I will give you twenty parcels of yarn; for we English spin it at lower cost than the Belgians."

But a customs officer who was there said: "My good man, trade with the Belgian, if you wish, but my orders are to keep you from trading with the Englishman."

"What!" exclaimed the countryman. "You want me to be content with fifteen parcels of yarn from Brussels, when I could have twenty from Manchester?"

"Certainly; do you not see that France would lose if you received twenty parcels instead of fifteen?"

"I find that hard to understand," said the vineyardist.

"And I find it hard to explain," replied the customs official;

---

* [A department of southwestern France along the estuary of the Gironde River, famed for such wines as Médoc, Sauternes, and Graves.—TRANSLATOR.]

"but it is a fact; for all our deputies, cabinet ministers, and journalists agree that the more a nation receives in exchange for a given quantity of its products, the poorer it becomes."

The farmer had to make his bargain with the Belgian. The farmer's daughter got only three-quarters of her trousseau, and these good people are still wondering how it happens that a person is ruined by receiving four parcels of yarn instead of three, and why a person is richer with three dozen towels than with four dozen.

9

An Immense Discovery!

At a time when everyone is trying to find a way of reducing the costs of transportation; when, in order to realize these economies, highways are being graded, rivers are being canalized, steamboats are being improved, and Paris is being connected with all our frontiers by a network of railroads and by atmospheric, hydraulic, pneumatic, electric, and other traction systems; when, in short, I believe that everyone is zealously and sincerely seeking the solution of the problem of *reducing as much as possible the difference between the prices of commodities in the places where they are produced and their prices in the places where they are consumed;* I should consider myself failing in my duty toward my country, toward my age, and toward myself, if I any longer kept secret the wonderful discovery I have just made.

Although the daydreams of inventors have been proverbially optimistic, I feel positively certain that I have discovered an infallible means of bringing to France the products of the whole world, and vice versa, at a considerable reduction in cost.

But its being infallible is only one of the advantages of my astounding discovery.

It requires neither plans nor estimates nor preparatory studies nor engineers nor mechanics nor contractors nor capital nor stockholders nor government aid!

It presents no danger of shipwreck, explosion, collision, fire, or derailment!

It can be put into effect in a single day!

Finally, and this will doubtless recommend it to the public, it will not add a centime to the budget; quite the contrary. It will not increase the staff of government officials or the requirements of the bureaucracy; quite the contrary. It will cost no one his freedom; quite the contrary.

It was not chance, but observation, that put me in possession of my discovery. Let me tell you how I was led to make it.

I had this question to resolve:

"Why should a thing made in Brussels, for example, cost more when it reaches Paris?"

Now, it did not take me long to perceive that the rise in price results from the existence of *obstacles* of several kinds between Paris and Brussels. First of all, there is the *distance;* we cannot traverse it without effort or loss of time, and we must either submit to this ourselves or pay someone else to submit to it. Then come rivers, marshes, irregularities of terrain, and mud; these are just so many more *impediments* to overcome. We succeed in doing so by raising causeways, by building bridges, by laying and paving roads, by laying steel rails, etc. But all this costs money, and the commodity transported must bear its share of the expenses. There are, besides, highway robbers, necessitating a constabulary, a police force, etc.

Now, among these *obstacles* between Brussels and Paris there is one that we ourselves have set up, and at great cost. There are men lying in wait along the whole length of the frontier, armed to the teeth and charged with the task of putting difficulties in the way of transporting goods from one country to the other. They are called *customs officials.* They act in exactly the same way as the mud and the ruts. They delay and impede commerce; they contribute to the difference that we have noted between the price paid by the consumer and the price received by the producer, a difference that it is our problem to reduce as much as possible.

And herein lies the solution of the problem. Reduce the tariff.

You will then have, in effect, constructed the Northern Railway without its costing you anything. Far from it! You will effect such enormous savings that you will begin to put money in your pocket from the very first day of its operation.

Really, I wonder how we could have ever thought of doing anything so fantastic as to pay many millions of francs for the purpose of removing the *natural obstacles* that stand between France and other countries, and at the same time pay many other millions for the purpose of substituting *artificial obstacles* that have exactly the same effect; so that the obstacle created and the obstacle removed neutralize each other and leave things quite as they were before, the only difference being the double expense of the whole operation.

A Belgian product is worth twenty francs at Brussels, but thirty francs when taken to Paris, because of transportation charges. The same article made in Paris is worth forty francs. How do we handle the problem?

First, we impose a customs duty of at least ten francs on the Belgian product, in order to raise its sales price at Paris to forty francs, and we pay numerous inspectors to see that it does not escape this tariff; with the result that, in transit, it is charged ten francs for transportation and ten francs for the tax.

Having done this, we reason as follows: This transportation charge of ten francs from Brussels to Paris is excessive. Let us spend two or three hundred millions for railroads, and we shall cut it in half. Yet clearly, all that we shall gain is that the Belgian product will be sold in Paris for thirty-five francs, to wit:

20 francs	its price at Brussels
10 francs	customs duty
5 francs	reduced transportation cost by railroad
35 francs	total, or sales price at Paris

Now, should we not have achieved the same result by lowering the tariff to five francs? We should then have:

20 francs	price at Brussels
5 francs	reduced customs duty
10 francs	transportation cost by ordinary routes
35 francs	total, or sales price at Paris

And this proceeding would save us the 200 millions the railroads would cost us, plus the costs of customs inspection, which will necessarily be reduced, since the lower tariff will constitute less of an incentive to smuggle.

But, it will be said, the tariff is necessary to protect Parisian industry. So be it; but do not, then, destroy its effectiveness by your railroad.

For if you persist in demanding that the Belgian product, like that of Paris, cost forty francs, you will have to raise the tariff to fifteen francs, so as to have:

20 francs	price at Brussels
15 francs	protective tariff
5 francs	railroad transportation charges
40 francs	total at equalized prices

But then, I venture to ask, what, in that case, is the good of the railroad?

Frankly, is it not somewhat humiliating for the nineteenth century to provide future ages with the spectacle of such childish behavior carried on with such an air of imperturbable gravity? To be hoodwinked by someone else is not very agreeable; but to use the vast apparatus of representative government to hoodwink ourselves, not just once, but twice over—and that, too, in a little matter of arithmetic—is surely something to temper our pride in being the *century of enlightenment.*

10

Reciprocity

We have just seen that whatever makes transportation more expensive acts in the same way as a protective tariff; or, if you prefer, that a protective tariff acts in the same way as anything that makes transportation more expensive.

It is thus accurate to say that a protective tariff is like a marsh, a rut, a gap in the route, or a steep hill—in a word, it is an *obstacle* whose effect is to increase the difference between the price the producer receives and the price the consumer pays. It is likewise incontestable that marshes and bogs are, in effect, protective tariffs.

There are people (a small number, it is true, but there are some) who are beginning to understand that obstacles are no less obstacles for being artificial, and that we have more to gain from free trade than from a policy of protectionism, for precisely the same reason that a canal is more favorable to traffic than a "hilly, sandy, difficult road."*

But, they say, free trade must be reciprocal. If we lowered the barriers we have erected against the admission of Spanish goods, and if the Spaniards did not lower the barriers they have erected against the admission of ours, we should be victimized. Let us therefore make *commercial treaties* on the basis of exact reciprocity; let us make concessions in return for concessions; let us make the *sacrifice* of buying in order to obtain the advantage of selling.

People who reason in this way, I regret to say, are, whether they

* [This is a partial quotation from La Fontaine's fable, *The Coach and the Fly* (*Le Coche et la mouche*): "Over a sandy, hilly, and difficult road, / Exposed to the sun on all sides / Six strong horses were drawing a coach."—TRANSLATOR.]

realize it or not, protectionists in principle; they are merely a little more inconsistent than the pure protectionists, just as the latter are more inconsistent than the advocates of total and absolute exclusion of all foreign products.

The following fable will demonstrate my point.

Stulta and Puera*

Once upon a time there were, no matter where, two cities, Stulta and Puera. At great expense they built a highway from one to the other. When it was completed, Stulta said to herself: "Here is Puera flooding us with her products; we must do something about it." Consequently, she created and salaried a corps of *Obstructors,* so called because their function was to set up obstacles in the way of traffic from Puera. Soon afterward, Puera also had a corps of *Obstructors.*

At the end of several centuries, during which there had been great advances in knowledge, Puera became sufficiently enlightened to see that these mutual obstacles could only be mutually harmful. She sent a diplomat to Stulta, who, except for official phraseology, spoke in this wise: "First we built a highway, and now we are obstructing it. That is absurd. It would have been better to have left things as they were. We should not, in that case, have had to pay, first for the highway, and then for the obstructions. In the name of Puera, I come to propose to you, not that we remove all at once the obstacles we have erected against each other —for that would be acting in accordance with a principle, and we despise principles as much as you do—but that we lessen these obstacles a little, taking care to balance equitably our respective *sacrifices* in this regard."

Thus spoke the diplomat. Stulta asked for time to consider the proposal. She consulted by turns her manufacturers and her farmers. Finally, after several years, she declared that she was breaking off the negotiations.

On receiving this news, the inhabitants of Puera held a meeting. An old man (it has always been suspected that he was secretly in

* [These names contain the roots of the Latin words meaning "foolish" and "childish."—TRANSLATOR.]

the pay of Stulta) rose and said: "The obstacles created by Stulta are a hindrance to the sale of our goods to her. That is a misfortune. Those that we ourselves have created are a hindrance to our purchases from her. That too is a misfortune. There is nothing we can do about the first situation, but we can do something about the second. Let us deliver ourselves at least from that one, since we cannot eliminate them both. Let us remove our *Obstructors* without demanding that Stulta do the same. Some day, no doubt, she will come to know her own interests better."

A second councillor, a practical man of affairs, undefiled by principles and reared on the venerable experience of his ancestors, replied: "Do not listen to this dreamer, this theorist, this innovator, this utopian, this economist, this *Stultophile*. We should all be lost if the obstacles on the highway between Stulta and Puera were not equalized and kept in perfect balance. It would be more difficult to *go* than to *come,* and to *export* than to *import.* We should be, in relation to Stulta, in the same situation of inferiority in which Le Havre, Nantes, Bordeaux, Lisbon, London, Hamburg, and New Orleans find themselves in relation to the cities located at the headwaters of the Seine, the Loire, the Garonne, the Tagus, the Thames, the Elbe, and the Mississippi; for it is more difficult to go upstream than downstream."

A voice: "The cities at the mouths of rivers have prospered more than those at the headwaters."

"That is impossible."

Same voice: "But it is a fact."

"Very well, then they have prospered *against the rules.*"

Reasoning so conclusive convinced the assembly. The orator followed up his victory by speaking of national independence, national honor, national dignity, domestic industry, inundation by foreign products, tribute paid to foreigners, and murderous competition; in short, his motion in favor of the maintenance of obstacles was carried; and if you are at all curious about the matter, I can take you into a certain country where you will see with your own eyes highway maintenance men and obstructors working side by side in the most friendly way in the world, under laws enacted by the same legislative assembly, and at the expense of the same taxpayers, the former to clear the road, and the latter to block it.

11

Money Prices

Do you wish to decide between free trade and protectionism? Do you wish to appreciate the significance of an economic phenomenon? Inquire into the extent of its effects *upon the abundance or the scarcity of commodities,* and *not upon a rise or a fall in prices.* Beware of thinking in terms of *money prices;* they will only lead you into an inextricable labyrinth.

M. Mathieu de Dombasle,* having proved that a policy of protectionism makes things more expensive, adds:

The increase in price raises the cost of living and *consequently* the price of labor, and everyone receives from the increase in the price of what he sells compensation for the increase in the cost of what he buys. Thus, if everyone pays more as a consumer, everyone also receives more as a producer.

It is clear that one could reverse the argument and say: "If everyone receives more as a producer, everyone pays more as a consumer."

Now, what does this prove? Nothing, except that a policy of protectionism uselessly and unjustly *redistributes* wealth. Plunder does the same thing.

Nevertheless, before we can argue that such an elaborate mechanism has this simple counterbalancing effect, we must accept M. de Dombasle's "consequently" and be sure that the price of

* [Christophe Joseph Alexandre Mathieu de Dombasle (1777–1843), a farmer and agronomist noted for his developments of farm machinery, and the author of various works on taxation setting forth his protectionist ideas.—Translator.]

labor does actually rise with the price of protected commodities. This is a question of fact in regard to which I defer to M. Moreau de Jonnès;* let him be good enough to ascertain whether wage rates have advanced as much as the price of shares in the mines of the Anzin Company. I, for my part, do not think so; for I believe that the price of labor, like all other prices, is governed by the relation between supply and demand. Now, it is clear to me that *restrictive measures* diminish the supply of coal and, as a result, raise its price; but it is not so clear to me that they increase the demand for labor and thereby result in higher wage rates. What renders such consequences unlikely is the fact that the quantity of labor demanded depends on the amount of capital available. Now, protection may well be able to redistribute capital by shifting it from one industry to another, but it cannot increase the total amount of capital by a single centime.

But this question, which is of the greatest interest, will be examined elsewhere. So far as money prices are concerned, I maintain that there are no absurdities that one cannot render plausible by reasoning such as that of M. de Dombasle.

Let us assume that there is an isolated nation, possessing a given quantity of specie, that amuses itself every year by burning half of all the commodities that it produces. I shall undertake to prove, using M. de Dombasle's theory, that it will not as a consequence be any the less rich.

In fact, as a result of the fire, everything that remains will double in price; so that an inventory taken after the disaster will show exactly the same *nominal* value as one taken before. But, in that case, who will have lost? If John buys cloth at a higher price, he also sells his wheat at a higher price; and if Peter loses on the purchase of wheat, he recovers his loss by the sale of his cloth. "Everyone receives from the increase in the price of what he sells [I shall say] compensation for the total increase in the cost of what he buys; and if everyone pays more as a consumer, everyone also receives more as a producer."

* [Alexandre Moreau de Jonnès (1778–1870), a French economist, statistician, and author, Director of the Statistical Bureau in the Ministry of Trade, 1834–1852.— TRANSLATOR.]

All this is sheer rigmarole, and not science. The truth, reduced to its simplest terms, is this: Whether men destroy cloth and wheat by burning them or by using them, the effect *on prices* is the same, but not *on wealth;* for it is precisely the potentiality of using things that constitutes wealth or well-being.

Similarly, restrictive measures, while reducing the abundance of things, can raise their prices to such an extent that, if you will, every person is, *in monetary terms,* just as rich as he was before. Whether an inventory shows three hectoliters of wheat at twenty francs, or four hectoliters at fifteen francs, the result will be sixty francs in either case; but are the two quantities the same from the point of view of their ability to satisfy wants?

This is the point of view of the consumer, and it is the consumer's point of view that I shall never cease calling to the attention of the protectionists; for consumption is the goal of all our efforts, and it is only by adopting the point of view of the consumer that we shall find the solution to all our problems.[1] The argument I address to them will always be the same: Is it not true that restrictive measures, by impeding exchange, by limiting the division of labor, by forcing workers to compensate for hardships due to geographic situation and climatic conditions, ultimately diminish the quantity produced by a given amount of labor? And what difference does it make that the lesser quantity produced under the protective system has the same *nominal value* as the greater quantity produced under conditions of free trade? Man does not live on *nominal values,* but on commodities actually produced; and the more he has of these commodities, regardless of their price, the richer he is.

I did not expect, in writing the foregoing, that I should ever come upon an antieconomist logically consistent enough to conclude explicitly that the wealth of nations depends upon the monetary value of things apart from their abundance. Yet here is what I find in the book of M. de Saint-Chamans* (page 210):

---

* [Auguste, Vicomte de Saint-Chamans (1777–1861), a Deputy and Councillor of State, a protectionist, and a proponent of the balance of trade. The quotation is from his *Du Système impôt fondé sur les principes d'économie politique.*—TRANSLATOR.]

If fifteen million francs' worth of goods sold abroad are taken from the normal production, estimated at fifty million francs, the remaining thirty-five million francs' worth of goods, being no longer capable of satisfying normal demand, will increase in price and rise to the value of fifty million francs. In that case, the income of the country will increase by fifteen million. . . . . There will thus be an increase in the national wealth of fifteen million francs, exactly the amount of the specie imported.

This is a really delightful way of looking at things! If a nation's agriculture and industry produce annually fifty million francs' worth of goods, it has only to sell a quarter of these products abroad to be a fourth richer! Thus, if it sold half of them, it would increase its fortune by half; and if it exchanged for cash its last thread of wool and its last kernel of wheat, it would raise its income to 100 millions! What a singular way of enriching oneself, by producing infinitely high prices by means of absolute scarcity!

Do you still insist on making a comparison between the two doctrines? Submit them to the test of exaggeration.

According to the doctrine of M. de Saint-Chamans, the French would be just as rich—that is to say, as well provided with everything—with a thousandth part of their present annual output, because it would be worth a thousand times as much.

According to our doctrine, the French would be infinitely rich if their annual output were infinitely abundant, and consequently had no monetary value at all.[2]

12

Does Protectionism Raise
Wage Rates?

An atheist was railing against religion, against priests, and against God. "If you keep on like this," said one of his listeners, who was not very orthodox himself, "you are going to make a pious man of me."

Similarly, when I hear our callow scribblers, our novelists, our reformers, our perfumed, mincing pamphleteers, gorged with ices and champagne, stuffing their portfolios with gilt-edged securities,* or getting richly paid for their tirades against the egoism and individualism of our age; when I hear them declaiming against the harshness of our institutions and bewailing the lot of wage earners and proletarians; when I see them raising to the heavens eyes full of tears at the sight of the poverty of the toiling masses—a poverty with which they never have any contact except to paint lucrative pictures of it; I am tempted to tell them: "If you go on like this, you are going to make me indifferent to the fate of the workers."

Oh, what affectation! It is the nauseating malady of our age! Workers, if a serious man, a sincere humanitarian, paints a true picture of your misery, and if his book makes any impression at all, a mob of reformers at once pounces on it. They turn it this

* [Bastiat here refers by name to certain securities that enjoyed wide public confidence at the time: those of the Comptoir Ganneron, a bank in which, at the height of the speculation, almost four hundred million francs were invested; those of the fur-trading company founded by Sir Alexander MacKenzie and later amalgamated with the original Hudson's Bay Company; and those of the Northern Railway of France.—TRANSLATOR.]

way and that; they exploit it; they distort it; they exaggerate it; they carry its ideas to ridiculous or disgusting extremes. They have a remedy for all your woes, and they are always ready to prescribe for you with big words like "association" or "organization"; they flatter you and fawn upon you so obsequiously that soon you will be in the same predicament as the slaves: earnest men will be ashamed to embrace your cause openly, for how can anyone introduce some sensible ideas in the midst of these mawkish declamations?

But I refuse to adopt an attitude of such cowardly indifference, which could not be justified even by the affectation that provokes it.

Workers, yours is a strange situation! People plunder you, as I shall show in a moment. . . . . No; I take back that word. Let us banish from our language every violent and possibly false expression—false, that is, in the sense that plunder, enveloped and disguised by sophisms, is carried on, one is constrained to believe, against the will of the plunderer and with the consent of the plundered. But after all, people do rob you of what is justly due you for your labor, and nobody concerns himself with seeing that you receive justice. Oh, if all you needed to console you was a clamorous appeal for philanthropy, for ineffectual charity, for degrading alms; if only big words—*organization, communism, phalanstery*—were enough, people would not stint themselves on your behalf. But *justice,* pure and simple *justice,* that is something no one dreams of giving you. And yet would it not be *just* if, after a hard day's ill-paid work, you could exchange the little you had received for the greatest amount of satisfaction that you could obtain freely from any man on the face of the earth?

Some day, perhaps, I shall speak to you also about association and organization, and we shall then see what you can expect of these idle fancies that you have allowed to lead you astray.

Meanwhile, let us see whether people are not doing you an *injustice* by passing laws that specify not only the persons from whom you are to buy the things you must have, such as bread, meat, linens, and woolens, but the price you are to pay for them.

Is it true that the policy of protectionism, which admittedly makes you pay higher prices for everything and in that respect harms you, also brings about a proportional increase in your wages?

What do wage rates depend on?

One of your fellow workers has put it very neatly: When two workers run after one employer, wages fall; they rise when two employers run after one worker.

For the sake of brevity, let me state this more scientifically, though perhaps not quite so clearly: Wage rates depend upon the supply of and the demand for labor.

Now, what does the *supply* of workers depend on?

On the number that there are on the market; and protectionism has no control over this.

What does the *demand* for labor depend on?

On the amount of domestic capital available for investment. But does the amount of capital increase because the law says: "People shall no longer get such and such a product from abroad; they shall make it at home"? Not in the least. It may force capital out of one branch of production and into another, but it does not add a centime to the total capital available. Therefore, it does not increase the demand for labor.

People point with pride to a certain factory. Did the capital that established it and that maintains it fall from the moon? No, it had to be withdrawn from agriculture, from shipping, or from wine production. And that is why, since we have had protective tariffs, there have been more workers in our mines and in the suburbs of our industrial cities, but there have been fewer sailors in our ports, and fewer farmers and vineyardists in our fields and on our hillsides.

I could expatiate at length on this subject, but I prefer to elucidate my meaning by way of an example.

A countryman had a farm of twenty arpents,* in which he invested 10,000 francs. He divided his land into four parts and rotated his crops on them in the following order: first, corn; second, wheat; third, clover; fourth, rye. He and his family needed only a very modest share of the grain, meat, and dairy products that the

* [An old French measure of area differing in value according to locality but being about an acre.—TRANSLATOR.]

farm provided, and he sold the surplus to buy oil, flax, wine, etc. The whole of his capital was spent each year on wages and payments to hired hands living in the neighborhood. This investment was recovered in the proceeds from his sales, and his capital even grew from year to year; and our countryman, well aware that money produces nothing unless it is put to work, benefited the working classes by devoting these annual surpluses to fencing off and clearing land and to improving his agricultural implements and buildings. He even had some savings on deposit with the banker in the neighboring town, but the latter did not let these funds lie idle in his vaults; he lent them to shipowners and to entrepreneurs engaged in useful industries, so that the money was constantly being paid out in the form of wages.

In the meantime, the countryman died; and his son, as soon as he came into his inheritance, said to himself: "It must be confessed that my father was victimized all his life. He bought olive oil and thus paid *tribute* to Provence, whereas our land could, in a pinch, be made to grow olive trees. He bought flax, wine, and oranges, and paid *tribute* to Brittany, Médoc, and the Hyères Islands,* whereas hemp, vines, and orange trees could, somehow or other, be made to yield some produce in our own fields. He paid *tribute* to the miller and the weaver, when our servants could easily weave our linen and grind our wheat. He ruined himself, and, besides, he let outsiders earn the wages that it would have been so easy for him to distribute here at home."

Fortified by this logic, the rash young man changed the system of crop rotation on the farm. He divided it into twenty fields. On one he cultivated olive trees; on another, mulberry trees; on a third, flax; on a fourth, grapes; on a fifth, wheat; etc., etc. In this way he succeeded in providing his family with everything they needed and in making himself *independent*. He no longer took anything out of the general circulation of goods, but he no longer put anything into it either. Was he any the richer on that account? No, because his land was unsuited for the cultivation of grapes; the climate was

* [Provence is an old province of southeastern France along the Mediterranean. Médoc is a farming district southwest of the Gironde River. The Hyères Islands are in the Mediterranean off Provence.—TRANSLATOR.]

unfavorable for the successful growing of olive trees; and, in the long run, the family was less well provided with all the things it needed than in the days when the father acquired them by way of exchange.

As for the hired hands, there was no more work for them than before. There were, to be sure, five times as many fields to cultivate, but they were only one-fifth as large; the farm produced olive oil, but less wheat was raised on it; the farmer no longer bought flax, but he no longer sold rye. Moreover, he could pay out in wages no more than the amount of his capital; and his capital, far from increasing as a result of the new system of crop rotation, kept on steadily decreasing. A great part of his capital was invested in buildings and the large assortment of agricultural implements necessary for carrying on a complex operation of this kind. As a result, the supply of labor remained the same, but as there was less money to pay the workers with, wages inevitably fell.

This is a picture, on a small scale, of what happens when a country isolates itself behind tariff walls. Granted that it multiplies the number of its industries, it at the same time diminishes their importance. It adopts, so to speak, a system of *industrial rotation* that is more complicated, yet no more fruitful. Indeed, the contrary is the case, since the same amount of capital and labor has to contend with a greater number of natural difficulties. A larger share of its circulating capital, which constitutes the wages fund, must be converted into fixed capital. No matter how varied the employment given to the remainder, its total quantity is not increased, any more than the water of a pond becomes more abundant when it is distributed in a number of reservoirs; precisely because it covers more ground and presents a greater surface to the sun, more water is absorbed, evaporated, and lost.

The productivity of a given quantity of capital and labor is inversely proportional to the obstacles with which both are confronted. It is indubitable that as international barriers force capital and labor in each country into channels where they encounter greater difficulties of climate and temperature, the general result must be a diminution in production, or—what amounts to the same thing—fewer goods capable of satisfying the wants of the consumers.

Now, if there is a general reduction in the quantity of goods capable of satisfying people's wants, how is the share of the workers to be increased? Is it to be supposed that the wealthy, who make the law, will arrange things in such a way that they will not only share proportionately in the total diminution, but will even allow their already diminished share to be reduced still further by all that is added, they say, to the workers' share? This is hardly possible or credible. Such suspect generosity the workers would be wise to reject.[1]

13

Theory and Practice

We advocates of free trade are accused of being theorists, of not taking practice sufficiently into consideration.

"In what a frightfully prejudicial light M. Say* is put," observes M. Ferrier,[1] "by that long line of distinguished administrators and that imposing band of writers who disagreed with his views! And M. Say was not unaware of it. Let us see how he deals with it:

"People have asserted, in support of long-standing errors, that there must really be some truth in ideas so generally accepted in all countries. Should we not mistrust observations and conclusions that run counter to opinions that up to our own day have been held to be well-founded, and that have been regarded as certain by so many persons who are esteemed for their knowledge and disinterestedness? This argument, I admit, is very plausible and might well cast doubt even on the most indisputable matters, were it not for the fact that the most erroneous opinions—whose falsity is now generally recognized—were successively accepted and propagated by everybody for century after century. It was not very long ago that all nations, from the most barbarous to the most enlightened, and all men, from the lowliest porter to the wisest philosopher, accepted it as true that there are four elements. No one would have dreamed of disputing this doctrine, which, nevertheless, is false; so much so that there is not a naturalist's assistant who would not bring himself into disrepute if he regarded earth, water, and fire as elements."

Upon this, M. Ferrier makes the following observation:

* [Jean-Baptiste Say (1767–1832), a French professor of political economy and a free-trade advocate. His ideas had great influence on Bastiat.—TRANSLATOR.]

If M. Say thinks that this comment constitutes an adequate reply to the very strong objection he raises, he is singularly mistaken. It is understandable that men otherwise very well-informed should have been in error for several centuries concerning some point or other in natural history. This fact, in itself, proves nothing. Whether or not water, air, earth, and fire are elements, they are not less useful to man. Such errors are of no consequence; they do not lead to riots; they do not unsettle men's minds; above all, they do not have an adverse effect on anyone's well-being, and that is why they could endure for thousands of years without occasioning the slightest inconvenience. The physical world goes on as if they did not exist. But can the same be said of errors that attack the moral world? Is it to be supposed that an absolutely wrong, and consequently harmful, system of government could be maintained for several centuries and among many nations with the general approval of all educated men? Can it be explained how such a system could be compatible with the constantly increasing prosperity of these nations? M. Say concedes that the argument he is combatting is very plausible. Indeed it is, and it retains its plausibility, for M. Say has increased rather than destroyed it.

Now let us hear what M. de Saint-Chamans has to say on this subject:

It was not until the middle of the eighteenth century—that age in which no subject or principle was exempt from discussion—that these purveyors of *speculative* ideas, which were applied to everything without being applicable to anything, began writing on political economy. The system of political economy that existed previously was not put in written form, but was *practiced* by governments. Colbert,* it is said, was its inventor, and it was the system that prevailed in all the nations of Europe. What is even more extraordinary, it still does so today, in spite of the abuse and the scorn directed against it, and in spite of all the discoveries made by modern economics. This system, which our authors have called the *mercantilist system,* consisted in . . . . banning,

---

* [Jean-Baptiste Colbert (1619–1683), French statesman, chief economic and financial advisor to King Louis XIV, under whom he served as Controller-General of Finances. He is credited with introducing the mercantilist system in conjunction with the many industries that he promoted.—TRANSLATOR.]

whether by outright exclusion or by the imposition of customs duties, foreign products that could destroy our industries by their competition. . . . . Economists of all schools have pronounced this system inept, absurd, and likely to impoverish the whole country;[2] it has been banished from all their books and forced to take refuge in the *practice* of every nation; and they cannot conceive why, in what concerns the wealth of nations, governments should not rely upon the advice of learned authors rather than trust to their *long experience* with a system, etc. . . . . Above all, they cannot understand why the French government should, ... in matters of political economy, go on obstinately resisting the advance of knowledge and retaining in its *practice* those inveterate errors which all our writers on economics have exposed. . . . . But enough of this mercantilist system, which has nothing in its favor *but the facts,* and which is not defended by any writer![3]

Words such as these might lead one to suppose that the economists, in demanding for everyone the *freedom to dispose of his property,* have, like the Fourierists, excogitated a new social order, visionary and bizarre—a sort of phalanstery without precedent in the annals of the human race. Yet it seems to me that if anything is contrived or contingent, it is not free trade, but protectionism; it is not the freedom to engage in voluntary exchange, but the use of the tariff to upset artificially the natural order in the pricing process.

However, our concern here is not to compare or evaluate the two systems, but to inquire which of the two is based on experience.

Now, in regard to this question, which is all that interests us for the moment, you advocates of monopoly contend that the *facts* are on your side, and that we have only *theories* on ours.

You even flatter yourselves that the long series of governmental actions, the *long* experience of Europe, which you invoke, has seemed to M. Say to carry a certain weight; and I concede that he has not refuted you protectionists on this point with his customary acumen. But I do not concede your claim that the *facts* are in your favor; for the only facts on your side are isolated cases resulting from the exercise of compulsion, whereas on our side we have the universal practice of mankind, the free and voluntary actions of all men.

What do we say, and what do you say?

We say:

"It is better to buy from another what it would be more costly to make oneself."

And you say:

"It is better to make things oneself, even if it would be less expensive to buy them from another."

Now, gentlemen, setting aside theory, demonstration, and reasoning, all of which seem to fill you protectionists with disgust, which of these two assertions enjoys the sanction of *universal practice?*

Visit fields, workshops, mills, and stores; look around you everywhere; examine what is done in your own household; observe your own actions at every moment; and then say which principle it is that guides these farmers, workers, industrialists, and merchants, not to mention your own personal *practice.*

Does the farmer make his own clothes? Does the tailor raise the wheat that he consumes? Does your housekeeper continue to bake bread at home when she finds she can buy it more cheaply at the bakery? Do you propose to give up the pen for the shoebrush in order to avoid paying *tribute* to the bootblack? Does not the whole economy of society depend on the division of labor, i.e., on *exchange?* And what is exchange but the calculation that induces us, so far as possible, to discontinue direct production whenever indirect acquisition enables us to effect a saving in time and effort?

It is not you, therefore, who are the *practical* men, for you could not point to a single person on the face of the earth who acts according to your principle.

But, you may say, we never intended to make our principle a guide for individual relations. We fully understand that this would be to break the bonds of society and to force men to live like snails, each in his own shell. We mean only that this is the prevailing *practice* in the relations that have been established among different groups of men.

Well, this assertion too is erroneous. The family, the commune,

the canton,* the department, the province, are just so many groups
that all, without any exception, reject your principle *in practice*
and have never even dreamed of acting on it. All procure for themselves by way of exchange whatever it would cost them more to
procure by way of direct production. And nations would do the
same if you did not prevent them by *force.*

It is therefore we who are the practical men; we are the ones
who base our principles on experience; for, in order to oppose the
restrictions that you have chosen to place upon a certain part of
international trade, we base our argument on the practice and experience of every individual and every group of individuals whose
acts are voluntary and can therefore be adduced as evidence. You,
on the other hand, begin by *coercing* or by *impeding*, and then
you seize upon *forced* or *prohibited* acts to support your case: "See;
practice proves us in the right!"

You inveigh against our *theory*, and even against *theory* in general. But, when you put forward a principle antagonistic to ours,
did you perchance imagine that you were not framing a *theory?*
Disabuse yourselves, gentlemen. You are theorists no less than we;
but between your theory and ours there is this difference:

Our theory consists only in observing universal *facts*, universal
attitudes, calculations, and procedures, and at most in classifying
and co-ordinating them so as to understand them better.

Our theory is so little opposed to practice that it is nothing else
than *practice explained*. We observe that men are motivated by
the instinct for self-preservation and a desire for progress, and
what they do freely and voluntarily is precisely what we call
political economy or the economy of society. As we never cease to
point out, each man is *in practice* an excellent economist, producing or exchanging according as he finds it more advantageous to
do the one or the other. Everyone gains a knowledge of this science
through experience; or rather, the science itself is only this same
experience accurately observed and methodically interpreted.

You, on the other hand, may properly be called *theorists* in the
pejorative sense of the word. The procedures you invent are not

* [An administrative unit in France, between the commune and the department.—
Translator.]

sanctioned by the practice of any man on earth, and so you find it necessary to resort to coercion in order to *compel* men to produce what they find it *more advantageous* to purchase. What you want is that they should renounce this *advantage* and act in accordance with a doctrine that is essentially self-contradictory.

I defy you to extend this doctrine, which you yourselves must admit would be absurd if applied to the relations among individuals, to transactions among families, communities, or provinces. By your own admission, it is applicable only to international relations.

And that is why you are reduced to repeating every day:

"There are no absolute principles. What is *good* for an individual, a family, a commune, or a province is *bad* for a nation. What is *good* on a small scale—to purchase rather than to produce, when purchasing is more advantageous than producing—is *bad* on a large scale; the political economy of individuals is not that of nations," and other nonsense of the same kind.

And what purpose does it all serve? Face up to it frankly. You want to prove that we consumers are your property! That we belong to you, body and soul! That you have an exclusive right over our stomachs and our limbs! That it is your prerogative to feed and clothe us at your price, whatever may be your incapacity, your greed, or the economic disadvantages of your situation!

No, you are not practical men; you are impractical visionaries—and extortionists.[4]

14

Conflict of Principles

One thing that confuses me is this:

Sincere political theorists, after studying economic problems solely from the producers' point of view, arrive at the following two conclusions:

"Governments should compel the consumers who are subject to their laws to do what is beneficial for domestic industry.

"Governments should make foreign consumers subject to their laws in order to compel them to do what is beneficial for domestic industry."

The first of these policies is called *protectionism;* the second, *opening up markets* for our products.

The premise on which both are based is what is called the *balance of trade:*

"A nation impoverishes itself when it imports, and enriches itself when it exports."

For, if every purchase from abroad is a *tribute paid* and a national loss, it is quite natural to restrict, and even to prohibit, imports.

And if every sale to a foreign country is a *tribute received* and a national profit, it is quite natural to *open up markets* for our products, even by force.

The *protectionist system* and the *colonial system* are, then, simply two aspects of one and the same theory. *Preventing* our fellow citizens from buying from foreigners and *forcing* foreigners to buy from our fellow citizens are simply two consequences of one and the same principle.

Now, it is impossible not to recognize that, according to this doctrine—if it is true—the general welfare depends upon *monopoly,* or domestic plunder, and *conquest,* or foreign plunder.

I enter one of the cottages that cling to the French side of the Pyrenees.

The head of the family receives only a slender wage for his work. His half-naked children shiver in the icy north wind; the fire is out, and there is nothing on the table. On the other side of the mountain there are wool, firewood, and corn; but these goods are forbidden to the family of the poor day-laborer, for the other side of the mountain is not in France. Foreign spruce will not gladden the cottage hearth; the shepherd's children will not know the taste of Biscayan maslin;* and wool from Navarre will never warm their numbed limbs. All this is, we are told, in the interest of the general welfare. Very well. But then it must be admitted that in this instance the general welfare is in conflict with justice.

To regulate consumers by law and limit them to the products of domestic industry is to encroach upon their freedom by forbidding them an action—exchange—that in itself is in no way contrary to morality; in short, it is to do them an *injustice.*

And yet, we are told, this is necessary if production is to be maintained and the prosperity of the country is not to receive a fatal blow.

The writers of the protectionist school thus reach the melancholy conclusion that there is a radical incompatibility between justice and the general welfare.

On the other hand, if it is in the interest of all nations to *sell* and not to *buy,* a succession of violent actions and reactions must be the natural state of their relations; for each will strive to impose its products on all, and all will attempt to reject the products of each.

In reality, a sale implies a purchase; and since, according to this doctrine, to sell is to profit, and to buy is to lose, every interna-

---

* [In French, *la méture,* a rather rare dialect word. Maslin is a mixture of different kinds of grain, usually wheat and rye, or a bread baked from such a mixture. Biscay and Navarre are provinces of Spain just across the Pyrenees from France.— TRANSLATOR.]

tional transaction is to the advantage of one country and to the detriment of another.

But, on the one hand, men are irresistibly impelled toward what benefits them; on the other hand, they instinctively resist what harms them. Hence, the conclusion is inescapable that each nation contains within itself a natural tendency toward expansion and a no less natural tendency to resist encroachment on its own domain, and that both these tendencies are equally harmful to all other nations; or, in other words, that antagonism and war are the *natural* state of human society.

Thus, the theory that I am discussing may be summed up in these two axioms:

The general welfare is incompatible with justice at home.

The general welfare is incompatible with peace abroad.

Now, what astonishes me, what amazes me, is that a political theorist or a statesman who sincerely professes an economic doctrine whose basic principle runs so violently counter to other principles that are indisputable, can enjoy a moment's calm or peace of mind.

For my own part, I think that if my study of the science of economics had led me to such conclusions, if I did not clearly perceive that freedom, the general welfare, justice, and peace are not only compatible but also closely connected and, so to speak, identical, I should endeavor to forget all I had learned; and I should ask myself:

"How could God have willed that men should attain prosperity only through injustice and war? How could He have willed that they should renounce war and injustice only at the price of their well-being?

"Is this science not misleading me when it requires me to accept the frightful blasphemy that this dilemma implies? How can I dare take it upon myself to make such a doctrine the basis of the laws of a great nation? And when a long succession of illustrious scholars has drawn more reassuring conclusions from the same science after devoting their entire lives to its study; when they assert that freedom and the general welfare are perfectly compatible with justice and peace, and that all these great principles run parallel to one another and will do so through all eternity without ever coming into conflict, do they not have on their side the presumption that stems from all that we know of the goodness and wisdom of God, as manifested in the sublime harmony of the physical universe? In the face of such a presumption and so many impressive authorities, am I, after a merely cursory investigation, to believe that this same God saw fit to introduce antagonism and discord into the laws of the moral universe? No; before concluding that all the principles of social order run counter to and neutralize one another and are in anarchic, eternal, and irreconcilable conflict; before imposing on my fellow citizens the impious system to which my reasoning has led me; I intend to review every step in the argument and make sure that there is not some point along the route where I have gone astray."

If, after an unprejudiced investigation, repeated twenty times over, I always arrived at the appalling conclusion that one must choose between material goods and the moral good, I should be so disheartened that I should reject this science, I should bury myself in voluntary ignorance, and, above all, I should decline to participate in any way in public affairs, leaving to men of another character the burden of, and the responsibility for, so painful a choice.[1]

15

Reciprocity Again

M. de Saint-Cricq inquires: "Are we sure that foreigners will buy from us as much as they sell to us?"

M. de Dombasle would like to know: "What reason have we to believe that English producers will look to our country, rather than to any other, for the products they may need, or that the value of what they import from us will equal that of their exports to us?"

I marvel how men who call themselves *practical* above everything else can employ reasoning so completely divorced from all practice!

In practice, is there one exchange in a hundred, in a thousand, in possibly even ten thousand, that involves the direct barter of one product for another? Ever since there has been money in the world, has any farmer said to himself: "I wish to purchase shoes, hats, counsel, and lessons only from the shoemaker, the hatter, the lawyer, or the teacher who will buy my wheat from me for exactly the equivalent value"? Why, then, should nations impose such an inconvenience upon themselves?

How is business actually transacted?

Suppose that a nation does not trade with the rest of the world, and that one of its inhabitants has produced some wheat. He sells it in the *domestic* market at the highest price he can get, and in exchange he receives . . . . what? Money, that is, warrants or drafts that are infinitely divisible, by means of which he may lawfully withdraw from the supply of domestic goods, whenever he deems it opportune, and subject to due competition, as much as he may need or want. Ultimately, at the end of the entire operation, he will have withdrawn from the total precisely the equivalent of what he put into it, and, in value, *his consumption will exactly equal his production.*

If the exchanges of this nation with the outside world are free, it is no longer the *domestic* market, but the *general* or world market, to which each individual sends his products and from which each withdraws the means of satisfying his wants and needs. It is no concern of his whether what he sends to the market is purchased by a fellow countryman or by a foreigner; whether the money he receives comes to him from a Frenchman or an Englishman; whether the commodities for which he afterwards exchanges this money in order to satisfy his needs were produced on this or the other side of the Rhine or the Pyrenees. For each individual there is always an exact balance between what he puts into and what he withdraws from the great common reservoir; and if this is true of each individual, it is true of the nation as a whole.

The sole difference between the two cases is that in the latter each unit has a wider market in which to buy and sell, and it consequently has more opportunities for carrying on both operations advantageously.

But, it may be objected, if everyone agrees not to buy the products of a given individual when they are brought to market, he cannot, in his turn, buy anything from anyone else. The same is true of nations.

The reply to this is that, if a nation cannot buy anything from any other nation, it will no longer sell anything on the world market; it will work for itself. It will be forced in that case to submit to what you want to impose on it from the outset, i.e., *isolation.*

And this will realize the ideal of the protectionist system.

Is it not ridiculous that you are now inflicting such a system upon the nation for fear that we might otherwise run the risk of coming to it some day without your interference?

16

Obstructed Rivers as Advocates for the Protectionists

Some years ago I was in Madrid, where I attended a session of the Cortes.* The subject under discussion was a treaty with Portugal for improving navigation on the Douro.† One of the deputies rose and said: "If the Douro is canalized, shipping rates for cargoes traveling on it will be reduced. Portuguese grain will consequently sell at a lower price in the markets of Castile and will provide formidable competition for our *domestic industry.* I oppose the project, unless our cabinet ministers agree to raise the customs duty so as to redress the balance." The assembly found this argument unanswerable.

Three months later I was in Lisbon. The same question was up for discussion in the Senate. A great hidalgo‡ said: "Mr. President, the project is absurd. At great cost you have set guards along the banks of the Douro to prevent an invasion of Portugal by Castilian grain, and at the same time you propose, again at great cost, to facilitate that invasion. It is an inconsistency to which I cannot assent. Let us leave the Douro to our children in just the same condition as our forefathers left it to us."

Later, when the question of improving the Garonne was being discussed, I remembered the arguments of these Iberian orators,

* [The Spanish legislature.—TRANSLATOR.]
† [A river rising in Spain and flowing through Portugal into the Atlantic.—TRANSLATOR.]
‡ [A member of the inferior nobility.—TRANSLATOR.]

and I said to myself: If the deputies from Toulouse were as good economists as those from Palencia, and the representatives from Bordeaux as skillful logicians as those from Oporto,* certainly they would leave the Garonne

To drowse in the soothing murmur of its overflowing wave.†

For the canalization of the Garonne would favor, to the injury of Bordeaux, its *invasion* by products from Toulouse, and, to the detriment of Toulouse, its *inundation* by products from Bordeaux.

---

* [Toulouse is a French city on the Garonne well upstream from Bordeaux. Palencia is a Spanish city on a tributary of the Douro; and Oporto, a Portuguese city at the mouth of the Douro.—TRANSLATOR.]

† [A modified version of the personification of the Rhine in the *Fourth Epistle* of the French poet Nicolas Boileau-Despréaux (1636–1711).—TRANSLATOR.]

17

A Negative Railroad

I have said that as long as one has regard, as unfortunately happens, only to the interest of the producer, it is impossible to avoid running counter to the general interest, since the producer, as such, demands nothing but the multiplication of obstacles, wants, and efforts.

I find a remarkable illustration of this in a Bordeaux newspaper.

M. Simiot* raises the following question:

Should there be a break in the tracks at Bordeaux on the railroad from Paris to Spain?

He answers the question in the affirmative and offers a number of reasons, of which I propose to examine only this:

There should be a break in the railroad from Paris to Bayonne at Bordeaux; for, if goods and passengers are forced to stop at that city, this will be profitable for boatmen, porters, owners of hotels, etc.

Here again we see clearly how the interests of those who perform services are given priority over the interests of the consumers.

But if Bordeaux has a right to profit from a break in the tracks, and if this profit is consistent with the public interest, then Angoulême, Poitiers, Tours, Orléans, and, in fact, all the intermediate points, including Ruffec, Châtellerault, etc., etc., ought also to demand breaks in the tracks, on the ground of the general interest —in the interest, that is, of domestic industry—for the more there

* [Alexandre Étienne Simiot, author of *Gare du chemin de fer de Paris à Bordeaux* (Bordeaux: Durand, 1846), and subsequently representative of the Gironde in the Constituent Assembly.—TRANSLATOR.]

are of these breaks in the line, the greater will be the amount paid for storage, porters, and cartage at every point along the way. By this means, we shall end by having a railroad composed of a whole series of breaks in the tracks, i.e., a *negative railroad*.

Whatever the protectionists may say, it is no less certain that the *basic principle of restriction* is the same as the *basic principle of breaks in the tracks:* the sacrifice of the consumer to the producer, of the end to the means.

18

There Are No Absolute Principles

We cannot but be astonished at the ease with which men resign themselves to ignorance about what it is most important for them to know; and we may be certain that they are determined to remain invincibly ignorant if they once come to consider it as axiomatic that there are no absolute principles.

Attend a session of the legislature and listen to a debate over the question whether the law should prohibit international exchange or permit free trade.

A deputy rises and says:

"If you permit these exchanges, foreigners will flood you with their goods—the English with textiles, the Belgians with coal, the Spanish with woolens, the Italians with silks, the Swiss with cattle, the Swedes with iron, and the Prussians with wheat, so that no industry will any longer be possible in our country."

Another replies:

"If you prohibit these exchanges, you will not be able to share in the various bounties that Nature has lavished on different countries. You will not share in the mechanical skill of the English, the wealth of the Belgian mines, the fertility of the Polish soil, the fruitfulness of Swiss pastures, the low cost of Spanish labor, or the warmth of the Italian climate; and you will have to produce for yourselves under adverse conditions what you could have obtained, by exchange, on easier terms."

One of these deputies must certainly be mistaken. But which one? It is worth the trouble to find out, for this is not a merely academic question. You stand at a crossroads; you must decide which direction to take; and one of them leads inescapably to *poverty*.

To avoid the dilemma, people say that there are no absolute principles.

This axiom, which is so fashionable nowadays, not only encourages indolence, but also ministers to ambition.

Whichever theory, protectionism or the doctrine of free trade, should come to prevail, our entire economic code would, in either case, be comprised in one very brief law. In the first case, it would declare: *All exchanges with foreign countries are prohibited;* in the second: *All exchanges with foreign countries are permitted,* and many distinguished personages would lose some of their importance.

But if exchange has no peculiar character of its own; if it is governed by no natural law; if it is sometimes beneficial and sometimes injurious; if its incentive is not to be found in the good that it does, and its limit in the good that it ceases to do; if its effects are beyond the comprehension of those who engage in it; in a word, if there are no absolute principles, then we must weigh, balance, and regulate every transaction, we must equalize the conditions of production and strive to keep profits at an average level— a colossal task well calculated to provide those who undertake it with big salaries and to invest them with great authority.

On coming to Paris for a visit, I said to myself: Here are a million human beings who would all die in a few days if supplies of all sorts did not flow into this great metropolis. It staggers the imagination to try to comprehend the vast multiplicity of objects that must pass through its gates tomorrow, if its inhabitants are to be preserved from the horrors of famine, insurrection, and pillage. And yet all are sleeping peacefully at this moment, without being disturbed for a single instant by the idea of so frightful a prospect. On the other hand, eighty departments have worked today, without co-operative planning or mutual arrangements, to keep Paris supplied. How does each succeeding day manage to bring to this gigantic market just what is necessary—neither too much nor too little? What, then, is the resourceful and secret power that governs the amazing regularity of such complicated movements, a regularity in which everyone has such implicit faith, although his prosperity and his very life depend upon it? That power is an *absolute principle,* the principle of free exchange. We put our faith in that inner light which Providence has placed in the hearts of all men, and to which has been entrusted the preservation and the unlimited improvement of our species, a light we term *self-interest,* which is so illuminating, so constant, and so penetrating, when it is left free of every hindrance. Where would you be, inhabitants of Paris, if some cabinet minister decided to substitute for that power contrivances of his own invention, however superior we might suppose them to be; if he proposed to subject this prodigious mechanism to his supreme direction, to take control of all of it into his own hands, to determine by whom, where, how, and under what conditions everything should be produced, transported, exchanged, and consumed? Although there may be much suffering within your walls, although misery, despair, and perhaps starvation, cause more tears to flow than your warm-hearted charity can wipe away, it is probable, I dare say it is certain, that the arbitrary intervention of the government would infinitely multiply this suffering and spread among all of you the ills that now affect only a small number of your fellow citizens.

If we all have faith in this principle where our domestic transactions are concerned, why should we not have faith in the same principle when it affects our international transactions, which are certainly less numerous, less delicate, and less complicated? And if there is no need for the local government of Paris to regulate our industries, to balance our opportunities, our profits, and our losses, to concern itself with the draining off of our currency, or to equalize the conditions of production in our domestic commerce, why should it be necessary for the customhouse to depart from its fiscal duties and to undertake to exercise a protective function over our foreign commerce?[1]

19

National Independence

Among the arguments that have been advanced in favor of the protectionist system, we must not forget the one that is founded on the idea of *national independence.*

"What shall we do in case of war," people ask, "if we have put ourselves at the mercy of England for iron and coal?"

The English monopolists for their part do not fail to exclaim:

"What will happen to Great Britain in time of war if she makes herself dependent on France for food?"

The one thing that people overlook is that the sort of dependence that results from exchange, i.e., from commercial transactions, is a *reciprocal* dependence. We cannot be dependent upon a foreigner without his being dependent upon us. Now, this is what constitutes the very essence of *society.* To sever natural interrelations is not to make oneself independent, but to isolate oneself completely.

And observe, too, that one isolates oneself in anticipation of war, but that the very act of isolating oneself is a beginning of war. It makes war easier to wage, less burdensome, and consequently less unpopular. If nations remain permanently in the world market; if their interrelations cannot be broken without their peoples' suffering the double discomfort of privation and glut; they will no longer need the mighty navies that bankrupt them or the vast armies that weigh them down; the peace of the world will not be jeopardized by the caprice of a Thiers or a Palmerston;* and war will disappear for lack of materials, resources, motives, pretexts, and popular support.

* [Louis Adolphe Thiers (1797–1877), French statesman and historian, opponent of free trade and, in Bastiat's time, advocate of an aggressively anti-English policy

I am well aware that I shall be reproached (it is the fashion nowadays) for basing the brotherhood of nations on anything so mean and prosaic as self-interest. There are those who would prefer it to have its roots in charity, in love, even in a little self-denial, and, by impairing somewhat men's material well-being, to have the merit of a generous sacrifice.

When shall we ever have done with these childish declamations? When shall we finally rid science of cant? When shall we cease interposing this nauseating inconsistency between what we preach and what we practice? We deride and revile *self-interest*—that is to say, we execrate what is useful and good (for to say that something is in the interest of all nations is to say that it is good in itself), as if self-interest were not the necessary, eternal, and indestructible motive force to which Providence has entrusted the improvement of mankind. Are we not all being represented as angels of disinterestedness? And is not the public surely beginning to see with disgust that this affected language disfigures the pages of the very writers that are most highly paid? Oh, affectation, thou art truly the canker of our times!

What! Because well-being and peace are correlative, because it has pleased God to establish this beautiful harmony in the moral sphere, am I not to admire and adore His decrees and to accept gratefully laws that make justice the necessary condition of happiness? You want peace only in so far as it conflicts with well-being, and free trade is burdensome to you because, you say, it imposes no sacrifices on you. But if you find self-sacrifice so attractive, what prevents you from practicing it in your private affairs? Society will be grateful to you for it, since at least someone will reap its fruits; but to seek to impose it upon mankind as a principle is the height of absurdity, because self-sacrifice by everyone means the sacrifice of everyone; it is evil elevated to the dignity of a moral theory.

But, thank heaven, a great deal of this bombast can be written and read without the world's ceasing on that account to be im-

for France. Henry John Temple, Viscount Palmerston (1784–1865), British statesman, Foreign Secretary when *Economic Sophisms* was written, and an opponent of France.—TRANSLATOR.]

pelled by its natural motive force, which is, whether one likes it or not, *self-interest.*

It is, after all, rather strange to see sentiments of the most lofty self-denial invoked in support of plunder itself. For that, in the end, is what all this ostentatious disinterestedness comes to. These men, so delicately fastidious that they do not want peace itself if it is based on the mean *self-interest* of mankind, are not averse to putting their hands into someone else's pocket, especially that of the poor; for what article in the tariff law protects the poor? Gentlemen, do as you like with your own property, but allow us to do likewise with the fruits of our toil, to use them or to exchange them as we wish. Declaim as much as you like on the virtue of self-renunciation; that is all very fine and noble; but at the same time, at least be honest.[1]

20

Human vs. Mechanical Labor and Domestic vs. Foreign Labor

Destroying machinery and interdicting the entry of foreign goods are alike in being both founded on the same doctrine.

Those who at the same time applaud the appearance of a great invention and nevertheless advocate protectionism are most inconsistent.

What is their objection to free trade? They charge it with encouraging foreigners who are more skillful than we are, or who live under more advantageous economic conditions than we do, to produce things that, in the absence of free trade, we should produce ourselves. In short, they accuse it of injuring *domestic labor*.

But then, should they not, for the same reason object to machinery of every kind, since, in enabling us to accomplish, by means of physical instruments, what, in their absence, we should have to do with our bare hands, it necessarily hurts *human labor?*

In effect, is not the foreign worker who lives under more advantageous economic conditions than the French worker a veritable *economic machine* that crushes him by its competition? And, in like manner, is not a machine that performs a particular operation at lower cost than a certain number of workers a veritable *foreign competitor* that hamstrings them by its rivalry?

If, therefore, it is expedient to protect *domestic labor* from the competition of *foreign labor*, it is no less expedient to protect *human labor* from the competition of *mechanical labor*.

Therefore, whoever supports the protectionist system, should, in all consistency, not stop at interdicting the entry of foreign products; he should also outlaw the products of the shuttle and the plow.

And that is why I much prefer the logic of those who, in denouncing the *invasion* of foreign goods, have at least the courage to denounce also the *overproduction* due to the inventive power of the human mind.

Such a one is M. de Saint-Chamans. "One of the strongest arguments against free trade and the excessive use of machinery," he says, "is that many workingmen are deprived of employment, either by foreign competition, which depresses manufacturing, or by the machines that take the place of men in the workshops."[1]

M. de Saint-Chamans has grasped perfectly the analogy—or, rather, the identity—that exists between *imports* and *machines;* that is why he outlaws both of them. It is indeed a pleasure to deal with those who are consistent in their reasoning, for even when they are in error, they boldly carry their argument to its logical conclusion.

But just see the difficulty that is waiting for them!

If it is true, a priori, that the domain of *invention* and that of *labor* cannot expand save at each other's expense, then it must be in the places where there are the most *machines*—in Lancashire, for example—that one should expect to find the fewest *workers.* And if, on the contrary, it is proved that *in fact* machinery and manual labor coexist to a greater degree among rich nations than among savages, the conclusion is inevitable that these two types of production are not mutually exclusive.

I cannot understand how any thinking being can enjoy a moment's rest in the face of the following dilemma:

Either man's inventions do not lessen his opportunities for employment, as the facts in general attest, since there are more of both among the English and the French than among the Hurons and the Cherokees; and, in that case, I am on the wrong track, though I know neither where nor when I lost my way. I should be committing the crime of treason to humanity if I were to introduce my mistake into the legislation of my country.

Or else, the discoveries of the human mind do limit the opportunities for the employment of manual labor, as certain facts would seem to indicate, since every day I see some machine replacing twenty or a hundred workers; and then I am obliged to acknowledge the existence of a flagrant, eternal, and irremediable antithesis between man's intellectual and his physical capacities—between his progress and his well-being—and I am forced to conclude that the Creator should have endowed man either with reason or with physical strength, either with force of character or with brute force, but that He mocked him by endowing him at the same time with faculties that are mutually destructive.

The problem is an urgent one. But do you know how we extricate ourselves from the dilemma? By means of this remarkable maxim:

In political economy, there are no absolute principles.

In plain and simple language, this means:

"I do not know which is true and which is false; I have no idea what constitutes general good or evil. I do not trouble myself about such questions. The immediate effect of each law on my personal well-being is the only principle that I consent to recognize."

There are no absolute principles! You might as well say there are no facts; for principles are only formulas that summarize a whole array of facts that have been fully established.

Machines and imports certainly do have some effects. These effects may be either good or bad. On this point there may well be differences of opinion. But, whichever position one adopts, it is expressed by one of these two *principles:* Machinery is a good; or, machinery is an evil. Imports are beneficial; or, imports are injurious. But to say that there are no principles, is certainly to exhibit the lowest depth to which the human mind can descend; and I confess that I blush for my country when I hear so monstrous a heresy expressed in the presence of the members of the French legislature, with their approval, that is, in the presence and with the approval of the elite of our fellow citizens; and this in order to justify their imposing laws upon us in utter ignorance of their consequences.

But, I may be reminded, all this does not constitute a refutation of the *sophism.* It still has to be proved that machines do not injure *human labor,* and that imports do not injure *domestic labor.*

In a work of this kind, such demonstrations cannot be really exhaustive. My purpose is rather to state difficulties than to resolve them, and to stimulate reflection rather than to satisfy the thirst for knowledge. The mind never fully accepts any convictions that it does not owe to its own efforts. I shall try, nevertheless, to put the reader on the right track.

The mistake made by the opponents of imports and machinery is in evaluating them according to their immediate and temporary effects instead of following them out to their general and ultimate consequences.

The immediate effect of an ingenious machine is to make a certain quantity of manual labor superfluous for the attainment of a given result. But its action does not stop there. Precisely because this result is obtained with less effort, its product is made available to the public at a lower price; and the total savings thus realized by all purchasers enables them to satisfy other wants, that is, to encourage manual labor in general to exactly the same extent that it was saved in the particular branch of industry that was recently mechanized. The result is that the level of employment does not fall, even though the quantity of consumers' goods has increased.

Let us give a concrete example of this whole chain of effects.

Suppose that the French people buy ten million hats at fifteen francs each; this gives the hatmaking industry an income of 150 million francs. Someone invents a machine that permits the sale of hats at ten francs. The income of this industry is reduced to 100 million francs, provided that the demand for hats does not increase. But the other fifty million francs are certainly not for that reason withdrawn from the support of *human labor.* Since this sum has been saved by the purchasers of hats, it will enable them to satisfy other wants and consequently to spend an equivalent amount for goods and services of every kind. With these five francs saved, John will buy a pair of shoes; James, a book; Jerome, a piece of furniture, etc. Human labor, taken as a whole, will thus continue to be supported to the extent of 150 million francs; but this sum will provide the same number of hats as before, and, in addition, satisfy other needs and wants to the extent of the fifty million francs that the machine will have saved. These additional goods are the net gain that France will have derived from the invention. It is a gratuitous gift, a tribute that man's genius will have exacted from Nature. We do not deny that in the course of the transformation a certain amount of labor will have been *displaced;* but we cannot agree that it will have been destroyed or even lessened.

The same is true of imports. Let us revert to our hypothesis.

Let us say that France has been making ten million hats whose sales price was fifteen francs. Foreigners invade our market by supplying us with hats at ten francs. I maintain that opportunities for *domestic labor* will in no way be thereby lessened.

For it will have to produce only to the extent of 100 million francs in order to pay for ten million hats at ten francs apiece.

And then, each buyer will have available the five francs saved per hat, or, in all, fifty millions, which will pay for other commodities, that is to say, other kinds of labor.

Therefore, the total of employment will remain what it was, and the additional commodities produced by the fifty millions saved on the hats will comprise the net profit from imports under a system of free trade.

And people should not try to frighten us with a picture of the sufferings that, on this hypothesis, the displacement of labor would involve.

For, if the restrictive measures had never been imposed, labor on its own initiative would have allocated itself in accordance with the law of supply and demand so as to achieve the highest ratio of result to effort, and no displacement would have occurred.

If, on the contrary, restrictive measures have led to an artificial and unproductive allocation of labor, then they, and not free trade, are responsible for the inevitable displacement during the transition from a poor to a good allocation.

At least let no one argue that, because an abuse cannot be suppressed without injuring those who profit from it, the fact that it has existed for a time gives it the right to last forever.

21

Raw Materials

It is said that the most advantageous of all branches of trade is that in which one exchanges manufactured goods for raw materials. For these raw materials are the staff of life for *domestic labor.*

Hence, the conclusion is drawn that the best tariff law would be the one that would most facilitate the importation of *raw materials* and would erect the most obstacles to the entry of finished goods.

There is, in political economy, no sophism more widely accepted than this. It is dear not only to the protectionist school but also, and above all, to the self-styled liberal school; and this is regrettable, for the worst thing that can happen to a good cause is, not to be skillfully attacked, but to be ineptly defended.

Freedom of exchange will probably share the fate of freedom in general: it will become a part of our laws only after having taken possession of our minds. But if it is true that a reform must be generally accepted in order to be firmly established, it follows that nothing can delay it so much as that which misleads public opinion; and what is better fitted to mislead it than works that, while advocating free trade, are themselves based on the doctrines of monopoly?

A few years ago three large French cities—Lyons, Bordeaux, and Le Havre—rebelled against the protectionist system. The nation —indeed, the whole of Europe—was stirred on seeing raised what they took for the banner of free trade. Alas, it was still the banner of monopoly—of a monopoly a little more grasping and a great deal more absurd than the one the rebels were apparently trying to overthrow. By using the *sophism* that I am going to try to unmask, the petitioners did nothing more than reproduce, with an additional inconsistency, the doctrine of *protection for domestic labor.*

What, really, is the protectionist system? Let us hear what M. de Saint-Cricq has to say on this subject:

"Labor constitutes the wealth of a nation, because labor alone creates the material objects that our wants demand, and because universal well-being consists in the abundance of these objects." So much for the premise of the argument.

"But this abundance must be the product of *domestic labor.* If it were the product of foreign labor, domestic labor would at once be disemployed." Here lies the error. (*See the preceding chapter.*)

"What, then, should an agricultural and industrial country do? Secure its market for the products of its own soil and its own labor." This is the end to be attained.

"And, to this end, restrict by means of tariffs and, if need be, exclude entirely the products of the soil and the labor of other nations." These are the means to be employed.

Let us compare this system with that proposed in the Bordeaux petition.

It divided goods into three classes.

"The first comprises food and *raw materials on which no human labor has been bestowed. In principle, a wise economic system would require that this class of goods enter duty-free."* Here, as there is no labor, there is no need of protection.

"The second is composed of articles that have undergone *preliminary fabrication.* This preliminary fabrication warrants *the levying of some duties."* Here protection begins, because, according to the petitioners, *domestic labor* starts contributing to the product.

"The third includes finished goods, which can in no way provide employment for domestic labor; we consider this class the most dutiable." Here labor, and with it protection, reach their maximum.

It is clear that the petitioners are arguing that foreign labor harms domestic labor; this is the *error* of the protectionist system.

They are demanding that the French market be secured for French *labor;* this is the *end* aimed at by the protectionist system.

They are requiring that foreign labor be subjected to restrictions and taxes. This is the *means* employed by the protectionist system.

What difference, therefore, is it possible to detect between the petitioners from Bordeaux and M. de Saint-Cricq, the leader of the protectionist chorus?

Only one: the breadth of the meaning given the word *labor.*

M. de Saint-Cricq extends it to everything. Therefore he insists on *protecting* everything.

"Labor constitutes *all* the wealth of a nation," he says; "protect agricultural industry, *all* agricultural industry; protect manufacturing industry, *all* manufacturing industry—that is the cry which will be heard again and again in this Chamber."

The petitioners consider as labor only what is performed in connection with manufacturing; hence, they would confer the privileges of protection only on manufactured goods.

"Raw materials are *those on which no human labor has been bestowed.* In principle, they should not be dutiable. Finished goods can no longer provide employment for domestic labor; we consider them the most dutiable."

It is not our task here to investigate whether protection for domestic labor is reasonable. On this point M. de Saint-Cricq and the Bordeaux petitioners agree, and we, as the reader has seen in previous chapters, differ with both of them.

Our task is to ascertain which of them—M. de Saint-Cricq or the Bordeaux petitioners—uses the word *labor* in its proper sense.

Now, on this ground, we must say that the position taken by M. de Saint-Cricq is a thousand times better founded, for here is the dialogue that might take place between them:

M. de Saint-Cricq: "You grant that the products of domestic labor should be protected. You grant that no products of foreign labor can be introduced into our market without destroying an equal quantity of job opportunities for our domestic labor. But you allege that there are many goods which are possessed of *value,* since they are sold, and on which, nevertheless, *no human labor has been bestowed.* And among these you include wheat, flour, meat, cattle, bacon, salt, iron, copper, lead, coal, wool, pelts, seeds, etc.

"If you will prove to me that the *value* of these things is not due to labor, I shall agree that it is useless to protect them.

"But, on the other hand, if I prove to you that there is as much labor in 100 francs' worth of wool as in 100 francs' worth of textiles, you will have to admit that protection is as obligatory for the one as it is for the other.

"Now, why is this sack of wool *worth* 100 francs? Is it not precisely because that is its sales price? And what is the sales price but the total amount that had to be paid out, in wages, salaries, interest, and profits, to all the workers and capitalists who co-operated in the production of the article?"

The Petitioners: "As regards the wool, you may be right. But can it be said that a sack of grain, an ingot of iron, a quintal of coal, are products of labor? Are they not *created* by Nature?"

M. de Saint-Cricq: "Undoubtedly, Nature creates the elements of all these things, but it is labor that produces their *value.* I myself was wrong in saying that labor *creates* material objects, and this faulty expression has led me into many other errors. It is not within the capability of man to *create,* to make something out of nothing, whether he is an industrialist or a farmer; and if by *production* is meant *creation,* all our labors must be considered unproductive, and yours, as merchants, more so than all the others, save perhaps my own.

"The farmer, then, cannot rightly claim to have *created* wheat, but he can rightly claim to have created its *value*—I mean, by his labor and that of his domestic servants, his cowherds, and his reapers, to have changed into wheat some substances that in no way resembled it. What more is there in the action of the miller who transforms it into flour, or of the baker who shapes it into bread?

"For man to be able to clothe himself, a great many operations are necessary. Prior to the application of any human labor, the real *raw materials* of clothing are air, water, heat, carbon dioxide, light, and the minerals that must enter into its composition. These are the *raw materials* of which it may truly be said that *no human labor has been bestowed on them,* since they have no *value,* and I should not dream of protecting them. But the first application of *labor* transforms these substances into fodder, a second into wool, a third into yarn, a fourth into cloth, and a fifth into a finished garment. Who will be so bold as to say that any part of this whole enterprise is not *labor,* from the first furrow cut by the farmer's plow to the last stitch of the tailor's needle?

"And because the labor involved is spread over several branches of industry for the sake of greater speed and better quality in the manufacture of the finished product, which in this case is a piece of clothing, do you want, by an arbitrary distinction, to rank the importance of these operations in terms of the order in which they follow one another, so that the first in the sequence does not deserve even the name of labor, while the last, which is pre-eminently worthy of the appellation, alone merits the privileges of protection?"

The Petitioners: "Yes, we are beginning to see that wheat, like wool, is not entirely a product on which *no human labor has been bestowed.* But the farmer has not, at least, like the manufacturer, done everything himself or with the assistance of his workers. Nature too has helped him; and if labor is involved in the production of wheat, it is not solely the product of labor."

M. de Saint-Cricq: "But the *value* of everything resides exclusively in the labor needed to produce it. I am glad that Nature contributed to the physical production of the wheat. I could even wish that this were the achievement of Nature alone. But you must admit that I have, by my labor, compelled Nature to come to my assistance; and when I sell you wheat, please observe that it is not *Nature's labor* that I ask you to pay for, but *my own.*

"Indeed, from your mode of reasoning it would follow that manufactured goods are not exclusively the products of labor either. For does not the manufacturer summon Nature to his assistance? Does he not assist the steam engine by availing himself of the weight of the atmosphere, just as I avail myself of its humidity to assist the plow? Are the laws of gravitation, of the transmission of energy, or of the affinity of chemical elements his handiwork?"

The Petitioners: "Very well. This case is analogous to that of wool. But coal is surely the work of Nature, and of Nature alone. It is really a product on which *no human labor has been bestowed.*"

M. de Saint-Cricq: "Yes, Nature created coal, but *labor created its value.* During the millions of years when it lay buried and unknown under a hundred feet of earth, the coal had no *value.* Someone had to go there and search for it: that was a form of *labor.* Someone had to bring it to the market: that too was a form of *labor.* Thus, as we have said, the price that you pay for it on the market is nothing but the remuneration for the labor involved in its extraction and transportation."[1]

It is evident that up to this point M. de Saint-Cricq has had the better of the argument; that the value of raw materials, like that of manufactured goods, represents the costs of production, that is, of the *labor* involved in rendering them marketable; that it is not possible to conceive of an object which has *value* but *without having had any human labor bestowed on it;* that the distinction the petitioners are making is futile in theory and would be iniquitous in practice, for the unequal distribution of *economic advantages* that would result from its application would permit the one-third of the French people that are engaged in manufacturing to enjoy the privileges of monopoly on the ground that they produce by *laboring,* whereas the other two-thirds—that is, the farm population—would be abandoned to competition, on the pretext that they produce *without laboring.*

No doubt the reply to this will be that it is more advantageous for a nation to import what are called *raw materials,* whether produced by labor or not, and to export manufactured goods.

This is an opinion very often expressed and widely accepted.

"The more abundant raw materials are," says the Bordeaux petition, "the more manufacturing will multiply and expand."

"Raw materials," it adds, "provide unlimited opportunities for employment for the inhabitants of the country into which they are imported."

"Since raw materials are essential for labor," says the Le Havre petition, "they must be subjected *to different treatment and gradually* admitted at the *lowest* customs rates."

The same petition holds that protection for manufactured goods should be reduced, *not gradually,* but after an indefinite lapse of time; not to the *lowest* rate, but to twenty per cent.

"Among other items that must be cheap and abundant," says the Lyons petition, "the manufacturers include *all raw materials.*"

All this is based on an illusion.

We have seen that all *value* represents labor. Now, it is quite true that manufacturing labor multiplies tenfold, sometimes a hundredfold, the *value* of an unfinished product; that is, it distributes ten times, or even a hundred times, more in earnings throughout the nation. Hence, people are led to reason as follows: The production of a quintal of iron earns only fifteen francs for all classes of workers. The transformation of this quintal of iron into watch springs raises their earnings to 10,000 francs. Will anyone venture to say that the nation does not have a greater interest in receiving 10,000 francs than fifteen francs for its labor?

This mode of reasoning disregards the fact that exchange, whether international or interpersonal, is not carried on in terms of equal quantities of weight or measure. People do not exchange a quintal of iron ore for a quintal of watch springs, or a pound of unwashed wool for a pound of cashmere shawls; but rather a certain value of one of these things *for an equal value* of another. Now, to exchange a value for an equal value is to exchange a quantity of labor for an equal quantity of labor. Hence, it is not true that the nation that sells textiles or watch springs for 100 francs gains more than one that sells wool or iron for 100 francs.

In a country where no law may be voted and no tax may be levied save with the consent of those whom the law is to govern and upon whom the tax is to fall, the public can be robbed only if it is first deceived. Our ignorance is the *raw material* of every extortion that is practiced upon us, and we may be certain beforehand that every *sophism* is the precursor of an act of plunder. My friends, when you detect a sophism in a petition, get a good grip on your wallet, for you may be sure that this is what the petitioners are aiming at.

Let us see, then, just what is the ulterior motive of the ship-owners of Bordeaux and Le Havre and the manufacturers of Lyons that they are concealing behind their distinction between agricultural products and manufactured goods.

"It is mainly this first class [that comprising raw materials, *on which no human labor has been bestowed*]," say the Bordeaux petitioners, "that constitutes the *chief support of our merchant marine*. . . . . In principle, a wise economic system would require that this class be duty-free. . . . . The second [semifinished goods] can be *taxed to a certain extent*. The third [finished goods requiring no further labor], we regard as *the most dutiable*."

The Le Havre petitioners are of the opinion "that it is imperative for us to reduce gradually the duties on raw materials *to the lowest rate*, so that industry can successively put to work the *maritime facilities* that will provide it with the primary and indispensable means for the employment of its labor."

The manufacturers were not long in returning the shipowners' courtesy. Accordingly, the Lyons petition demands the duty-free entry of raw materials "in order to prove," as it says, "that the interests of manufacturing cities are not always opposed to those of maritime cities."

No; but it must be said that the interests of both, understood in the sense in which the petitioners use the term, are directly opposed to the interests of farmers and of consumers in general.

This, gentlemen, is what you are really aiming at! This is the actual goal of your nice economic distinctions! You want the law to keep *finished* goods from crossing the ocean, so that the far more costly transportation of raw materials in the coarse state in which a good part of their bulk still consists of impurities and wastes may provide more employment for your merchant marine and put your *maritime facilities* to work on a larger scale. This is what you call a *wise economic system*.

Why not, then, on the same principle, demand that pine trees be brought from Russia with their branches, bark, and roots; gold from Mexico in its mineral state; and hides from Buenos Aires still attached to the bones of their stinking carcasses?

I shortly expect to see railroad stockholders, as soon as they manage to gain a majority in the Chambers, pass a law forbidding the production at Cognac of the brandy that is consumed in Paris. Would not a law requiring the transportation of ten barrels of wine for every barrel of brandy furnish Parisian industry with the *indispensable means for the employment of its labor* and, at the same time, put our locomotive resources to work?

How long will people shut their eyes to such a simple truth?

Industry, maritime facilities, and labor have as their goal the general welfare, the common good; to create useless industries, to favor superfluous transportation facilities, to foster needless labor, not for the good of the public, but at the expense of the public, is to begin at the wrong end of the stick. What is desirable in itself is not labor, but consumption; all nonproductive labor is a dead loss. Paying sailors for carrying useless wastes across the seas is like paying them for skimming pebbles over the surface of the water. Thus, we reach the conclusion that all *economic sophisms,* despite their infinite variety, are alike in confusing the *means* with the *end* and in enlarging the one at the expense of the other.[2]

22

Metaphors

Sometimes a sophism expands until it permeates the whole fabric of a long and elaborate theory. More often it contracts and shrinks, assumes the form of a principle, and takes cover behind a word or a phrase.

Paul-Louis* used to pray, "May the good Lord deliver us from the snares of the devil—and of the metaphor!" And indeed, it would be hard to say which does more mischief in this world. It is the devil, you say; he puts the spirit of plunder into the hearts of all of us, frail creatures that we are. Yes, but he leaves the repression of abuses entirely to the counteraction of those who suffer from them. What paralyzes this counteraction is *sophistry*. The sword that *malice* puts into the hand of the assailant would be powerless if *sophistry* did not shatter the shield on the arm of the man who is assailed; and Malebranche† was right when he wrote on the frontispiece of his book: *Error is the cause of man's misery.*

Let us see how this takes place. Ambitious hypocrites may have some evil objective, such as, for instance, planting the seeds of international discord in the mind of the public. These fateful seeds may germinate, lead to general warfare, arrest the progress of civilization, cause torrents of blood to be shed, and inflict on the country that most dreadful of all catastrophes—*invasion.* In any case, and aside from this, these feelings of hostility lower us

* [Paul-Louis Courier de Méré (1772–1825), French army officer, scholar, and publicist. The quotation is from his political satire, the *Pamphlet des pamphlets.*—TRANSLATOR.]
† [Nicolas de Malebranche (1638–1715), theologian and philosopher, author of *La Recherche de la vérité.*—TRANSLATOR.]

116

in the estimation of other nations and compel Frenchmen who have retained any sense of justice to blush for their country. These are undoubtedly great evils; and for the public to protect itself against the machinations of those who would expose it to such risks, it needs no more than a clear insight into their nature. How has it been deprived of this insight? By the use of *metaphors.* Twist, stretch, or pervert the meaning of three or four words, and the whole job is done.

The word *invasion* itself is a good example of this.

A French ironmaster says: "We must protect ourselves from the *invasion* of English iron!" An English landlord cries: "We must repel the *invasion* of French wheat!" And they urge the erection of barriers between the two nations. Barriers result in isolation; isolation gives rise to hatred; hatred, to war; war, to *invasion.* "What difference does it make?" say the two *sophists.* "Is it not better to risk the possibility of invasion than to accept the certainty of invasion?" And the people believe them, and the barriers remain standing.

And yet, what analogy is there between an exchange and an *invasion?* What possible similarity can there be between a warship that comes to vomit missiles, fire, and devastation on our cities, and a merchant vessel that comes to offer us a voluntary exchange of goods for goods?

The same is true of the word *flood.* This word is customarily used in a pejorative sense, for floods often ravage fields and crops. If, however, what they deposited on our soil was of greater value than what they washed away, like the floods of the Nile, we should deify and worship them, as the Egyptians did. Before crying out against the *floods* of foreign goods, before putting up onerous and costly obstacles in their way, do people ask themselves whether these are floods that ravage or floods that fertilize? What should we think of Mohammed Ali* if, instead of spending great sums to raise dams across the Nile so as to extend the area covered by its *floods,* he used his piastres to dredge out a deeper channel for it, so that Egypt would not be soiled by this *foreign* slime brought

* [Also known as Mehemet Ali (1769–1849), viceroy of Egypt, who reformed Egypt to some extent according to European principles.—TRANSLATOR.]

down from the Mountains of the Moon?* We display exactly the same degree of wisdom and judgment when we try, by spending millions of francs, to protect our country—from what? From being flooded by the blessings that Nature has bestowed upon other lands.

Among the *metaphors* that conceal an altogether pernicious theory, none is more widespread than that which is contained in the words *tribute* and *tributary*.

These words have become so common that people treat them as synonymous with *purchase* and *purchaser,* and use either the one pair or the other indiscriminately.

However, a *tribute* is as different from a *purchase* as a *theft* is from an *exchange;* and I should as lief hear it said that Cartouche† broke into my strongbox and *purchased* a thousand crowns from it, as hear it reiterated in our legislative chambers that we have paid Germany *tribute* for the thousand horses she sold us.

For what differentiates the action of Cartouche from a *purchase* is that he has not put into my strongbox, and with my consent, a value equivalent to that which he took out of it.

And what differentiates the payment of 500,000 francs that we have made to Germany from a *tribute* is precisely the fact that she has not received the money for nothing, but has delivered to us in exchange a thousand horses that we ourselves have judged to be worth over 500,000 francs.

Is it really necessary to subject such linguistic abuses to serious criticism? Why not, since they figure seriously in newspapers and books?

And it should not be supposed that these are mere slips of the pen on the part of certain ignorant writers. For every writer that refrains from using such expressions I can name you ten that employ them, including the cleverest—the D'Argouts, the Dupins, the

* [The Mountains of the Moon, in east-central Africa, are the traditional source of the Nile. However, the Nile-borne sediment in Egypt comes from Ethiopia via the Blue Nile.—TRANSLATOR.]

† [Louis Dominique Cartouche (1693–1721), a celebrated Parisian outlaw, as synonymous with "highway robber" to the French as Jesse James is to Americans.—TRANSLATOR.]

Villèles,* peers, deputies, cabinet ministers—men, in short, whose word is law, and whose most glaring sophisms serve as the basis on which the country is governed.

A celebrated modern philosopher has added to the categories of Aristotle the sophism that consists in begging the question by the use of a single word. He cites several examples of it. He could have added the word *tributary* to his list. The question actually at issue here is whether purchases made abroad are advantageous or harmful. They are harmful, you say. Why? Because they make us tributaries of foreigners. But this is simply to use a word that already presupposes the fact in question.

How did this deceptive figure of speech come to be introduced into the rhetoric of the monopolists?

Money *leaves the country* to satisfy the greed of a victorious enemy. Money *also leaves the country* to pay for imports. The two events are treated as analogous by taking into account only the respects in which they resemble each other and disregarding those in which they differ.

However, the latter, that is, the nonreimbursement in the first case, and the reimbursement voluntarily agreed to in the second, establishes between these two events such a difference that it is not really possible to put them in the same category. It is one thing to *be forced* to hand over a hundred francs to one who has you by the throat, and quite another to do so *willingly* to one who supplies you with what you want. You might as well say that it makes no difference whether you throw bread into the river or eat it, because the bread is *destroyed* in either case. What is wrong with this reasoning, as with that involving the word *tribute,* is that it treats two events as alike in every respect simply because of their resemblance in one respect and disregards the respects in which they differ.

* [J. P. G. M. A. Seraphin, Comte de Villèle (1773–1854), French statesman, an extreme conservative, in Bastiat's time a member of the Chamber of Peers.—TRANSLATOR.]

Conclusion

All the sophisms that I have so far attacked concern only the question of the policy of protectionism; and even of those, out of pity for the reader, "I pass over some of the best":* *acquired rights, practical difficulties in the way, depletion of the currency,* etc., etc.

But political economy is not confined within this narrow circle. Fourierism, Saint-Simonianism, communism, mysticism, sentimentalism, false humanitarianism, affected aspirations for an imaginary equality and fraternity; questions relating to luxury, wages, machinery; to the so-called tyranny of capital; to colonies, outlets, conquests, population, emigration, association, taxes, and loans, have crowded the field of the science with a host of parasitic arguments, of *sophisms,* that call for the hoe and the mattock of the diligent economist.

It is not that I fail to see the defect in my plan, or rather in my absence of plan. To attack, one by one, so many incoherent sophisms, which sometimes are in conflict with one another and more often are included in one another, is to condemn oneself to a disorderly and capricious struggle and to expose oneself to perpetual repetitions.

I should so much prefer simply to state how things *are,* without concerning myself about the thousand aspects under which ignorance *sees* them! To set forth the laws under which society prospers or perishes is virtually to destroy all sophisms at once. When La-

* [In French, *"j'en passe, et des meilleurs,"* a line from the famous and controversial play, *Hernani,* by Victor Hugo (1801–1885). It was spoken by the Spanish grandee, Don Ruy Gomez de Silva, as he exhibited the portraits of his ancestors.— TRANSLATOR.]

place* described all that could be known up to his time about the movements of the heavenly bodies, he dispelled—even without naming them—all the astrological fantasies of the Egyptians, the Greeks, and the Hindus, much more surely than he could have done by refuting them directly in innumerable volumes. Truth is one; the book that sets it forth is an imposing and durable structure:

> Bolder than the pyramids
> And more durable than brass,
> It defies greedy tyrants.

Error is manifold and ephemeral: the work that combats it cannot in itself be either great or permanent.

But if I have lacked the strength and perhaps the opportunity[1] to proceed in the manner of Laplace and of Say, I cannot but believe that the form I have here adopted also has its modest usefulness. It seems to me particularly well adapted to the needs of the age, which is able to devote only occasional fleeting moments to study.

A treatise doubtless has an incontestable superiority, but on the one condition that it be read, pondered, and thoroughly examined. It is addressed only to a select few. Its mission is first to establish, and then to expand, the domain of acquired knowledge.

The refutation of commonplace prejudices cannot have such a lofty function. It aims only at clearing the way for truth, at preparing men's minds to understand it, at correcting public opinion, at breaking dangerous weapons in the hands of those who misuse them.

It is above all in political economy that this hand-to-hand struggle, this ever reviving combat with popular error, has real practical value.

The sciences can be arranged in two categories.

* [Pierre Simon, Marquis de Laplace (1749–1827), French astronomer and mathematician, whose great achievement was to solve the problem of apparent instability in the solar system.—TRANSLATOR.]

Some can be known, in a strict sense, only by scholars. These are the ones whose practical application is confined to particular professions. Despite his ignorance, the common man benefits from them. Although he knows nothing of mechanics or astronomy, he nonetheless enjoys the utility of a watch; with nothing but his faith in the engineer or the pilot, he is nonetheless transported by the locomotive or the steamship. We walk according to the laws of equilibrium without our being aware of them, just as M. Jourdain produced prose without knowing it.*

But there are, on the other hand, sciences that influence the public only in proportion to the understanding of them that the public itself has, and that derive all their efficacy, not from the knowledge accumulated by a few exceptionally learned men, but from that diffused among mankind in general. These include ethics, hygiene, political economy, and, in countries where men are their own masters, politics. It is probably above all these sciences of which Bentham could say: "It is better to disseminate them than to advance them." What difference does it make that a great man, or even God Himself, has promulgated the rules of ethics, so long as men, imbued with wrong ideas, mistake virtue for vice and vice for virtue? What difference does it make that Smith,† Say, and—according to M. de Saint-Chamans—the economists *of every school* have proclaimed, with respect to business transactions, the superiority of *freedom* over *coercion,* if those who make the laws and those for whom they are made are convinced of the contrary?

These sciences, which have been rightly called *social,* also have this peculiarity: precisely because their practical application concerns everyone, no one admits ignorance of them. If someone needs to solve a problem in chemistry or geometry, he does not pretend to have an innate knowledge of the science, nor is he

---

* [In *The Would-Be Gentleman* (*Le Bourgeois gentilhomme*), by J. B. P. Molière (1622–1673), M. Jourdain, a bourgeois being trained in the manners of gentlemen, had never realized that common speech could have the high-sounding name of "prose."—TRANSLATOR.]

† [Adam Smith (1723–1790), Scottish moral philosopher and economist, probably the most influential of all writers and thinkers in the realm of economic freedom.—TRANSLATOR.]

ashamed to consult M. Thénard or to seek for information in the pages of Legendre or Bezout.* But in the social sciences, people acknowledge scarcely any authorities. Since each person every day acts upon his own ideas, whether good or bad, reasonable or absurd, of ethical conduct, of hygiene, of economics, and of politics, each one feels himself competent to expound, discuss, decide, and settle these matters. Are you ill? There is not a good old lady in the country who is not prepared to tell you at once both the cause and the cure for your ills: "These are humors," she asserts; "what you need is a cathartic." But what are humors? And are there such things as humors at all? These are questions she does not trouble herself about. I immediately think of this good old lady whenever I hear all the ailments of society explained in such banal phrases as: overproduction, the tyranny of capital, excessive industrial capacity, and other nonsense of which one cannot even say *Verba et voces, praetereaque nihil,* for these are just so many fateful errors.†

From what precedes, two conclusions can be drawn: (1) *Sophisms* must be more abundant in the social sciences than in any others, for they are the ones in which each person consults only his own opinion or his own instinctive feelings; and (2) it is in these sciences that *sophisms* are especially harmful, because they mislead public opinion in a field in which public opinion is authoritative —is, indeed, law.

Thus, these sciences require two kinds of books: those that expound them and those that propagate them, those that set forth the truth and those that combat error.

It seems to me that the inherent shortcoming in the form of this brief work, *repetition,* is what gives it its chief utility.

In regard to the question that I have been dealing with, each sophism doubtless has its own phraseology and its particular meaning, but all have a common root: *the disregard of men's interests in their capacity as consumers.* To show that this sophism is the *starting point* for a thousand roads to error is to teach the public

* [L. J. Thénard (1777–1857), a chemist; A. M. Legendre (1752–1834), a geometrist; Étienne Bezout (1730–1783), a mathematician.—TRANSLATOR.]
† [Latin, "Mere words and sounds, and nothing more."—TRANSLATOR.]

to recognize it, to understand it, and to mistrust it under all circumstances.

After all, my aim is not to inspire convictions, but to raise doubts.

It is not my expectation that when the reader puts down this book he will cry out, "I know!" Would to heaven that he might honestly say to himself, "I don't know!"

"I don't know, for I am beginning to fear that there may be something illusory about the alleged blessings of scarcity." (Sophism I.)

"I am no longer so enthusiastic about the wonderfully beneficial effects of *obstacles*." (Sophism II.)

"*Effort without result* no longer seems to me so desirable as *result without effort*." (Sophism III.)

"It may well be that the key to success in business is not, as in dueling (according to the definition of it given by the fencing master in *Le Bourgeois gentilhomme*),* *to give and not to receive*." (Sophism VI.)

"I understand that an article gains in *value* in proportion to the amount of work that is done upon it; but, for the purposes of an exchange, do two *equal* values cease to be equal because one comes from the plow and the other from a Jacquard loom?"†

"I confess I am beginning to find it odd that man improves by being fettered and becomes rich by being taxed; and frankly, I should be relieved of a great anxiety, I should experience a sense of pure elation, if it were proved to me, as the author of the *Sophisms* asserts, that there is no incompatibility between prosperity and justice, between peace and freedom, between the expansion of job opportunities and the advancement of knowledge." (Sophisms XIV and XX.)

"Therefore, without considering myself altogether satisfied by

* [In *The Would-Be Gentleman*, the fencing master assures M. Jourdain that dueling is not at all dangerous, for all M. Jourdain need do is hit his adversary and not be hit in return.—TRANSLATOR.]

† [A complex and efficient weaving apparatus developed over a lengthy period; one of the numerous contributors to this development was J. M. Jacquard (1752–1834), a businessman and inventor of Lyons, France.—TRANSLATOR.]

his arguments, which I am not sure whether to regard as well reasoned or as paradoxical, I shall consult the experts in this science."

Let us conclude this monograph with one last and important observation.

The world is not sufficiently aware of the influence that *sophistry* exerts over it.

When the *rule of the stronger* was overthrown, *sophistry* transferred the empire to *the more subtle,* and it would be hard to say which of these two tyrants has been the more disastrous for mankind.

Men have an immoderate love of pleasure, influence, prestige, power—in a word, wealth.

And, at the same time, they are driven by a powerful impulse to obtain these things for themselves at the expense of others.

But these *others,* who constitute the public, are impelled no less powerfully to keep what they have acquired, provided that they *can* and that they *know how.*

Plunder, which plays such an important role in the affairs of the world, has but two instruments: *force* and *fraud,* and two impediments: *courage* and *knowledge.*

The annals of mankind are replete with instances of force employed for plunder. To retrace its history would be to reproduce almost entirely the history of all nations: Assyrians, Babylonians, Medes, Persians, Egyptians, Greeks, Romans, Goths, Franks, Huns, Turks, Arabs, Mongols, Tartars, not to speak of that of the Spaniards in America, the English in India, the French in Africa, the Russians in Asia, etc., etc.

But, at least among civilized nations, the men that produce wealth have become numerous and *strong* enough to defend it. Does this mean that they are no longer being plundered? Not at all; they are being plundered just as much as ever, and, what is more, they are plundering one another.

The only difference is that the instrument of plunder has changed; it is no longer by *force,* it is by *fraud,* that the public is being despoiled of its wealth.

To rob the public, it is necessary to deceive it. To deceive it is to persuade it that it is being robbed for its own benefit, and to induce it to accept, in exchange for its property, services that are fictitious or often even worse. This is the purpose of *sophistry,* whether it be theocratic, economic, political, or monetary. Thus, ever since brute force has been held in check, the *sophism* has been not merely a species of evil, but the very essence of evil. It must, in its turn, be held in check. And, to this end, the public must be made more *subtle* than the subtle, just as it has already become *stronger* than the strong.

Good people, it is with this idea in mind that I address this first essay to you—although the Preface is strangely misplaced and the Dedication somewhat delayed.[2]

Second Series[1]

> The request of industry to government is as modest as that of Diogenes to Alexander: "Get out of my light."
> —Bentham.

1

The Physiology of Plunder[1]

Why do I keep dwelling on that dry science, political economy?

Why? The question is a reasonable one. All labor by its very nature is so repugnant that one has the right to ask what purpose it serves.

Let us investigate and see.

I do not address myself to those philosophers who profess to adore poverty, if not in their own name, at least in the name of mankind.

I speak to whoever holds *wealth* in some regard; and I understand by this word, not the opulence of the few, but the comfort, the well-being, the security, the independence, the education, the dignity, of all.

There are only two ways of obtaining the means essential to the preservation, the adornment, and the improvement of life: *production* and *plunder*.

Some people say: *"Plunder* is a fortuitous event, a purely local and transient evil, condemned by moral philosophy, punished by law, and unworthy of the attention of *political economy."*

Yet however well disposed or optimistic one may be, one is compelled to recognize that *plunder* is practiced in this world on too vast a scale, that it is too much a part of all great human events, for any social science—political economy least of all—to be able to ignore it.

I go further. What keeps the social order from improving (at least to the extent to which it is capable of improving) is the constant endeavor of its members to live and to prosper at one another's expense.

Hence, if *plunder* did not exist, society would be perfect, and the social sciences would be without an object.

I go still further. When *plunder* has become a way of life for a group of men living together in society, they create for themselves in the course of time a legal system that authorizes it and a moral code that glorifies it.

It suffices to name some of the more obvious forms of *plunder* to indicate the position it holds in human affairs.

The first is *war*. Among savages, the conqueror kills the conquered in order to acquire hunting rights that, if not incontestable, are at least *uncontested*.

Next is *slavery*. When man learns that labor can make the earth fruitful, he arranges to share with his brother on the following terms: "Yours the toil; mine the harvest."

Then comes *theocracy*. "According as you give me, or refuse me, what is yours, I will open to you the gates of heaven or of hell."

Finally, *monopoly* makes its appearance. Its distinguishing characteristic is to permit the continued existence of the great law of society: *service for service*, but to introduce force into the negotiations, and, consequently, to upset the just balance between *service received* and *service rendered*.

Plunder always carries within itself the germ that ultimately kills it. It is rarely that the many plunder the few; for, in such a case, the latter would promptly be so reduced in number as no longer to be capable of satisfying the greed of the former, so that plunder would come to an end from want of sustenance.

Almost always it is the many that are oppressed by the few; yet plunder is none the less doomed to come to an end.

For if it makes use of force, as in war and slavery, in the long run force will naturally pass to the side of the many.

And if fraud is the means, as in theocracy and monopoly, it is natural, unless intelligence is to count for nothing, that the majority should eventually become aware of it.

There is, besides, another providential law whose operation is no less fatal, in the end, to the success of every system of plunder: Plunder not only *redistributes* wealth; it always, at the same time, *destroys* a part of it. War annihilates many values. Slavery paralyzes many capabilities. Theocracy diverts many energies toward childish or injurious ends. Monopoly too transfers wealth from one pocket to another, but much of it is lost in the process.

This is an admirable law. Without it, provided that there were a balance of power between oppressors and oppressed, plunder would have no end. Thanks to this law, the balance is always tending to be upset; either because the plunderers come to realize that too much wealth is being destroyed, or, in the absence of this realization, because the evil is constantly worsening, and it is in the nature of whatever keeps on worsening to come to an end.

In fact, there comes a time when the progressively accelerating destruction of wealth goes so far that the plunderer is poorer than he would have been if he had remained honest. Such is the case when a war costs a nation more than the booty is worth; when a master pays more for slave labor than for free labor; when a theocracy has so stupefied the people and so sapped their energies that it can no longer exact anything from them; when a monopoly increases its efforts to absorb in proportion as there is less to absorb, just as it takes more effort to milk a cow as the udder becomes empty.

Monopoly is evidently a species of the genus plunder. There are several varieties—among others, sinecures, privileges, and trade restrictions.

Some of the forms it may assume are simple and naive, like feudal rights. Under this system the masses were plundered and knew it. The system involved the abuse of force and fell with it.

Other forms are more complicated. Often the masses are plundered and do not know it. It may even happen that they believe they owe everything to plunder, not only what they are allowed to keep, but also what is taken away from them and what is lost in the operation. Moreover, I assert that, in the course of time, thanks to so ingenious a mechanism as *custom*, many people become plunderers without knowing it and without intending it. Monopolies of this kind are engendered by fraud and nourished on error.

They flourish in the darkness of ignorance and vanish only in the light of knowledge.

I have said enough to show that political economy has an evident practical utility. It is the torch that, by exposing fraud and dispelling error, destroys that form of social disorder called plunder. Someone—I believe a woman—has rightly defined it as "the safety lock on the savings of the people."

Commentary

If this little book were fated to last three or four thousand years, to be read and reread, pondered and studied, sentence by sentence, word by word, and letter by letter, from generation to generation, like a new Koran; if it were to fill all the libraries in the world with avalanches of annotations, explanations, and paraphrases; I might abandon the foregoing remarks to their fate, without misgivings concerning their rather obscure succinctness. But since they need a commentary, I believe the wiser course is to provide it myself.

The true and just rule for mankind is the *voluntary exchange of service for service*. Plunder consists in prohibiting, by force or fraud, freedom of exchange, in order to receive a service without rendering one in return.

Forcible plunder is effected by waiting until a man has produced something, and then taking it from him by violence.

It is specifically forbidden by the Commandment: *Thou shalt not steal.*

When practiced by one individual on another, it is called *theft* and is punishable by imprisonment; when practiced by one nation on another, it is called *conquest* and leads to glory.

Why this difference? It is worth while to seek for the cause. It will reveal to us an irresistible power, public opinion, which, like the atmosphere, envelops us so completely that we no longer notice it. Rousseau never spoke more truly than when he said: "It takes a great deal of scientific insight to discern the facts that are closest to us."*

* [This quotation is from Part One of the *Discourse on Inequality* by J. J. Rousseau (1712–1778), a French philosopher. Bastiat was so impressed by it that he referred to it five times in his *Economic Harmonies*.—TRANSLATOR.]

The *thief,* precisely because he acts alone, has public opinion against him. He frightens everyone about him. However, if he has a few comrades, he boasts to them about his exploits, and here one may begin to notice the power of public opinion; for it takes merely the approval of his accomplices to relieve him of the feeling that he is doing anything wrong and even to make him proud of his dishonor.

The *warrior* lives in a different world. The public opinion that vilifies him is elsewhere, in the conquered nations; he does not feel its pressure. But the opinion of those around him approves of him and sustains him. He and his comrades have a strong sense of the common interest that unites them. The fatherland, which has created enemies and dangers for itself, finds it necessary to extol the courage of its children. It bestows honors, fame, and glory on the most intrepid among them, on those who have expanded its frontiers and brought it the most loot. Poets sing their exploits, and women braid garlands for them. And such is the power of public opinion that it separates the idea of injustice from plunder and frees the plunderer of even the consciousness of having done any wrong.

The public opinion that reacts against military plunder, since it arises, not in the plundering nation, but among the plundered, has very little influence. Yet it is not entirely ineffectual, and it gains in importance as nations come into contact with one another and come to understand one another better. In this connection, it is evident that the study of languages and freedom of communication among different nations tend to give the prevailing influence to the opinion that opposes this sort of plunder.

Unfortunately, it often happens that those who live in the vicinity of a plundering nation themselves become plunderers when they can, and thenceforth become imbued with the same prejudices.

When this happens, there is only one remedy: time. People have to learn, through hard experience, the enormous disadvantage there is in plundering one another.

Some may propose another form of restraint: moral influence. But the purpose of moral influence is to encourage virtuous actions. How, then, can it restrain acts of plunder when public opinion ranks these acts among the noblest virtues? Is there a more powerful moral influence than religion? Has there ever been a religion more favorable to peace and more widely accepted than Christianity? And yet what have we witnessed for eighteen centuries? The spectacle of men warring with one another not only in spite of religion, but in the very name of religion.

A conquering nation is not always waging offensive warfare. It, too, falls on evil days when its soldiers find themselves obliged to defend their homes and property, their families, their national independence, and their liberty. At such times war takes on the character of a great crusade. The flag, consecrated by the ministers of the Prince of Peace, symbolizes everything that is holy on earth; people revere it as the living image of the fatherland and of the homage due to it; and martial virtues are extolled above all others. But after the danger has passed, public opinion remains the same; and by a natural reaction of that spirit of revenge which is confused with patriotism, people love to parade their cherished flag from one capital city to another. It seems that Nature has thus prepared its punishment for the aggressor.

It is the fear of this punishment, and not our increased knowledge, that keeps weapons in our arsenals, for it cannot be denied that the most highly civilized nations wage war and concern themselves very little about justice when they do not have to fear any reprisals. The Himalayan, the Atlas, and the Caucasus Mountains attest to this.

If religion has been powerless, if knowledge is powerless, how, then, is war to cease?

Political economy demonstrates that, even in the case of the victors, war is always waged in the interest of the few and at the expense of the many. All that is needed, then, is that the masses should clearly perceive this truth. The weight of public opinion, which is still divided, will then fall entirely on the side of peace.[2]

Forcible plunder also takes another form. Instead of waiting until a man has produced something in order to take it away from him, the plunderer takes possession of the man himself, deprives him of his freedom, and compels him to work. The plunderer does not say to him: "If you do this for me, I shall do that for you"; but: "Yours all the toil, mine all the enjoyment." This is slavery, which always implies the misuse of power.

Now, it is an important question whether it is not in the very nature of an incontestably dominant power to be misused. For my part, I put no faith in it at all, and I might just as well expect a falling stone to contain the power that will halt its fall as to rely upon force to impose restraints upon itself.

I should like, at least, to be shown a country or an era in which slavery was abolished by the free and voluntary action of the masters.

Slavery furnishes a second and striking example of the impotence of religious and humanitarian sentiments in a conflict with the powerful force of self-interest. This may seem regrettable to certain modern schools of thought that expect self-denial to be the principle that will reform society. Let them begin, then, by reforming the nature of man.

In the Antilles,* the masters, from father to son, have been professing the Christian religion ever since slavery was established there. Several times a day they repeat these words: "All men are brothers; to love thy neighbor is to fulfill the whole of the law." And yet they have slaves, and nothing seems to them more natural or legitimate. Do the modern reformers expect that their ethical principles will ever be as universally accepted, as well-known, as authoritative, or as often on the lips of everyone, as the Gospel? And if the Gospel has been unable to pass from the lips to the heart, over or through the great barrier of self-interest, how do they expect their ethical principles to perform this miracle?

Is slavery, then, indestructible? No. *Self-interest,* which created it, will destroy it, provided that the special interests that have inflicted the wound are not protected in such a way as to nullify the general interests that tend to heal it.

Another truth demonstrated by political economy is that free labor is essentially progressive, whereas slave labor is necessarily

---

* [The reference is to such French West Indian islands as Martinique and Guadeloupe, where slavery existed until 1848 or later.—TRANSLATOR.]

static. Hence, the triumph of the first over the second is inevitable. What has become of the cultivation of indigo by the Negroes?*

Free labor employed in the cultivation of sugar will lead to a continual reduction in its price. The slave will become proportionately less profitable to his master. Slavery would have collapsed of its own weight long ago in America if European laws had not kept the price of sugar artificially high. Therefore we see the masters, their creditors, and their legislative representatives making vigorous efforts to keep these laws in force, for they are today the pillars of the whole edifice of slavery.

Unfortunately, these laws still have the support of people among whom slavery has disappeared; from this it is clear that here, too, public opinion is sovereign.

If it is sovereign even in the domain of force, it is still more so in the domain of fraud. This, in fact, is the domain in which public opinion is most efficacious. Fraud consists in the misuse of the intellect; public opinion becomes progressively more enlightened as men's intellectual attainments are enlarged. These two forces are at least of the same nature. Imposture on the part of the plunderer implies credulity on the part of the plundered, and the natural antidote for credulity is truth. It follows that by enlightening men's minds we deprive this kind of plunder of the food that nurtures it.

I shall briefly review some of the kinds of plunder that are carried out by fraud on a grand scale.

The first is plunder by theocratic fraud.

In what does it consist? In inducing men to give one actual services, in the form of food, clothing, luxuries, prestige, influence, and power, in exchange for fictitious services.

If I tell a man, "I am going to render you an immediate service," I am obliged to keep my word; otherwise this man would soon know what to expect, and my fraud would be quickly unmasked.

But suppose I say to him, "In exchange for services from you, I shall confer immense services upon you, not in this world but in the next. Whether, after this life, you are to be eternally happy or

* [More efficient (and humane) methods of production in India had resulted in a sharp drop in indigo production by slave labor in the West Indies.—TRANSLATOR.]

wretched depends entirely upon me; I am an intermediary between God and man, and can, as I see fit, open to you the gates of heaven or of hell." If this man believes me, he is at my mercy.

This sort of imposture has been widely practiced since the beginning of the world, and the extent of the power which the Egyptian priests attained by such means is well known.

It is easy to understand how impostors operate. It is enough to ask yourself what you would do in their place.

If, with designs of this sort, I were to find myself among an ignorant people, and if, by some extraordinary and apparently miraculous deed, I were to succeed in passing myself off as a supernatural being, I should profess to be a messenger from God, with absolute power to control the future destinies of men.

Next, I should forbid any examination of my claims. I should go further: since reason would be my most dangerous enemy, I should forbid the use of reason itself, at least as applied to this awesome subject. I should render this question, and all questions related to it, *taboo,* as the savages say. To answer them, to ask them, even to think of them, would be an unpardonable crime.

It would certainly be the acme of ingenuity thus to set up a *taboo* as a barrier to all intellectual avenues that might lead to the discovery of my imposture. What could better guarantee its permanence than to make even doubt an act of sacrilege?

However, to this fundamental guarantee I should add some auxiliary ones. For instance, so that knowledge might never be diffused among the masses, I should confer upon myself, as well as upon my accomplices, a monopoly over all the sciences; I should hide them under the veil of a dead language and a hieroglyphic alphabet; and, in order never to be caught unawares by any danger, I should take care to devise some institution that would allow me to penetrate, by day, into the hidden recesses of every man's conscience.

It would not be amiss for me to satisfy some of the real needs of my people, especially if, by doing so, I were able to increase my influence and authority. For instance, men have a great need for education and morality, and I should make myself the source of both. In that way I should guide as I wished the minds and hearts of my people. I should establish an indissoluble connection between morality and my authority by representing them as unable to exist without one another, so that if anyone dared to raise a tabooed question, the whole of society, which cannot survive without morality, would feel the earth tremble beneath its feet and would turn its wrath upon this rash innovator.

When things reached such a point, these people would evidently belong to me more than if they were my slaves. The slave curses his chains; my people would bless theirs, and I should have succeeded in stamping the seal of servitude, not on their brows, but on their very hearts and consciences.

Public opinion alone can knock down such an edifice of iniquity; but where is it to begin, if every stone is tabooed? This must be the work of time and the printing press.

God forbid that I should seek here to disturb those comforting beliefs that view this life of sorrows as but a prelude to a future life of happiness! But that the irresistible yearning that impels us to accept such beliefs has been shamefully exploited, no one, not even the Pope, could deny. There is, it seems to me, one sign by which it is possible to determine whether or not people have been victimized in this way. Examine the religion and the priest, and see whether the priest is the instrument of the religion, or the religion is the instrument of the priest.

If *the priest is the instrument of the religion,* if his only thought is to disseminate everywhere its ethical principles and its beneficial influence, he will be gentle, tolerant, humble, charitable, and zealous; his life will resemble that of his divine model; he will preach freedom and equality among men, and peace and brotherhood among nations; he will resist the temptations of temporal power, since he will want no ties with that which, of all things in this world, has the greatest need of restraint; he will be a man of the people, a man of good counsel and tender consolation, a man whose opinion is esteemed, and a man obedient to the Gospel.

If, on the contrary, *the religion is the instrument of the priest,* he will treat it as one does an instrument that one modifies, bends, or twists to his own purposes, so as to derive from it the greatest possible advantage for oneself. He will multiply the number of

tabooed questions; he will adjust his moral principles to suit changing times, men, and circumstances. He will try to awe the populace
with his studied gestures and poses; a hundred times a day he will
mumble words that have long since lost all their meaning and have
become mere empty *conventionalities*. He will traffic in relics, but
only just enough not to shake people's faith in their sanctity; and
he will take care that the more perceptive the people become, the
less obvious his trafficking will be. He will involve himself in
worldly intrigues; and he will always side with those in power on
the sole condition that those in power side with him. In brief, from
every one of his acts it will be clear that what he is aiming at is,
not to advance religion by means of the clergy, but to advance the
clergy by means of religion; and since so much effort implies an
end, and as this end, according to our hypothesis, can be nothing
other than power and wealth, the conclusive proof that the people
have been duped is that the priest is rich and powerful.

Quite clearly, one can misuse a true religion as well as a false
one. Indeed, the more worthy of respect its authority is, the greater
is the danger that it may be improperly employed. But there is a
great deal of difference in the consequences. The abuse of such authority always outrages the sound, enlightened, self-reliant members of the population. Their faith cannot but be shaken, and the
weakening of a true religion is far more lamentable than the
crumbling of a false one.

The extent to which this method of plunder is practiced is always in inverse proportion to the perspicacity of the people, since
it is in the nature of abuses to go as far as they can. Not that high-
minded and dedicated priests cannot be found in the midst of the
most ignorant people; but what is to stop a knave from donning
the cassock and seeking to wear the miter? Plunderers conform to
the Malthusian law: they multiply with the means of existence;
and the means of existence of knaves is the credulity of their dupes.
Seek as one will, there is no substitute for an informed and enlightened public opinion. It is the only remedy.

Another sort of plunder is known as *commercial fraud,* a term
that seems to me much too restricted, for the guilty ones include
not only the merchant who adulterates his goods or gives short

weight, but also the quack doctor and the pettifogging lawyer. In such cases, one of the two services exchanged consists of debased coin; but since the service received was first voluntarily agreed upon, it is evident that plunder of this kind should diminish as the public becomes better informed.

Next comes the misuse of *government services*—an immense field for plunder, so immense that we can only glance at it.

If God had made man a solitary animal, everyone would labor for himself. Individual wealth would be in proportion to the services that each man performed for himself.

But, *since man is a social creature, services are exchanged for services*—a proposition whose terms you can transpose, if you are so minded.

The members of society have certain needs that are so general, so universal, that provision is made for them by organizing *government services*. Among these requirements is the need for security. People agree to tax themselves in order to pay, in the form of *services* of various kinds, those who perform the service of seeing to the common security.

This arrangement in no way conflicts with the principle of exchange as formulated in political economy: *Do this for me, and I will do that for you.* The essence of the transaction is the same; only the method of payment is different; but this fact is very important.

In ordinary, private transactions each party remains the sole judge both of the service he receives and of the service he performs. He can always either decline the exchange or make it elsewhere; hence the need of offering in the market only such services as will find voluntary acceptance.

This has not been true of the state, especially prior to the establishment of representative government. Whether or not we need its services, whether they are real or spurious, we are always obliged to accept what it provides and to pay the price that it sets.

Now, it is the tendency of all men to exaggerate the services that they render and to minimize the services they receive; and chaos would reign if we did not have, in private transactions, the assurance of a *negotiated price*.

This assurance is completely, or almost completely, lacking in our transactions with the government. And yet the state, which, after all, is composed of men (although nowadays this is denied, at least by implication), obeys the universal tendency. It wants to serve us a great deal—more, indeed, than we desire—and to make us accept as *real* services what are often far from being such, and all this for the purpose of exacting some *services* from us in return in the form of taxes.

The state too is subject to the Malthusian law. It tends to expand in proportion to its means of existence and to live beyond its means, and these are, in the last analysis, nothing but the substance of the people. Woe to the people that cannot limit the sphere of action of the state! Freedom, private enterprise, wealth, happiness, independence, personal dignity, all vanish.

For there is one circumstance that must be noted: Among the services that we demand of the state, the chief is *security*. To assure us this, it must have at its command a force capable of overcoming all individual or collective, domestic or foreign forces that might imperil it. In combination with that fatal disposition that we have observed among men to live at the expense of others, this fact makes for a situation that is obviously fraught with danger.

To appreciate this, one has only to consider on what a vast scale, throughout history, plunder has been practiced by way of the abuses and excesses of government. One has only to ask oneself what services were performed for the people, and what services were exacted from them, by the governments of Assyria, Babylon, Egypt, Rome, Persia, Turkey, China, Russia, England, Spain, and France. The enormous disparity between the one and the other in each case staggers the imagination.

At last, representative government was established, and one might have supposed, a priori, that all this would come to an end as if by magic.

In fact, such governments are based on the following principle:

"The people themselves, through their representatives, will determine the nature and extent of the functions that they regard as proper to be established as *government services,* and the amount they propose to pay in remuneration for these *services.*"

The tendency to appropriate the property of others was thereby placed in direct confrontation with the tendency to defend one's own property. There was every reason to expect that the latter would overcome the former.

To be sure, I am convinced that in the long run the system of representative government will succeed. Yet it must be admitted that up to now it has not done so.

Why? For two quite simple reasons: Governments have had too much discernment, and people have had too little.

Governments are very adroit. They act methodically, step by step, according to a well-contrived plan that is constantly being improved by tradition and experience. They study men and their passions. If they perceive, for instance, that the people are inclined to war, they incite and inflame this calamitous propensity. By their diplomacy they surround the nation with dangers, and, as a natural consequence, they demand that it provide soldiers, sailors, arsenals, and fortifications. Often, in fact, they do not need to go to the trouble of making such demands, for everything they want is offered to them. Then they have jobs, pensions, and promotions to distribute. All this requires a great deal of money; hence, they impose taxes and float loans.

If the nation is open-handed, the government offers to cure all the ills of mankind. It promises to restore commerce, make agriculture prosperous, expand industry, encourage arts and letters, wipe out poverty, etc., etc. All that is needed is to create some new government agencies and to pay a few more bureaucrats.

In a word, the tactic consists in initiating, in the guise of actual services, what are nothing but restrictions; thereafter the nation pays, not for being served, but for being disserved. Governments, assuming gigantic proportions, end by absorbing half of the national income. The people are astonished to find that, while they hear of wonderful inventions that are to multiply goods without end, they are working as hard as ever and are still no better off than before.

The trouble is that, while the government has been acting with so much ability, the people have shown practically none. Thus, when called upon to choose those who are to be entrusted with the powers of government, those who are to determine the sphere of and the payment for governmental action, whom do they choose? Government officials. They entrust the executive authority itself with the power to fix the limits of its own activities and requirements. They act like Molière's would-be gentleman, who, for the selection and the number of his suits, relied upon—his tailor.[3]

In the meanwhile, things go from bad to worse, and at last people open their eyes, not to the remedy (for they have not yet progressed to that point), but to the evil.

Governing is so pleasurable a profession that everyone aspires to engage in it. Hence, the demagogues never cease telling the people: "We are aware of your sufferings, and we deplore them. Things would be different if we were governing you."

This period, which is ordinarily quite long, is one of rebellions and insurrections. If the people are conquered, the costs of the war are added to their tax burden. If they are the conquerors, the government changes hands, and the abuses continue.

And this goes on until the people learn to recognize and defend their true interests. Thus, we always reach the same conclusion: The only remedy is in the progressive enlightenment of public opinion.

Certain nations seem particularly liable to fall prey to governmental plunder. They are those in which men, lacking faith in their own dignity and capability, would feel themselves lost if they were not *governed and administered* every step of the way. Without having traveled a great deal, I have seen countries in which the people think that agriculture can make no progress unless the government supports experimental farms; that soon there will no longer be any horses, if the government does not provide studs; that fathers will not have their children educated, or will have them taught only immorality, if the government does not decide what it is proper to learn; etc., etc. In such countries, revolutions may come in rapid succession, with governments falling one after another; but the governed are none the less governed at the discretion and the mercy of the rulers (for the propensity that I am discussing here is the very stuff of which governments are made), until the people finally come to realize that it is better to leave the greatest possible number of *services* to be exchanged by the interested parties *at a freely negotiated price.*[4]

We have seen that society consists in the *exchange of services.* It should be an exchange of only good and honest services. But we have also shown that men have a great interest in, and consequently an irresistible inclination toward, exaggerating the relative value of the services they perform. I cannot, indeed, see any other limit to these pretensions than the voluntary acceptance or rejection of the exchange on the part of those to whom the services are offered.

Hence, certain men have recourse to the law in order to abridge the natural prerogatives of this freedom on the part of other men. This kind of plunder is called privilege or monopoly. Let us be very clear about its origin and character.

Everyone knows that the services that he offers in the general market will be evaluated and remunerated in proportion to their scarcity. Everyone, therefore, will seek the enactment of a law that will keep from the market all those prepared to offer services similar to his own; or, what amounts to the same thing, if the employment of some means of production is indispensable for the performance of the service, he will ask the law for exclusive possession of it.[5]

I shall say little about this variety of plunder here, limiting myself to one comment only.

An isolated case of monopoly never fails to enrich those to whom the law has granted it. It may then happen that each class of producers, instead of seeking to destroy this monopoly, will demand for itself a similar monopoly. This kind of plunder, thus reduced to a system, then becomes the most ridiculous practical joke on everybody, and the ultimate result is that each person thinks he is getting *more* out of a general market in which *the supply of everything is being lessened.*

It is needless to add that this extraordinary system also sows the seeds of universal discord among all classes, all professions, and all nations; that it requires the constant, but always unpredictable, interference of the government; that it therefore abounds in the type of abuses described in the preceding paragraph; that it renders every industrial enterprise desperately insecure, and accustoms men to making the law, and not themselves, responsible for their livelihood. It would be difficult to imagine a more prolific source of social disturbance.[6]

Justification

It may be asked: "Why this ugly word *plunder?* Besides being crude, it is offensive and irritating; it only turns calm and temperate men against you and embitters the whole controversy."

I submit that I do respect individuals; I do believe in the sincerity of practically all the advocates of protectionism; and I do not arrogate to myself the right to question the personal honesty, scrupulosity, or humanitarianism of anyone. I repeat that protectionism is the consequence—the fateful consequence—of a common error of which all men, or at least the great majority of them, are at once victims and accomplices. But, after all, I cannot prevent things from being as they are.

Imagine a sort of Diogenes thrusting his head out of his tub and saying, "Athenians, you force slaves to serve you. Has it never occurred to you that you are practicing upon your brothers the most iniquitous kind of plunder?"

Or imagine a tribune speaking as follows in the Forum: "Romans, you have based your whole way of life on the successive pillaging of all other nations."

To be sure, they would only have been expressing incontestable truths. Must we therefore conclude that Athens and Rome were inhabited exclusively by dishonest people, and that Socrates and Plato, Cato and Cincinnatus were despicable individuals?

Who could harbor such a thought? After all, these great men lived in an environment that made them unconscious of their injustice. It is well known that Aristotle could not even conceive of the idea of a society that would be capable of existing without slavery.

In modern times, slavery has continued to our own day without causing the plantation owners many qualms of conscience. Armies have served as instruments for large-scale conquests—in other words, for acts of plunder on a large scale. Does this mean that they are not well provided with officers and men as individually scrupulous as, and perhaps more scrupulous than, the ordinary run of men engaged in industrial pursuits—men who would blush at the very thought of theft, and who would face a thousand deaths rather than stoop to a single disgraceful action?

It is not individuals who are to blame, but the general tendency of public opinion that blinds and misleads them—a tendency of which the whole of society is guilty.

The same is true of monopoly. I accuse the system, and not individuals; society as a whole, and not any of its members in particular. If the greatest philosophers were incapable of seeing the iniquity of slavery, how much easier it is for farmers and manufacturers to deceive themselves concerning the nature and effects of protectionism!

2

Two Systems of Ethics

Having arrived—if he does arrive—at the end of the preceding chapter, the reader may well exclaim:

"Well, was I wrong to accuse economists of being dry and cold? What a portrait of mankind! Plunder is represented as an omnipresent force, almost a normal phenomenon, assuming every guise, practiced under any pretext, legal or extralegal, perverting to its own purposes all that is most sacred, exploiting weakness and credulity by turns, and constantly growing by what it feeds on! Could any more depressing picture of the world be imagined?"

But the question is, not whether it is depressing, but whether it is true. History says that it is.

It is rather odd that those who denounce political economy (or *economism,* as they are pleased to call this science) for studying man and the world just as they are, take a far gloomier view, at least of the past and the present, than the economists do. The books and newspapers of the socialists are full of such bitterness and hatred toward society that the very word *civilization* has come to be for them synonymous with injustice, civil disorder, and anarchy. So little confidence do they have in the natural capacity of the human race to improve and progress of its own accord that they have even gone so far as to condemn *freedom,* which, as they see it, is every day driving mankind closer to the edge of doom.

It is true that they are optimists in regard to the future. For, although mankind, in itself incompetent, has been on the wrong track for six millennia, a prophet has come who has shown men the way to salvation; and if the flock will only be docile enough to follow the shepherd, he will lead it into the promised land where prosperity may be attained without effort, and where order, security, and harmony are the easy reward of improvidence.

All that men have to do is to permit the reformers to change, as Rousseau said, *their physical and moral constitution.*

Political economy has not been given the mission of finding out what society would be like if it had pleased God to make man different from what he is. It may be regrettable that Providence, at the beginning, neglected to seek the advice of some of our modern social reformers. And just as the celestial mechanism would have been quite different if the Creator had consulted Alfonso the Learned;* so too, if He had not disregarded the advice of Fourier, the social order would have borne no resemblance to the one in which we are obliged to live, breathe, and move about. But, since we are in it, since we do live, move, and have our being in it, our only recourse is to study it and to understand its laws, especially if the improvement of our condition essentially depends upon such knowledge.

We cannot prevent an endless succession of unsatisfied desires from springing up in men's hearts.

We cannot render it possible for these desires to be satisfied without labor.

We cannot close our eyes to the fact that labor is as repugnant to mankind as its fruits are attractive.

We cannot prevent men, since they are so constituted, from engaging in a constant effort to increase their share of the fruits of labor, while throwing upon one another, by force or fraud, the burden of its pains.

It is not within our competence to erase the whole record of human history, or to silence the voice of the past, which attests that this is the way things have been since the beginning of time. We cannot deny that war, slavery, serfdom, theocracy, the excesses of government, privileges, frauds of every kind, and monopolies have

---

* [Alfonso X (the Learned), ruler of Castile from 1252 until 1284, a weak king but a man of encyclopedic interests. He is supposed once to have observed, as Bartlett's *Familiar Quotations* has it: "Had I been present at the Creation, I would have given some useful hints for the better ordering of the universe."—TRANSLATOR.]

been the indisputable and terrifying manifestations of these two sentiments united in the heart of man: *fondness for the fruits of toil and repugnance to its pains.*

"In the sweat of thy face shalt thou eat bread." But everyone wants as much bread and as little sweat as possible. History provides conclusive proof of this.

Thank heaven, history also shows that the distribution of the fruits and the pains among the members of the human race is approaching ever more nearly to equality.

Unless one is prepared to deny the obvious, it must be admitted that at least in this respect society has made some progress.

In that case, there must exist in society some natural and providential force, some law that causes iniquity progressively to decline and justice no less inexorably to prevail.

We say that this force exists within society, and that God has put it there. If it were not already there, we should be reduced, like the utopians, to resorting to artificial means for producing it, by arrangements that would require the preliminary alteration of the *physical and moral constitution* of man; or rather, we should consider the effort to produce such a force useless and vain, because we cannot understand how a lever can operate without a fulcrum.

Let us try, therefore, to identify the beneficent force that tends progressively to overcome the maleficent force which we call plunder, and whose existence is all too well demonstrated by reason and proved by experience.

Every maleficent action necessarily has two termini: its point of origin and its point of impact; the man who performs the action, and the man upon whom the action is performed; or, in the language of the schools, the *agent* and the *patient.*

There are, thus, two possible ways of preventing the maleficent action from taking effect: the *agent* may voluntarily abstain, or the *patient* may resist.

This fact gives rise to two systems of ethics that, far from contradicting each other, concur in their conclusions: religious or philosophical ethics and utilitarian ethics, which I shall permit myself to call *economic.*

Religious ethics, in order to prevent a maleficent action, addresses its author—man in his *active* role. It says to him: "Reform and purify thyself; cease to do evil; do good; subdue thy passions; sacrifice thine own interests; do not oppress thy neighbor, for it is thy duty to love and to comfort him; be first just and then charitable." This code of ethics will always be the more beautiful and the more moving of the two, the one that displays the human race in all its majesty, that better lends itself to impassioned eloquence, and is better fitted to arouse the admiration and sympathy of mankind.

The economic, or utilitarian, system of ethics has the same end in view, but above all addresses itself to man in his *passive* role. Merely by showing him the necessary consequences of his acts, it stimulates him to oppose those that injure him, and to honor those that are useful to him. It strives to disseminate enough good sense, knowledge, and justifiable mistrust among the oppressed masses to make oppression more and more difficult and dangerous.

It should be noted that utilitarian ethics is not without its influence upon the oppressor as well. A maleficent action produces both good and evil effects: evil for him who is subjected to it; and good for him who performs it, or else it would not have been performed. But the good effects by no means compensate for the evil. The evil is always, and necessarily, greater than the good, because the very act of oppressing involves a waste of energy, creates dangers, provokes reprisals, and demands costly precautions. The mere demonstration of these effects not only stimulates a reaction on the part of the oppressed, but attracts to the side of justice all those whose hearts have not been corrupted and disturbs the security of the oppressors themselves.

But it is easy to understand that this system of ethics, which is more implicit than explicit; which, after all, is only a scientific demonstration; which would even lose some of its efficacy if it changed its character; which addresses itself, not to the heart, but to the mind; which seeks, not to persuade, but to convince; which gives, not counsel, but proofs; whose mission is, not to arouse, but to enlighten; and which wins over evil no other victory than that of denying it sustenance—it is easy to understand, I say, that this system of ethics has been accused of being dry and prosaic.

The reproach is true, but unfair. It amounts to saying that political economy does not tell us everything, does not include everything, is not the universal science. But who in the world has ever made so sweeping a claim for it?

The accusation would be justified only if political economy pretended that its procedures gave it exclusive dominion over the entire moral realm, and if it had the presumption to forbid philosophy and religion the use of their own direct methods of working for the improvement of mankind.

Let us welcome, then, the concurrent action of moral philosophy properly so called and political economy—the one stigmatizing the evil deed in our conscience by exposing it in all its hideousness, and the other discrediting it in our judgment by the description of its effects.

Let us even concede that the triumph of the religious moralist, when it occurs, is more noble, more encouraging, and more fundamental. But at the same time it is difficult not to acknowledge that the triumph of economics is more easy to secure and more certain.

In a few lines that are worth more than many ponderous volumes, J. B. Say some time ago observed that there are two possible ways of bringing to an end the dissensions introduced by hypocrisy into a respectable family: *to reform Tartuffe* or *to make Orgon less of a fool.** Molière, that great depictor of the human heart, seems to have had constantly in mind the second procedure as the more efficacious.

The same is true on the world's stage.

Tell me what Caesar did, and I shall describe to you the Romans of his day.

Tell me what modern diplomacy accomplishes, and I shall describe for you the moral condition of the nations of the world.

We should not be paying close to two billions in taxes if we did not delegate the power of voting them to those that consume them.

We should not have all the difficulties and all the expenses of

---

* [In Molière's comedy, *Tartuffe, or the Impostor*, Tartuffe is the scheming hypocrite, and Orgon his well-meaning dupe.—TRANSLATOR.]

152 *Economic Sophisms*

the African problem if we were as well convinced that *two and two is four* in political economy as in arithmetic.*

M. Guizot would not have had occasion to say: "France is rich enough to pay for its glory," if France had not been infatuated with false glory.†

The same statesman would never have said, "Liberty is too precious for France to haggle over its price," if France really understood that *heavy government expenditures* and *liberty* are incompatible.

It is not, as people think, the monopolists, but the monopolized, that sustain the monopolies.

And, in regard to elections, it is not because there are corrupters that people are corruptible, but the reverse; and the proof consists in the fact that the latter pay all the costs of corruption. Is it not, then, their responsibility to bring it to an end?

Let religious ethics soften, if it can, the hearts of the Tartuffes, the Caesars, the colonialists, the sinecurists, the monopolists, etc. The task of political economy is to enlighten their dupes.

Of these two methods, which is the more efficacious in promoting social progress? If this question requires any answer at all, I should say it is the second. Mankind, I fear, cannot escape the necessity of first learning *a defensive system of ethics*.

In vain have I investigated, read, observed, and inquired: nowhere do I find any abuse, practiced to any considerable extent, that has perished by voluntary renunciation on the part of those who were profiting from it.

I see many, on the contrary, that are yielding to the manly opposition of those who suffer from them.

To describe the consequences of abuses is therefore the most efficacious means of destroying them. And this is true particularly in regard to abuses that, like the system of protectionism, while

* [The African problem constituted a series of costly military expeditions by the French to conquer Algeria.—TRANSLATOR.]
†François Pierre Guillaume Guizot (1787–1874), French statesman and historian, chief rival of Thiers for political power in the 1840's. He urged the French people to devote themselves to making money, opposed domestic reforms, and was friendly toward Britain.—TRANSLATOR.]

inflicting real hardships on the masses, prove only an illusion and a disappointment to those who expect to profit from them.

Does this mean that utilitarian ethics will, of itself, bring about all the social improvement that the sympathetic nature of the human soul and of its noblest faculties leads one to hope for and expect? I am far from making such a claim. Let us assume the universal diffusion of this *defensive system of ethics,* which is, after all, nothing but the acknowledgment that the rightly understood interests of all men are consonant with justice and the general welfare. A society based on such principles, although certainly well regulated, might not be very attractive; for it would be one in which there would no longer be any swindlers only because there would no longer be any dupes; where vice, always *latent* and, so to speak, enervated by famine, would need only a little sustenance to revive; where prudence on the part of everyone would be enjoined by the vigilance of everyone else; where, in short, reform, although regulating external acts, would not have penetrated beneath the surface to the consciences of men. We sometimes see such a society typified in one of those sticklers for exact justice who are prepared to resist the slightest infringement of their rights and are skillful at warding off encroachments from any quarter. You respect and may, perhaps, even admire him; you would choose him as your deputy, but you would not choose him as your friend.

These *two systems of ethics,* instead of engaging in mutual recriminations, should be working together to attack evil at each of its poles. While the economists are doing their work—opening the eyes of the credulous, uprooting prejudices, arousing justifiable and necessary mistrust of every type of fraud, studying and describing the true nature of things and actions—let the religious moralist, on his part, perform his more agreeable, but more difficult, task. Let him engage in hand-to-hand combat with iniquity; let him pursue it into the most secret recesses of the human heart; let him depict the delights of beneficence, self-denial, and self-sacrifice; let him tap the springs of virtue where we can but dry up the springs of vice—that is his task. It is a noble and glorious one. But why should he dispute the utility of the one that has devolved upon us?

Would not a society that, without being intrinsically virtuous, was nevertheless well regulated by the action of the *economic system of ethics* (by which I mean nothing more than knowledge of *political economy*), offer opportunities for the progress of religious morality?

Habit, it has been said, is a second nature.

A country in which everyone has been long unaccustomed to injustice solely as a result of the resistance of enlightened public opinion might still be a sorry place to live in. But it seems to me that it would at least be ready to receive precepts of a purer and higher order. To have become unaccustomed to doing evil is already to have taken a long stride toward becoming good. Men cannot remain stationary. Turned aside from the path of vice, which would lead only to ignominy, they would feel the attraction of virtue all the more.

Perhaps society must pass through this prosaic stage, in which men practice virtue out of self-interest, so that they may thence rise to the more poetic sphere in which they will no longer have need of such a motive.

3

The Two Hatchets

Petition of Jacques Bonhomme,* Carpenter, to
M. Cunin-Gridaine,† Minister of Commerce

Mr. Manufacturer and Cabinet Minister:

I am a carpenter, as Jesus was; I wield the hatchet and the adze to serve you.

Now, while I was chopping and hewing from dawn to dusk on the states of our lord the king, it occurred to me that my labor is as much a part of our *domestic* industry as yours.

And ever since, I have been unable to see any reason why protection should not come to the aid of my woodyard as well as your factory.

For after all, if you make cloth, I make roofs. We both, in different ways, shelter our customers from the cold and the rain.

Yet I have to run after my customers, whereas yours run after you. You have found a way of forcing them to do so by preventing them from supplying themselves elsewhere, while my customers are free to turn to whomever they like.

What is so astonishing about this? M. Cunin, the cabinet minister, has not forgotten M. Cunin, the textile manufacturer: that is only natural. But, alas, my humble craft has given no cabinet minister to France, although it did give a God to the world.

And in the immortal code this God bequeathed to man, there is not the slightest expression that could be interpreted as authoriz-

---

* [The nickname for French peasants as a class.—Translator.]

† [Laurent Cunin-Gridaine (1778–1859), a textile manufacturer, Deputy, Minister of Commerce, and extreme advocate of protectionist policies.—Translator.]

ing carpenters to enrich themselves at the expense of others, as you do.

Consider my position, then. I earn thirty sous a day, except Sundays and holidays. If I offer you my services at the same time as a Flemish carpenter offers you his, and if he is prepared to work for a sou less than I, you will prefer him.

But suppose I want to buy myself a suit of clothes? If a Belgian textile manufacturer offers his cloth on the market in competition with yours, you drive both him and his cloth out of the country.

Thus, forced to enter your shop, although it is the more expensive, my poor thirty sous are really worth only twenty-eight.

What am I saying! They are not worth more than twenty-six, for instead of expelling the Belgian manufacturer *at your expense* (which would be the very least you could do), you make me pay for the people whom, in your interest, you set at his heels.

And since a great number of your fellow legislators, with whom you have a perfect understanding, each takes from me a sou or two —one under the pretext of protecting iron; another, coal; this one, oil; and that one, wheat—I find, when everything is taken into account, that of my thirty sous I have been able to save only fifteen from being plundered.

You will doubtless tell me that these little sous, which pass in this way, without compensation, from my pocket to yours, provide a livelihood for the people around your castle and enable you to live in grand style. May I point out to you in reply that if you left the money in my hands, it would have provided a livelihood for the people around me.

Be that as it may, Mr. Cabinet Minister and Manufacturer, knowing that I should be ill-received, I do not come to you and demand, as I have a full right to do, that you withdraw the *restriction* you are imposing on your customers; I prefer to follow the prevailing fashion and claim a little *protection* for myself.

At this point, you will raise a difficulty for me: "My friend," you will tell me, "I should really like to protect you and others of your craft; but how are we to go about conferring tariff benefits upon the work of carpenters? Are we to forbid the importation of houses by land or by sea?"

This would quite obviously be absurd; but, by dint of much reflection on the matter, I have discovered another means of benefiting the sons of St. Joseph; and you will welcome it all the more readily, I hope, as it in no way differs from the means you employed in maintaining the privilege that you vote for yourself every year.

The wonderful means I have in mind consists in forbidding the use of sharp hatchets in France.

I maintain that this *restriction* would be no more illogical or more arbitrary than the one to which you subject us in the case of your cloth.

Why do you drive out the Belgians? Because they undersell you. And why do they undersell you? Because they are in some respect superior to you as textile manufacturers.

Between you and a Belgian, consequently, there is exactly the same difference as between a dull hatchet and a sharp hatchet.

And you are forcing me—me, a carpenter—to buy from you the product of a dull hatchet.

Look upon France as a workman who is trying, by his labor, to obtain everything he needs, including cloth.

There are two possible ways of doing this:

The first is to spin and weave the wool himself.

The second is to produce other commodities—for instance, clocks, wallpaper, or wine—and to exchange them with the Belgians for the cloth.

Of these two procedures the one that gives the better result may be represented by the sharp hatchet; the other, by the dull hatchet.

You do not deny that at present, in France, it requires *more labor* to obtain a piece of cloth directly from our looms (the dull hatchet) than indirectly by way of our vines (the sharp hatchet). You are so far from denying this that it is precisely because of this *additional toil* (which, according to you, is what wealth consists in) that you request, nay more, you *impose*, the use of the poorer of the two hatchets.

Now, at least be consistent; be impartial; and if you mean to be just, give us poor carpenters the same treatment you give yourself.

Enact a law to this effect:

"No one shall use beams or joists save those produced by dull hatchets."

Consider what the immediate consequences will be.

Where we now strike a hundred blows with the hatchet, we shall then strike three hundred. What we now do in one hour will take three hours. What a mighty stimulus to employment! Apprentices, journeymen, and masters, there will no longer be enough of us. We shall be in demand, and therefore well paid. Whoever wants to have a roof made will be henceforth obliged to accept our demands, just as whoever wants cloth today is obliged to submit to yours.

And if the *free-trade* theorists ever dare to call into question the utility of this measure, we shall know perfectly well where to find a crushing retort. It is in your parliamentary report of 1834. We shall beat them over the head with it, for in it you have made a wonderful plea on behalf of protectionism and of dull hatchets, which are simply two names for one and the same thing.

4

Subordinate Labor Council

"What! You have the effrontery to demand for all citizens the right to buy, sell, barter, and exchange, to render and receive service for service, and settle on the price among themselves, on the sole condition that they carry on these transactions honestly and pay their taxes? What are you trying to do—deprive working-men of their jobs, their wages, and their bread?"

This is what people say to us. I know what to think of it myself, but I wanted to know what the workers themselves think of it.

I had at hand an excellent instrument of inquiry.

It was not one of those *supreme industrial councils*, where big landlords who call themselves farmers, influential shipowners who think of themselves as sailors, and wealthy stockholders who pretend to be laborers, practice their well-known form of humanitarianism.

No; it was bona fide workingmen, *real* workingmen, as they say today—joiners, carpenters, masons, tailors, shoemakers, dyers, blacksmiths, innkeepers, grocers, etc., etc.—who in my village have established a *mutual-aid society*.

I transformed it, by my own personal authority, into a *subordinate labor council*, and I obtained from it a report that is worth quite as much as any other, though it is not crammed with figures and inflated to the dimensions of a quarto volume printed at government expense.

My aim was to interrogate these good people in regard to the way in which they are, or think they are, affected by the policy of protectionism. The president pointed out to me that this would

159

violate to some extent the principles on which the *association* was founded. For, in France, in this land of freedom, people who *associate* give up their right to discuss *politics*—that is, to take counsel together concerning their common interests. However, after a great deal of hesitation, he agreed to put the question on the agenda.

The council was divided into as many committees as there were groups representing different trades. Each was given a form to be filled out after fifteen days of discussion.

On the designated day, the venerable president took the chair (we are adopting the official style, for in fact it was nothing more than an ordinary kitchen chair), and took from the table (official style again, for it was a table of poplar wood) about fifteen reports, which he read one after another.

The first one submitted was that of the *tailors*. Here is an exact and authentic copy of its text:

Effects of Protection—Report of the Tailors

Disadvantages	*Advantages*
1. *As a result of the policy of protectionism,* we are paying more for bread, meat, sugar, wood, needles, thread, etc., which is equivalent in our case to a considerable loss of income.	None.[1]
2. *As a result of the policy of protectionism,* our customers also pay more for everything, which leaves them less to spend on clothing. This means less business for us, and therefore smaller profits.	
3. *As a result of the policy of protectionism,* cloth is expensive, so that people put off buying clothes for a longer time and make do with what they have. This again means less business for us and compels us to offer our services at a lower price.	[1] In spite of all our efforts, we found it impossible to discover any respect whatsoever in which the policy of protectionism is of advantage to our business.

Here is another report:

Effects of Protection—Report of the Blacksmiths

Disadvantages	*Advantages*
1. Every time we eat, drink, heat our homes, and buy clothing, the policy of protectionism imposes on us a tax that never reaches the treasury.	*None.*

2. It imposes a similar tax on all our fellow citizens who are not blacksmiths; and since they have that much less money, most of them use wooden pegs for nails and a piece of string for a latch, which deprives us of employment.

3. It keeps iron at such a high price that it is not used on farms for plows, gates, or balconies; and our craft, which could provide employment for so many people who need it, does not provide us even with enough for ourselves.

4. The revenue that the tax collector fails to realize from duties on foreign goods *that are not imported into the country* is added to the tax we pay on salt and postage.

As the same refrain recurs in all the other reports, I spare the reader their perusal. Gardeners, carpenters, shoemakers, clogmakers, boatmen, millers—all gave vent to the same grievances.

I regret that there were no farmers in our association. Their report would certainly have been very instructive.

But alas, in our section—the Landes*—the poor farmers, *well protected* though they are, do not have a sou, and after they have insured their livestock, they themselves lack the means of joining a *mutual-aid society*. The alleged benefits of protection do not prevent them from being the pariahs of our social order. What shall I say of the vineyardists?

What I find particularly noteworthy is the good sense which our villagers showed in perceiving not only the direct injury that the policy of protectionism inflicts on them, but also the indirect in-

* [A department in southwestern France.—Translator.]

jury that, after first affecting their customers, rebounds upon them.

This, I said to myself, is what the economists of the *Moniteur industriel* apparently do not understand.

And perhaps those—the farmers in particular—whose eyes are dazzled by a little protection would be willing to give it up if they could see this side of the question.

Perhaps they would say to themselves: "It is better to support oneself by one's own efforts and have customers who are well off than to be *protected* and have customers who are impoverished."

For to seek to enrich each industry in turn by creating a void around one after another is as futile an endeavor as trying to leap over one's own shadow.

5

High Prices and Low Prices[1]

I feel it my duty to present to the reader certain—alas, theoretical—comments on the illusions to which the expressions *high
prices* and *low prices* give rise. At first glance, I know, people may
be inclined to consider these comments a little abstruse; but the
question is, not whether they are abstruse, but whether they are
true. Now, I believe that they are not only perfectly true but particularly well suited to raise some doubts in the minds of those—
by no means few in number—who have a sincere faith in the efficacy of protectionism.

Whether we are advocates of free trade or proponents of restrictive measures, we are all obliged to make use of the expressions
high prices and *low prices*. The former proclaim themselves in
favor of low prices, with a view to the interests of the consumer;
the latter declare themselves in favor of high prices, having regard
for the interests of the producer. Others take a middle position
and say: "The producer and the consumer are one and the same
person"; thereby leaving it quite undecided whether the law
should aim at high prices or at low.

Faced with this conflict, the law, it would seem, has only one alternative, and that is to permit prices to be arrived at naturally.
But then one has to meet the objections of the implacable enemies
of laissez faire. They absolutely insist that the law intervene, even
without knowing in what direction. Yet it is incumbent upon those
who want to use the law for the purpose of creating artificially high
or unnaturally low prices to explain the grounds of their preference. The burden of proof rests exclusively upon them. Hence, it

follows that free trade is always to be deemed good until the contrary is proved, for free trade consists in allowing prices to be arrived at naturally.

But the roles have been reversed. The advocates of high prices have succeeded in making their system prevail, and it is incumbent upon the proponents of natural prices to prove the superiority of theirs. On both sides the argument turns on the meaning of two expressions, and it is therefore essential to ascertain just what these two expressions really mean.

But first we must call attention to a series of events that may well disconcert the champions of both camps.

In order to *raise* prices, the restrictionists have obtained protective tariffs; and, much to their surprise and disappointment, prices have fallen.

In order to *reduce* prices, the freetraders have sometimes succeeded in securing the adoption of their program, and, to their great astonishment, what followed was a rise in prices.

For example, in France, in order to favor agriculture, a duty of twenty-two per cent was imposed on foreign wool; and yet domestic wool has been selling at a lower price after the law than it did before.

In England, for the relief of the consumer, the duty on wool was reduced and finally removed entirely; and yet the price of English wool is higher than ever before.

And these are not isolated cases, for there is nothing unique about the price of wool that exempts it from the general law governing all prices. The same result is produced whenever the circumstances are analogous. Contrary to every expectation, a protective tariff has more often brought about a fall, and competition more often a rise, in commodity prices.

Then the debate reached the height of confusion with the protectionists saying to their adversaries: "It is our system that brings about these low prices of which you boast so much," and the latter replying: "It is free trade that brings about those high prices that you find so advantageous."[2]

Would it not be amusing to see *low prices* in this way become the password in the rue Hauteville, and *high prices* in the rue Choiseul?*

Evidently there is in all this a misunderstanding, an illusion, that needs to be dispelled, and this is what I shall now attempt to do.

Imagine two isolated nations, each containing a million inhabitants. Suppose that, other things being equal, one of them has twice as much of everything—wheat, meat, iron, furniture, fuel, books, clothing, etc.—as the other. Evidently, then, one is twice as rich as the other.

However, there is no reason to assert that *money prices* will differ in these two countries. They may even be higher in the richer country. It may be that in the United States everything is nominally more expensive than in Poland, and that the American people are nevertheless better provided in all respects; whence we see that what constitutes wealth is, not the money prices of goods, but their abundance. Hence, when we wish to compare protectionism and free trade, we should not ask which of the two produces low prices and which produces high prices, but which leads to abundance and which leads to scarcity.

For it should be noted that, when products are exchanged, a relative scarcity of everything and a relative abundance of everything leave the money prices of things at exactly the same point, but not the relative condition of the inhabitants of the two countries.

Let us enter a little more deeply into this subject.

When tariff increases and reductions are found to produce effects directly contrary to those expected of them—a fall in prices often following a higher duty, and a rise in prices sometimes accompanying the removal of a duty—it becomes the obligation of political economy to seek an explanation of phenomena that controvert all our accepted ideas; for, needless to say, science—if it is to be worthy of the name—is but the faithful description and correct explanation of events.

Now, the one that we are examining here can be quite satisfac-

* [Bastiat himself lived for some time in the rue Choiseul, while the Odier Committee (see *infra*, p. 167) was established in the rue Hauteville.—TRANSLATOR.]

torily accounted for by a circumstance that must never be lost sight of, namely, that high prices have *two causes,* and not just one.

The same is true of low prices.[3]

One of the best-established principles of political economy is that prices are determined by the relation between supply and demand.

There are, then, two factors that influence prices: supply and demand. These factors are inherently variable. They can work together in the same direction, or they can work in opposite directions, and in infinitely varied proportions in either case. Hence, prices are the resultant of an inexhaustible number of combinations of these two factors.

Prices may rise, either because the supply diminishes or because the demand increases.

They may fall, either because the supply increases or because the demand diminishes.

Hence, there are two types of high prices and two types of low prices.

High prices of the bad type are the results of diminution in the supply, for this implies scarcity and therefore *privation* (such as was experienced this year in regard to wheat); *high prices* of the good type result from an increase in demand, for this presupposes a rise in the general level of prosperity.

In the same way, *low prices* are desirable when they have their source in abundance, and are lamentable when they are caused by a cessation in demand resulting from the poverty of the consumer.

Now, please observe that a policy of protectionism tends to produce, at the same time, both the bad type of high prices and the bad type of low prices: the bad type of high prices, in that it diminishes the supply of goods—which, indeed, is its avowed purpose; and the bad type of low prices, in that it also reduces demand, since it encourages unwise investment of both capital and labor, and burdens the consumer with taxes and restrictions.

Hence, *so far as prices are concerned,* these two tendencies neutralize each other; and that is why this system, which restricts demand at the same time as supply, does not in the long run result even in the high prices that are its object.

But, so far as the condition of the population is concerned, these two tendencies do not neutralize each other; on the contrary, they co-operate in making it worse.

The effect of free trade is precisely the opposite. In its general consequences, it may likewise fail to result in the low prices it was intended to produce; for it, too, has two tendencies, the one toward a desirable reduction in prices effected by an increase in the supply, i.e., by way of abundance, and the other toward an appreciable rise in prices resulting from an increase in demand, i.e., in general wealth. These two tendencies neutralize each other in regard to *money prices;* but they co-operate in improving the well-being of the population.

In short, in so far as a policy of protectionism is put into effect, men retrogress toward a state of affairs in which both supply and demand are enfeebled; under a system of free trade, they advance toward a state of affairs in which both supply and demand increase together without necessarily affecting money prices. Such prices are not a good criterion of wealth. They may very easily remain the same, whether society sinks into the most abject poverty or advances to a high level of prosperity.

The following remarks may serve to illustrate this point briefly.

A farmer in the south of France thinks he has the treasures of Peru in his hand because he is protected by tariffs from foreign competition. It makes no difference that he is as poor as Job; he nonetheless believes that sooner or later the policy of protectionism will make him rich. In these circumstances, if the question is put to him, in the terms in which it was framed by the Odier Committee: "Do you want to be subject to foreign competition—yes or no?" his first reaction is to answer, "No," and the Odier Committee* proudly gives wide publicity to his answer.

However, one must probe a little more deeply into the matter. Unquestionably, foreign competition—and indeed, competition in general—is always irksome; and if one branch of industry alone

* [The Committee for the Defense of Domestic Industry, a protectionist organization of which Antoine Odier (1766–1853), President of the Chamber of Commerce of Paris, a Deputy, and later a Peer of France, was one of the leaders.—TRANSLATOR.]

could get rid of it, business in that branch would for some time be very profitable.

But protection is not an isolated privilege; it is a system. If it tends to create, to the profit of the farmer, a scarcity of grain and of meat, it tends also to create, to the profit of other producers, a scarcity of iron, of cloth, of fuel, of tools, etc.—that is, a scarcity of everything.

Now, if the scarcity of wheat tends to raise its price on account of the diminution in the supply, the scarcity of all the other commodities for which wheat is exchanged tends to lower the price of wheat on account of the diminution in demand; so that it is by no means certain that in the long run the price of wheat will be one centime higher than under a system of free trade. All that is certain is that, since there is less of everything in the country, everyone will be less well provided in every respect.

The farmer really ought to ask himself whether it would not be better for him if a certain quantity of wheat and livestock were imported from abroad, so long as, on the other hand, he was surrounded by a well-to-do population, able to consume and pay for all sorts of agricultural products.

Suppose there were a department in France in which the inhabitants were clothed in rags, dwelt in hovels, and lived on chestnuts. How could you expect agriculture to flourish there? What could you make the earth produce with any reasonable hope of fair return? Meat? It would form no part of their diet. Milk? They would have to be content to drink water. Butter? For them it would be a luxury. Wool? They would use as little of it as possible. Is it to be supposed that all these consumers' goods could be thus forgone by the masses without exerting a downward pressure on prices concomitantly with the upward pressure exerted by protectionism?

What we have said of the farmer is just as true of the manufacturer. Textile manufacturers assert that foreign competition will lower prices by increasing the supply. Granted; but will not these prices rise again as a result of an increase in demand? Is the consumption of cloth a fixed, invariable quantity? Does everyone have as much of it as he could and should have? And if the general level of prosperity was raised by the abolition of all these taxes and restrictions, would not the first use that people would make of the money be to clothe themselves better?

The problem—the eternal problem—then, is not whether protectionism favors this or that particular branch of industry; but whether, all things considered, restriction is, *by its very nature,* more productive than free trade.

Now, no one ventures to maintain this. Otherwise people would not always be granting that we are "right in principle."

If this is the case, if restriction is advantageous to each particular branch of industry only by impairing the general well-being to an even greater extent, we must conclude that money prices in themselves express a relation between each particular branch of industry and industry in general, between supply and demand, and, accordingly, that a *remunerative price,* which is the object of protectionism, far from being realized by such a policy, is actually rendered impossible by it.[4]

Addendum

The article that we published under the title, "High Prices and Low Prices," has brought us the following two letters, which we present here, together with our replies:

Dear Editor:

You are upsetting all my ideas. I used to be a staunch champion of free trade and found it very persuasive to use *low prices* as an argument. Everywhere I went, I used to say: "Under a system of free trade, bread, meat, wool, linen, iron, and fuel are going to be cheaper." This displeased those who sold these commodities, but pleased those who bought them. Now you are raising doubts about whether free trade will, in fact, result in *low prices.* If not, of what use is it? What will people gain by it, if foreign competition, which can injure them in their sales, brings them no advantage in their purchases?

Dear Freetrader:

Allow us to inform you that you only half read the article that inspired your letter. We said that free trade acts in the same way as roads, canals, railways, and everything else that facilitates com-

munication by removing obstacles. Its first tendency is to increase
the supply of the duty-free commodity, and consequently to lower
its price. But, by increasing at the same time the supply of everything else for which this commodity may be exchanged, it concomitantly increases the *demand* for it, and its price accordingly
goes up. You ask how people will gain by free trade. Suppose you
have a balance consisting of several scales, in each of which there
are a certain number of the items that you have enumerated. If
you add a little wheat to one scale, it will tend to tip the balance;
but if you add a little cloth, a little iron, and a little fuel to the
other scales, the equilibrium will be restored. So far as the beam is
concerned, nothing has changed. But so far as the people are concerned, they are evidently better fed, better clothed, and better
housed.

Dear Editor:

I am a textile manufacturer and a protectionist. I confess that your
article on "High Prices and Low Prices" is causing me to reconsider
my position. It has a certain plausibility about it that would require
only a conclusive proof to bring about a conversion.

Dear Protectionist:

We say that the object of your restrictive measures is something
evil, namely, *artificially high prices*. But we do not say that they
always realize the hopes of those who support them. It is certain
that they inflict on the consumer all the evil consequences of *high
prices*. But it is not certain that they invariably confer any of the
expected benefits on the producer. Why? Because while they
diminish the supply, they also diminish the demand.

This proves that in the economic arrangement of this world
there is a moral force, a healing power, that makes unjust ambition
ultimately meet with disappointment.

Be good enough to observe, sir, that one of the factors making
for the prosperity of each individual branch of industry is the general wealth of the community. The *price* of a house depends not
only on its original cost but also on the number and economic

status of the occupants. Do two houses that are exactly similar necessarily have the same price? Certainly not, if one is situated in Paris and the other in Lower Brittany. One should never speak of price without taking all the relevant *circumstances* into consideration, and one should recognize quite clearly that no undertaking is more futile than that of trying to base the prosperity of the parts on the ruination of the whole. And yet this is what the policy of protectionism seeks to do.

Competition always has been and always will be troublesome to those who have to meet it. That is why men have always and everywhere struggled to rid themselves of it. We (and perhaps you, too) are acquainted with a municipal council in which the resident merchants wage violent war on nonresident merchants. Their projectiles are their exactions for local permits to stall animals, for licenses to set up stands for the sale of goods, for bridge-tolls, etc., etc.

Now, consider what would have become of Paris if this war had been waged successfully there.

Suppose that the first shoemaker who established himself there had succeeded in keeping out all others; that the first tailor, the first mason, the first printer, the first watchmaker, the first hairdresser, the first doctor, and the first baker had all likewise been successful in maintaining a monopoly on their services. Paris today would still be a village of from 1,200 to 1,500 inhabitants. Instead, the market has been open to everyone (save those whom you still debar), and this is precisely what has made it the great metropolis it is today. For the enemies of competition it has meant only a long series of vexations; but it has made Paris a city of a million inhabitants. No doubt it has raised the general level of prosperity; but has it been detrimental to the individual prosperity of the shoemakers and the tailors? That is the essential question you have to ask yourself. As competitors arrived, you would have said, "The price of shoes is going to fall." But has it fallen? No; for if the *supply* has increased, the *demand* has increased as well.

The same will be true of cloth, sir; let it be imported duty-free. You will have more competitors, it is true; but you will also have more customers, and what is more, they will be richer. Has this never occurred to you on seeing nine-tenths of your fellow country-men in the winter obliged to do without that cloth which you weave so well?

If you wish to prosper, let your customer prosper. This is a lesson it has taken you a very long time to learn.

When people have learned this lesson, everyone will seek his individual welfare in the general welfare. Then jealousies between man and man, city and city, province and province, nation and nation, will no longer trouble the world.

6

To Artisans and Laborers[1]

Several newspapers have attacked me in your presence. Won't you please read my defense?

I am not a distrustful person. When a man writes or speaks, I take it for granted that he believes what he is saying.

And yet, as I read and reread the newspapers that have attacked me, I seem to find in them unfortunate evidence to the contrary.

What is the question at issue? It is that of determining which is more advantageous for you, protectionism or free trade.

I believe that it is free trade, and they believe that it is protectionism; it is incumbent upon each of us to prove his contention.

Was it necessary to insinuate that we are the agents of England, of the south of France, of the government?

Just see how easy it would be for us to retaliate in the same vein.

We are, they say, agents of the English, because some of us have used the words "meeting" and "freetrader"!

But do they not use the words "drawback" and "budget"?*

We are, it is said, imitating Cobden and English democracy!

And are they not parodying Bentinck and the British aristocracy?†

We are accused of borrowing from perfidious Albion the doctrine of free trade!

* [Words enclosed in quotation marks are in English in the original.—TRANSLATOR.]
† [Richard Cobden (1804–1865), English manufacturer, member of Parliament, and champion of free trade, known personally to Bastiat and much admired by him. Lord George Bentinck (1802–1848), known in Parliament almost exclusively for his leadership of the opposition to free trade.—TRANSLATOR.]

And are they not borrowing from her the quibbles of protectionism?

We are alleged to be yielding to pressure from Bordeaux and the South!

And do they not serve the greed of Lille and the North?*

We are charged with abetting the secret designs of the ministry, which is trying to divert public attention from its policy!

And are they not favoring the views of the civil service, which benefits more than anyone else in the world from the policy of protectionism?

You see very well that, if we were willing to stoop to character assassination of this kind, we should have no shortage of weapons.

But that is not what is in question.

The question, and I shall not lose sight of it, is this:

Which is better for the working classes—to be, or not to be, free to buy from abroad?

You workers are told: "If you are free to buy from abroad what you now produce yourselves, you will no longer produce it; you will be without employment, without wages, and without bread; it is therefore for your own good that we are limiting your freedom."

This argument takes all kinds of forms. For instance, it is said: "If we clothe ourselves in English fabrics, if we make our plows with English iron, if we cut our bread with English knives, if we dry our hands with English towels, what will become of French workingmen? What will become of our *domestic industry?*"

Tell me, workers, suppose a man were to stand on the dock at the port of Boulogne and say to each Englishman who landed, "If you will give me those English shoes, I will give you this French hat"; or "If you will give me that English horse, I will give you this French tilbury"; or, "Would you like to exchange that Birmingham machine for this French clock?" or, again, "Would it suit you to trade that Newcastle coal for this champagne?" and assuming that our man used good judgment in making his pro-

---

* [In France at this time, just as traditionally in the United States, there was an agricultural, free-trade South and an industrial, protectionist North.—TRANSLATOR.]

posals, can it be said that our *domestic industry,* taken as a whole, would be injured as a result?

Would it be any more so if there were twenty men offering exchanges at Boulogne instead of one, if there were a million such transactions instead of four, or if merchants and money were introduced in order to facilitate the whole process and indefinitely multiply the number of individual acts of exchange?

Now, whether one country buys wholesale from another in order to sell at retail, or buys at retail in order to resell wholesale, if we follow the transaction to its ultimate conclusion, we shall always find that *commerce* is nothing but a complex of *barter transactions* involving the exchange of *goods for goods* and *services for services.* If, then, a single barter transaction does no harm to *domestic industry,* since it involves just as much *domestic labor given* as *foreign labor received,* a hundred billion barter transactions will not harm it any the more.

But, you may ask, in what will the profit consist? The profit comes from making the best use of the resources of each country, so that the same amount of labor yields greater satisfaction and well-being everywhere.

There are some who resort to an unusual stratagem in dealing with you. They begin by conceding that free trade is superior to a policy of protectionism, doubtless in order to avoid having to defend themselves on that ground.

Then, they remark that, in the transition from one system to the other, there will be some *displacement* of labor.

Next, they expatiate on the sufferings that this *displacement* must, according to them, necessarily entail. They exaggerate these sufferings, enlarge upon them, make them the chief subject of discussion, representing them as the sole and final consequence of the proposed reform, and strive in this way to enlist you under the banner of monopoly.

This is, in fact, the very same stratagem that has been used to defend every kind of abuse; and I must frankly acknowledge that it always disconcerts the proponents of reforms, even of those most desirable for the people.

The reason for this is easily understood.

Once an abuse exists, everything is arranged on the assumption that it will last indefinitely; and, as more and more people come to depend upon it for their livelihood, and still others depend upon them, a superstructure is erected that soon comprises a formidable edifice.

The moment you try to tear it down, everybody protests; and the point to which I wish to call particular attention here is that those who protest always appear at first glance to be in the right, because it is easier to show the disorder that must accompany reform than the order that should follow it.

The supporters of the abuse are able to cite specific facts; they can name the particular persons, as well as their suppliers and workers, who will be injured by the reform—while the reformer, poor devil, can refer only to the *general good* that is to be gradually diffused among the masses. This does not produce nearly so great an effect.

Thus, if the question is that of abolishing slavery, "You poor men," they say to the Negroes, "who is going to feed you now? Your master may have you beaten, but he also provides you with cassava."

And the slaves miss their fetters, for they ask: "Where are we to get our cassava?"

They do not see that it is not the master who feeds them, but their own labor, which also feeds the master.

When the monasteries were being reformed in Spain, people would ask the beggars, "Where will you get your food and clothing? The prior is your good angel. Is it not convenient to be able to turn to him?"

And the beggars would say: "It's true. If the prior goes away, we see quite clearly what we stand to lose, but we do not see who will come to take his place in our lives."*

What they failed to see was that if the monasteries were bestowing alms, they were also living on them; so that the monks received more than they gave.

In the same way, workers, monopoly imperceptibly lays taxes on

* [In 1836 the monasteries in Spain were closed, and their property was confiscated by the government.—TRANSLATOR.]

the shoulders of all of you, and then, out of the income derived from these taxes, it gives you jobs.

And your false friends ask you, "If there were no monopolies, who would give you work?"

And you reply, "That's right. We can count on the jobs the monopolists obtain for us. But whether we can count on the promises of free trade is uncertain."

What you fail to see is that the monopolists first worm the money out of you, and then give you back a part of it for your labor.

You ask who will give you work? Good heavens! Do you not see that you give one another work? With the money that will no longer be taken away from you, the shoemaker will dress better and give work to the tailor. The tailor will buy new shoes more often and give work to the shoemaker. And the same thing will happen in all other branches of business.

It is said that under a system of free trade there will be fewer workers in the mines and textile mills.

I do not think so. But, if this does happen, it will be *necessarily* because a greater number of workers will be voluntarily employed at home or working above ground.

For if these mines and textile mills can support themselves, as is alleged, only with the help of taxes levied for their benefit on *everyone*, once these taxes are abolished, *everyone* will be more prosperous, and it is the prosperity of all that supports the labor of each.

Excuse me if I dwell a little longer on this point. I should so much like to see all of you on the side of free trade!

Suppose that the capital invested in French industry yields a profit of five per cent. But here is M. Mondor, who has put 100,000 francs into a mill that leaves him with a loss of five per cent. Between profit and loss, the difference is 10,000 francs. What is to be done? Quite stealthily, a small tax of 10,000 francs is imposed on you, and the proceeds are turned over to Mondor. You do not notice it, because the whole affair is very cleverly disguised. It is not the tax collector who comes to demand from you your share of the tax; instead you pay it to Mondor, the ironmaster, every time you buy your hatchets, your trowels, and your planes.

Then you are told: "If you do not pay this tax, Mondor will go out of business; his workers, Jack and Jim, will be out of work." Good heavens! If the tax were restored to you, would you not put one another to work, and for your own benefit too?

After that, rest assured, once this soft cushion of price-supports maintained by taxation is removed, Mondor will spare no effort to convert his loss into a profit, and Jack and Jim will not be discharged. Then *everyone* will profit.

Perhaps you will rejoin: "We quite understand that after the reform there will, on the whole, be more jobs than before; but meanwhile Jack and Jim will be out on the street."

To this, I reply:

1. When labor is displaced only so that jobs can multiply, any man who has a head and hands is not left long on the street.

2. There is nothing to hinder the state from earmarking certain funds to provide, during the transition, for the relief of unemployment, which I, for my part, do not think will occur.

3. Finally, if I know the workers, they are quite ready to endure some temporary hardships necessitated by a shift from one job to another if this means getting out of a rut and entering upon a life that will be better and, above all, fairer for everyone. Would that the same were true of their employers!

After all, just because you are workers, are you not intelligent and responsible? Your pretended friends seem to forget this. Is it not surprising that they should discuss such a question in your presence and talk of wages and profits, without even once uttering the word *justice*? Yet they are well aware that trade restrictions are *unjust*. Why, then, do they not have the courage to admit it and to tell you: "Workers, an injustice prevails in this country, but it is profitable for you, and it must be maintained." Why? Because they know that you would reply: "No."

But it is not true that this injustice is profitable to you. Give me your attention for a few more moments, and judge for yourselves.

What is being protected in France? Things made by big business—iron, coal, cloth, and textiles—and you are told that this is done, not in the interests of the entrepreneurs, but in yours, in order to guarantee you employment.

Yet every time *foreign labor* appears on our market in such a form that it could be harmful to you, but useful to the big businessmen, do they not let it enter?

Are there not twenty thousand Germans in Paris making clothes and shoes? Why are they permitted to establish themselves alongside of you, when cloth from abroad is barred from France? Because cloth is made in large mills belonging to manufacturers who are also legislators, whereas clothing is made by workers in their own homes. In the processing of wool into cloth, these gentlemen want no competition, because that is what they do for a living; but in the processing of cloth into clothing, they readily allow it, for that is what you do for a living.

When they built railroads, they prohibited the importation of English rails, but they brought over English workmen. Why? Well, it's quite simple: because English rails compete with those produced by our own big mills, whereas English labor competes only with your labor.

We ourselves do not ask that German tailors and English navvies be kept out of France. What we ask is that cloth and rails be free to enter. We demand justice for all, equality before the law for everyone!

It is ridiculous to tell us that tariff restrictions are imposed for your benefit. Tailors, shoemakers, carpenters, joiners, masons, blacksmiths, shopkeepers, grocers, clockmakers, butchers, bakers, upholsterers, milliners—I defy you all to cite me a single respect in which protectionism benefits you, and, any time you wish, I shall cite you four in which it harms you.

Let us see, after all, just how much truth there is in your journalists' accounts of the "self-sacrifice" practiced by the monopolists.

I think one may call the *natural rate of wages* that which would be established *naturally* under a system of free trade. When, therefore, you were told that protectionism is to your advantage, this was as good as being told that it adds a *surplus* to your *natural* wages. Now, a surplus *over and above the natural rate* of wages must come from somewhere; it does not fall from the moon, and it must come from those who pay it.

You are therefore led to the conclusion that, according to your self-styled friends, the policy of protectionism has been introduced and adopted so that the interests of the capitalists may be sacrificed to those of the workers.

Now, tell me, is that likely?

Where, then, is your seat in the Chamber of Peers? When have you had a voice at the Palais-Bourbon?* Who has ever asked your advice? Where did you get this idea of instituting a policy of protectionism?

I can hear you answer: "It was not we who instituted it. Alas, we are neither peers nor deputies nor councillors of state! It was the capitalists who did it."

Great God in heaven! They must have been in very good humor that day! What! The capitalists made the law; they instituted the policy of protectionism, and they did it so that you workers might profit at their expense!

But here is what is even more extraordinary.

How does it happen that your self-styled friends, who talk to you so much about the goodness, the generosity, and the self-sacrifice of the capitalists, never cease to commiserate with you on the fact that you are deprived of your political rights? From their point of view, what could you do with them even if you enjoyed them? The capitalists have a monopoly on legislation; that is true.† Thanks to this monopoly, they have conferred upon themselves a monopoly on iron, cloth, textiles, coal, wood, and meat—that is also true. But your self-styled friends tell you that by doing this the capitalists have impoverished themselves, without being under any obligation to do so, in order to enrich you, without your having any right to be rich! Surely, if you were voters and deputies, you could not manage your affairs better; indeed, you could not manage them so well.

If the currently prevailing industrial organization has been designed with your interests in view, then it is perfidious to demand political rights on your behalf; for these new-fangled democrats

---

* [Meeting-place, in Paris, of the Chamber of Deputies.—TRANSLATOR.]

† [In France at this time, out of a population of about thirty millions, perhaps as many as 200,000 men from the upper-income group were empowered to vote.—TRANSLATOR.]

will never escape the following dilemma: the law, as made by the middle classes, either gives you *more,* or it gives you *less,* than your natural wages. If it gives you *less,* they are deceiving you by inviting you to support it. If it gives you *more,* they are still deceiving you by urging you to demand political rights, when the middle classes are making sacrifices for you that you, in all honesty, would not dare to vote for yourselves.

Workers, God forbid that this tract should have the effect of sowing in your hearts any seeds of resentment against the wealthy classes! If self-interest, whether badly understood or genuinely alarmed, is still the mainstay of monopoly, let us not forget that it has its roots in *errors* common to both capitalists and workers. Thus, rather than incite them against one another, let us strive to draw them together. And what do we need to do to achieve this end? If it is true that natural social tendencies are conducive to the elimination of inequalities among men, we need only allow these tendencies to operate, remove the artificial obstacles that interfere with their effectiveness, and let the relations among the various classes be based upon justice, which is indistinguishable, at least in my mind, from the principle of freedom.[2]

7

A Chinese Tale

People bewail the greed and selfishness of our age!

I, for my part, find the world, especially Paris, peopled with Deciuses.*

Open the thousand books, the thousand newspapers, the thousand pamphlets, that the Parisian presses spew forth every day over the country. Are they not all the work of little saints?

What animation in the painting of the vices of our day! What moving concern for the masses! With what liberality the rich are invited to share with the poor, if not the poor with the rich! What a host of plans for social reforms, social improvements, social organizations! Is there any hack scribbler who is not devoting himself to the welfare of the toiling masses? For an advance of a few crowns,† he will find the opportunity to indulge himself in humanitarian lucubrations.

And yet people talk about the selfishness and individualism of our era!

There is nothing that does not pretend to serve the well-being and the edification of the people—nothing, not even the *customhouse*. You think, perhaps, that it is just another instrument of taxation, like the license bureau or the tollhouse at the end of the bridge? Nothing of the kind. It is essentially an institution for the ad-

---

* [The Deciuses referred to here were Publus Decius Mus, father and son, both military leaders of the Roman Republic between 350 and 275 B.C. Each is said to have performed an act of self-devotion by hurling himself into the enemy's midst when the Roman column he was leading was repulsed by the foe.—TRANSLATOR.]

† [Écus, obsolete French coins approximating in size the later silver five-franc piece. —TRANSLATOR.]

vancement of civilization, fraternity, and equality. What do you expect? To be in fashion today, one must show, or pretend to show, feeling, sentimental sensibility, everywhere, even at the customhouse window where they ask, "What do you have there, friend?"

But for realizing these humanitarian aspirations, the customhouse has, it must be confessed, some rather strange procedures.

It musters an army of directors, assistant directors, inspectors, deputy inspectors, superintendents, auditors, collectors, department heads, assistant department heads, clerks, supernumeraries, candidates for the jobs of supernumeraries, and candidates for the candidacy, to say nothing of those on *active service*—all with the object of exercising over the productive activities of the people the negative action that can be summed up in the word *bar*.

Notice that I do not say *tax*, but quite genuinely *bar*.

And to *bar*, not acts repugnant to morality or dangerous to public order, but transactions that are innocent and, as is admitted, conducive to peace and harmony among nations.

Nevertheless, mankind is so flexible and adaptable that in one way or another it always surmounts these *barriers*. It is just a matter of applying more labor.

If people are barred from importing their food from abroad, they produce it domestically. This is more laborious, but one must eat. If they are barred from passing through the valley, they climb over the mountains. This way is longer, but one must reach one's destination.

All this is regrettable, but it does have its ridiculous side. When the law has in this way created a certain number of obstacles, and when, in order to overcome them, mankind has diverted a corresponding amount of labor from other employments, you are no longer allowed to demand the reform of the law; for if you point out the *obstacle*, the jobs that it makes for are pointed out to you, and if you say, "These are not jobs that have been *created*, but *displaced*, by the obstacle," you are answered in the words of *L'Ésprit public:* "Only our impoverishment is certain and immediate; as for our enrichment, that is more than problematical."

This reminds me of a Chinese story.

Once upon a time there were, in China, two great cities: Chin and Chan. They were connected by a magnificent canal. The emperor judged it desirable to have enormous blocks of stone thrown into it, in order to put it out of service.

Seeing this, Kuang, his chief mandarin, said to him:

"Son of Heaven, you are making a mistake."

To which the emperor replied:

"Kuang, you are talking like a fool."

(Of course I am reporting here only the gist of their conversation.)

After three moons had passed, the celestial emperor sent for the mandarin and said to him:

"Kuang, look yonder."

And Kuang opened his eyes and looked.

And he saw, some distance from the canal, a multitude of men *at work*. Some were excavating, others were raising embankments, still others were leveling the ground, and others laying paving stones; and the mandarin, who was very well read, thought to himself: They are making a highway.

After three more moons had passed, the emperor summoned Kuang and said to him:

"Look yonder."

And Kuang looked.

And he saw that the highway was completed, and he noticed that at different points all along the road, inns were being built. A host of pedestrians, carts, and palanquins were coming and going; and innumerable Chinese, overcome with fatigue, were carrying heavy burdens from Chin to Chan and from Chan to Chin. And Kuang said to himself: "It was the destruction of the canal that provided jobs for these poor people." But it never occurred to him that their labor had been *diverted* from other employments.

And three more moons passed by, and the emperor said to Kuang:

"Look yonder."

And Kuang looked.

And he saw that the inns were always full of travelers, and, grouped around them, were the shops of butchers, bakers, and dealers in swallows' nests, to feed the hungry travelers. And, inasmuch as these worthy artisans could not go about naked, there had also settled among them tailors, shoemakers, and dealers in parasols and fans; and since people do not sleep out in the open air, even in the Celestial Empire, there were also carpenters, masons, and roofers. Then there were police officials, judges, and fakirs; in brief, a city with its suburbs had grown up around each inn.

And the emperor said to Kuang, "What do you think of it?"

And Kuang replied: "I should never have thought that the destruction of a canal could create jobs for so many people"; for it never occurred to him that these jobs had not been created, but *displaced,* and that the travelers used to eat just as well when they went along the canal as they did after they were forced to use the highway.

However, to the great astonishment of the Chinese, the emperor died, and this Son of Heaven was laid to rest.

His successor sent for Kuang and said: "Have the canal opened up."

And Kuang said to the new emperor:

"Son of Heaven, you are making a mistake."

And the emperor answered:

"Kuang, you are talking like a fool."

But Kuang persisted and said, "Sire, what do you have in mind?"

"I have in mind," the emperor said, "facilitating the movement of men and things between Chin and Chan by making transportation less expensive, so that the people may have tea and clothing at lower cost."

But Kuang was all prepared. The evening before, he had received several issues of the *Moniteur industriel,* a Chinese newspaper. Knowing his lesson well, he asked permission to reply; after obtaining it, he prostrated himself nine times and said:

"Sire, by facilitating transporation, you hope to reduce the price of consumers' goods, in order to put them within reach of the people, and to this end, you begin by making them lose all the jobs that the destruction of the canal gave rise to. Sire, in political economy, low prices . . ."

The emperor: "You seem to be reciting this from memory."

Kuang: "You are right; it will be more convenient for me to read it to you."

And, after unfolding *L'Ésprit public*, he read:

In political economy, low prices for consumers' goods are of only secondary importance. The real problem consists in establishing an equilibrium between the price of labor and that of the means of subsistence. The wealth of a nation consists in the amount of employment it provides its labor force, and the best economic system is that which provides the greatest possible number of jobs. The question is not whether it is better to pay four cash or eight cash for a cup of tea, five taels or ten taels for a shirt. These are childish considerations unworthy of a mature mind. No one disputes your thesis. The problem is whether it is better to have to pay more for a commodity, but to have, thanks to the abundance of jobs and the higher price of labor, more means of acquiring it; or whether it is better to limit the number of job opportunities, reduce the total quantity of domestic production, and transport consumers' goods by water, doubtless at lower cost, but at the same time denying some of our workers the possibility of buying them even at these reduced prices.

Since the emperor was still not entirely convinced, Kuang said to him: "Sire, deign to wait. I still have the *Moniteur industriel* to read to you."

But the emperor said:

"I do not need your Chinese newspapers to know that to create *obstacles* is to divert and displace labor. But that is not my mission. Go out there and clear the obstacles from the canal. After that, we'll reform the tariff."

And Kuang went off, tearing at his beard and lamenting: "O Fô! O Pê! O Lî! and all other monosyllabic, circumflected gods of Cathay, take pity on your people; for there has come to us an emperor of the *English school,* and I can see that before long we shall be in want of everything, since we shall no longer need to do anything "

8

Post Hoc, Ergo Propter Hoc*[1]

This is the most common and the most deceptive of all fallacies.

Real suffering is taking place in England.

It comes in the train of two other events:

1. The tariff reform.†

2. Two bad harvests in succession.

To which of these last two circumstances is the first to be attributed?

The protectionists have not failed to cry out: "It is this accursed
free trade that is causing all the trouble. It promised us no end of
blessings, we accepted it, and here the factories have closed, and
the people are suffering: *Cum hoc, ergo propter hoc.*"

Free trade distributes in the most uniform and equitable manner the fruits that Providence grants to the labor of man. If some
of these fruits are destroyed by a natural disaster, free trade nonetheless ensures the fair distribution of what remains. Men are, no
doubt, less well supplied; but should the blame be laid on free
trade, or on the natural disaster?

Free trade acts on the same principle as insurance. When a
disaster occurs, insurance spreads over a great number of men and
a great many years losses that, in its absence, would have had to be
borne by one individual all at one time. Now, is one ever justified
in saying that fire is no longer a calamity since the introduction of
insurance?

* [Latin, "after this; therefore, on account of it."—TRANSLATOR.]

† [In 1846 Parliament had taken the longest step toward introducing free trade by
ending the duties on imports of grain.—TRANSLATOR.]

In 1842, 1843, and 1844, England began reducing her tariffs. At the same time, her harvests were very abundant; and it is reasonable to conclude that these two circumstances contributed to the unprecedented prosperity that the country enjoyed during this period.

In 1845, the harvest was poor; in 1846, poorer still. As the price of food rose, the people had to spend more of their available resources just to feed themselves, and had to limit their consumption of other commodities accordingly. Clothing was less in demand, factories were not so busy, and wages showed a tendency to decline.

Fortunately, in that same year, the tariff barriers were lowered again, and an enormous quantity of food was able to enter the English market. Otherwise it is almost certain that a frightful revolution would have broken out in Great Britain at that time.

And yet free trade is blamed for disasters that it forestalled and at least partly redressed!

A poor leper was living in solitude. No one wanted to touch anything he had touched. Reduced to providing entirely for himself, he dragged out a miserable existence. One day a great doctor cured him. Now our recluse was able to enjoy all the benefits of *free trade*. What a beautiful future was opening up before him! He entertained himself by imagining the excellent use which, thanks to his relations with other men, he would now be able to make of his physical strength. But then he had the misfortune to break both his arms. Alas! Now his lot was more dreadful. The journalists of this country, witnessing his misery, said, "Look at what free trade has reduced him to! Really, he was less to be pitied when he lived as a recluse."

"Come now," replied the doctor, "do you take no account of his two broken arms? Have they nothing to do with his sorry plight? His misfortune comes from having lost the use of his arms, and not at all from being cured of leprosy. He would be much more pitiable if he had the use of but one arm and were leprous into the bargain."

Post hoc, ergo propter hoc; put no faith in that sophism.

9

Robbery by Subsidy[1]

People are finding my little book of *Sophisms* too theoretical, scientific, and metaphysical. Very well. Let us try the effect of a trivial, banal, and, if need be, a ruder style of writing. Convinced that the public has been *duped* into accepting the policy of protectionism, I have tried to prove it by an appeal to reason. But the public prefers to be shouted at. Therefore, let us vociferate:

Midas, King Midas, has the ears of an ass!*

A burst of plain speaking often works better than the most polished of circumlocutions. You remember Oronte and the difficulty that the misanthrope, utterly misanthropic though he is, has in convincing him of his fatuity.

> ALCESTE: One takes the chance of making oneself look
> ridiculous.
> ORONTE: And are you trying to tell me by these words
> That I am wrong in wanting. . . . ?
> ALCESTE: I don't say that.
> But. . . . .
> ORONTE: Do I write badly. . . . ?
> ALCESTE: I don't say that.
> But after all. . . . .

* [A reference to the ancient legend of King Midas, who, after preferring Pan's flute to Apollo's lyre in a musical contest, had a pair of ass's ears clapped on his head by Apollo.—TRANSLATOR.]

ORONTE: But can't I find out just what in my
         sonnet . . . . ?
ALCESTE: Frankly, you ought to hide it somewhere and
         forget it.*

Frankly, dear public, *you are being robbed.* This may be put
crudely, but at least it is clear.

The words *robbery, rob, and robber,* may appear to many people
to be in bad taste. I should ask them, as Harpagon asked Élise: "Is
it the word or the thing that makes you afraid?"†

"Whoever by fraud has taken possession of a thing that does not
belong to him is guilty of robbery." (Penal Code, art. 379.)

To rob: To appropriate by stealth or by force. (Dictionary of
the Académie française.)

Robber: He who exacts more than his due. (*Ibid.*)

Now, does not the monopolist who, by means of a law of his own
making, makes it necessary for me to pay him twenty francs for
what I could buy elsewhere for fifteen, take from me, by fraud,
five francs that belong to me?

Does he not appropriate them by stealth or by force?

Does he not exact more than his due?

He does, indeed, it may be said, take; he does appropriate; he
does exact; but not at all *by stealth* or *by force,* which are the
characteristics of robbery.

When our tax accounts contain a charge of five francs for the
subsidy that the monopolist takes, appropriates, or exacts, what
could be more *stealthy,* since so few of us suspect it? And for those
who are not dupes, what could be more *forced,* since at the first
sign of refusal the bailiff's man is at our door?

Still, the monopolists need have no anxiety on that score. Rob-

* [Excerpts from a scene in Molière's *Le Misanthrope,* in which Alceste, the misanthrope, is trying to tell Oronte, a silly nobleman, that a sonnet of Oronte's is
literarily worthless. The problem arises from the fact that Alceste, an upright man,
is severely limited by strict rules on his conduct and speech. He is, however, a
personal advocate of frankness, so that after several circumlocutions he bursts out
with the last line.—TRANSLATOR.]

† [In Molière's *L'Avare,* Harpagon, the miser, asks this question of Élise, his daughter, regarding "marriage."—TRANSLATOR.]

beries *by subsidy* or *by tariff*, though they violate equity quite as much as highway robbery does, do not violate the law; on the contrary, they are perpetrated by means of the law; this fact only makes them worse, but the *magistrates* have no quarrel with them.

Besides, willy-nilly, we are all both *robbers* and *robbed* in this respect. The author of this volume may well cry, "Stop thief!" when he buys, but people could just as well address the same cry to him when he sells;[2] if he differs very much from his fellow countrymen, it is only in the fact that he knows that he loses more at the game than he wins, and they do not; if they knew it, they would soon bring the game to an end.

Nor do I boast of being the first to call this practice by its proper name. Here is what Smith said of it more than sixty years ago:

People of the same trade seldom meet together, even for merriment and diversion, but the conversation ends in a conspiracy against the public, or in some contrivance to raise prices.*

Should this surprise us, when the public shows no concern about it?

Let us suppose that a council of industrialists is formed and holds a meeting for the purpose of setting a *general policy.* What takes place, and what decisions are reached?

Here, greatly abridged, are the minutes of the meeting.

"A SHIPOWNER: Our merchant marine is in a desperate situation [outburst of indignation]. No wonder! I can't build without iron. I find plenty of it at ten francs *on the world market;* but, by law, the French ironmaster compels me to pay fifteen francs for it; so there go five francs that he takes from me. I demand the freedom to buy where I think best.

"AN IRONMASTER: *On the world market,* I can have freight shipped for twenty francs. By law, the shipowner exacts thirty; so there go ten francs that he *takes* from me. He plunders me, and I plunder him; everything is as it should be.

"A STATESMAN: The shipowner has come to a most unwise conclusion. Let us, rather, encourage the close harmony that gives us

* [Adam Smith, *The Wealth of Nations,* Bk. I, chap. x, Pt. II.—TRANSLATOR.]

our strength; if we yield even a single point in the theory of protectionism, we may as well say farewell to the whole of it.

"THE SHIPOWNER: But protectionism has failed us; I repeat that our merchant marine is in desperate straits.

"A SHIPMASTER: Very well! Let us raise the *surtax,* and the shipowner, who is taking thirty francs from the public for their freight, can take forty.

"A CABINET MINISTER: The government will make the utmost possible use of the beautiful mechanism of the *surtax,* but even that, I am afraid, will not suffice.[3]

"A GOVERNMENT OFFICIAL: Here you are, all completely stymied by a minor detail. Is there no salvation except in the tariff? Are you not forgetting taxation? The consumer may be generous, but the taxpayer is no less so. Let us heap taxes upon him, and the shipowner will be content. I propose that a five-franc subsidy be paid to the shipwright out of the public treasury for every quintal of iron he uses.

"CONFUSION OF VOICES: Second the motion! Second the motion!

"A FARMER: A three-franc subsidy per hectoliter of wheat for me!

"A TEXTILE MANUFACTURER: A two-franc subsidy per meter of cloth for me! Etc., etc.

"THE CHAIRMAN: Then it's agreed; our meeting has instituted the system of *subsidies,* and that shall be its eternal glory. What industry can ever again suffer losses, now that we have two such simple means of converting losses into profits—the tariff and the subsidy? The meeting is adjourned."

Some supernatural intuition must have given me a premonition, in a dream, of the imminent appearance of the *subsidy* (who knows but that I may even have first suggested the idea to M. Dupin?) when, a few months ago, I wrote the following words:

It seems clear to me that neither the essence nor the consequence of protectionism would in any way be altered if it took the form of a direct tax levied by the state and distributed as subsidies to privileged industries by way of indemnification.

And, after comparing a protective tariff to a subsidy:

I frankly confess my preference for the latter system. It seems to me more just, more economical, and more honest: more just, because if society wants to pay bounties to certain of its members, everybody should contribute to them; more economical, because it will save much of the cost of collection and will eliminate many restrictions; finally, more honest, because the public would then see clearly the nature of the operation and realize what it is being made to do.[4]

Let us study this system of *robbery by subsidy*, since the opportunity for doing so has been so kindly offered to us. What can be said about it is equally applicable to *robbery by tariff*; and since the latter is a little better disguised, the system of direct pocket-picking will help us to understand the system of indirect pocket-picking. The mind will thus be led from the simple to the complex.

But is there not a type of robbery that is simpler still? Yes, indeed; there is *highway robbery;* it requires only to be legalized and monopolized, or—as they say today—*organized.*

Now, here is what I find in a book of travels I have been reading:

When we arrived in the kingdom of A . . . ., all branches of industry were saying that they were in a doleful state. The farmers were bewailing their lot, the manufacturers were complaining, the merchants were protesting, the shipowners were grumbling, and the government did not know whom to listen to. At first, it had the idea of levying a heavy tax on all the malcontents and then dividing the proceeds among them, after deducting a share for itself, very much on the same principle as that of the Spanish lottery that is so dear to us. There are a thousand of you, and the state takes one piaster from each; then it craftily skims off 250 piasters, and divides the remaining 750, in larger or smaller shares, among the players. The worthy hidalgo who receives three-fourths of a piaster, forgetting that he has contributed a whole piaster, cannot contain himself for joy and rushes off to spend his fifteen reals* at the nearest pothouse. This would have been something like what is happening in France. Be that as it may, uncivilized though the country was, the government did not think that the inhabitants were so stupid that they could be relied on to accept such strange methods of protection, and so it finally adopted the following plan.

The country was covered with a network of roads. The government had the kilometers marked off on them very exactly, and then it told the farmers: "Everything you can steal from those traveling between these two markers is yours; let it serve as your *subsidy,* your protection, your incentive." Then it assigned each manufacturer and each shipowner a portion of the road to exploit, according to the following formula:

> I give and grant you
> Power and authority to
>   Steal,
>   Plunder,
>   Thieve,
>   Cheat,
>   And swindle,
> With impunity along this whole
> Road.†

Now, it has come to pass that the natives of the kingdom of A . . . . have today become so used to this system, so accustomed to taking into account only what they have stolen, and not what is stolen from them, so thoroughly addicted to viewing plunder only from the viewpoint of the plunderer, that they regard the sum total of all individual thefts as *gross national profit* and refuse to give up a system of *protection* in the absence of which, they say, there is not a single branch of industry that could fend for itself.

* [This is the *real de vellón,* a base-silver coin, of which there were twenty to the piaster (peso). The *real de plata* was presumably of sterling and valued at one-eighth of a piaster, which consequently was a "piece of eight."—TRANSLATOR.]
† [Faithful to his promise to alter his literary style, Bastiat here indulges in a parody of Molière's parody on the conferring of the degree of Doctor of Medicine in his comedy, *The Imaginary Invalid* (*Le Malade imaginaire*). Molière says in macaronic Latin: "I give and grant you / Power and authority to / Practice medicine, / Purge, / Bleed, / Stab, / Hack, / Slash, / and Kill / With impunity / Throughout the whole world."—TRANSLATOR.]

Do you find this hard to believe? It is not possible, you protest, that a whole nation should agree in seeing an *increase in wealth* in what the inhabitants steal from one another.

And why not? We have completely accepted this view in France, and are continually devising and improving methods of *reciprocal robbery* under the name of subsidies and protective tariffs.

Still, let us not exaggerate. Let us agree that, with regard to the *method of collection* and all attendant circumstances, the system of the kingdom of A . . . . may be worse than ours; but we must at the same time acknowledge that, with respect to the essential principle and its necessary consequences, there is not an iota of difference among all these species of robbery instituted by law to provide additional profits for the various branches of industry.

It should also be observed that, if there are certain inconveniences in the perpetration of *highway robbery*, it also has advantages that are not to be found in *robbery by tariff*.

For example, it is possible to make an equitable division of its proceeds among all the producers. The same cannot be done in the case of customs duties. These by their very nature are incapable of protecting certain classes of society, such as artisans, tradesmen, men of letters, lawyers, military personnel, laborers, etc.

It is true that *robbery by subsidy* also lends itself to infinite subdivision of the proceeds, and in this respect is no less effective than *highway robbery;* but, on the other hand, it often leads to such bizarre and absurd consequences that the natives of the kingdom of A . . . . might well regard it as ridiculous. What the victim of a highway robbery loses, the robber gains. The stolen object at least remains in the country. But, under the system of *robbery by subsidy,* what the tax takes away from the French is often conferred upon the Chinese, the Hottentots, the Kaffirs, or the Algonquins. This is how it works:

Suppose a piece of cloth is worth a *hundred francs* at Bordeaux. It is impossible to sell it for less without a loss, and it is impossible to sell it for more, because *competition* among the sellers prevents the price from rising any higher. Under these circumstances, if a Frenchman wants to buy this cloth, he will have to pay a *hundred francs* or do without it. But if it is an Englishman who wants to buy the cloth, then the government intervenes and tells the merchant: "Sell your cloth; I shall make the taxpayers give you *twenty francs.*" The merchant, who neither demands nor can get more than a hundred francs for his cloth, sells it to the Englishman for eighty francs. This sum added to the twenty francs which *robbery by subsidy* has extorted makes his account exactly even. The result is, therefore, precisely the same as if the taxpayers had given twenty francs to the Englishman on condition that he buy French cloth at a twenty-franc discount, at twenty francs below the cost of production, at twenty francs below what it would cost us ourselves. Thus, *robbery by subsidy* has this peculiarity, that its *victims* live in the country that tolerates it, while the *robbers* are scattered over the face of the earth.

It is really astonishing that people still persist in considering it as an established truth that *everything that the individual steals from the common fund represents a general gain.* Perpetual motion, the philosopher's stone, the squaring of the circle, have long since ceased to occupy men's minds; but the theory of *progress through robbery* is still held in esteem. Yet a priori one might have thought that of all puerilities this was the least likely to survive.

There are those who ask us: "Are you, then, advocating a policy of *laissez passer?** Are you one of the economists of the superannuated school of Smith and Say? Is that why you are opposed to the *organization of industry?*" Well, gentlemen, organize industry as much as you please. But we, for our part, will take care to see that you do not organize *robbery.*

Others, more numerous, keep repeating: "*Subsidies* and *tariffs* have been allowed to go too far. They must be used with discretion, and not abused. What *judicious,* practical men advocate is a sensible amount of free trade combined with a moderate amount of protectionism. Let us beware of *absolute principles.*"

This, according to the Spanish traveler, is exactly what was being said in the kingdom of A. . . . . "Highway robbery," the

---

* [*Laissez passer:* "allow to pass," substantially equivalent to *laissez faire.*—TRANSLATOR.]

wise men said, "is neither good nor bad in itself; that depends on circumstances. All that needs to be done is to keep things *evenly balanced* and to pay us government officials well for this labor of balancing. Perhaps pillage has been allowed too much latitude; perhaps it has not been allowed enough. Let us see, let us examine, let us balance the account of each worker. To those who do not earn enough, we shall give a little more of the road to exploit. For those who earn too much, we shall reduce the hours, days, or months during which they will be allowed to pillage."

Those who spoke in this way acquired for themselves a great reputation for moderation, prudence, and wisdom. They never failed to rise to the highest offices in the state.

As for those who said: "Let us eliminate every injustice, for there is no such thing as a partial injustice; let us tolerate no *robbery*, for there is no such thing as a *half-robbery* or a *quarter-robbery*," they were regarded as idle visionaries, tiresome dreamers who kept repeating the same thing over and over again. Besides, the people found their arguments too easy to understand.. How can one believe that what is so simple can be true?

10

The Tax Collector

JAMES GOODFELLOW, a Vineyardist.
CLODPATE, a Tax Collector.

CLODPATE: You have laid in twenty tuns of wine?

JAMES GOODFELLOW: Yes, by dint of much toil and sweat.

C.: Be so kind as to give me six of the best.

J.G.: Six tuns out of twenty! Good heavens! You're trying to ruin me. And, if you please, what do you intend to do with them?

C.: The first will be given to the creditors of the state. When one has debts, the very least one can do is to pay the interest on them.

J.G.: And what has become of the principal?

C.: That would take too long to tell. A part of it was once invested in cartridges, which produced the most beautiful smoke in the world. Another part went to pay those who became crippled in foreign lands that they had laid waste. Then, when these expenditures of ours led to an invasion of our land by our good friends, the enemy, they were unwilling to leave without taking away some money, which we had to borrow.

J.G.: And what benefit do I derive from it today?

C.: The satisfaction of saying:

> How proud I am to be a Frenchman
> When I behold the triumphal column!*

* [An adaptation from a popular song, author unknown. The "column" refers to the Vendôme Column standing in the heart of Paris, made from the brass of the cannons captured by Napoleon at the Battle of Austerlitz in 1805.—TRANSLATOR.]

J.G.: And the humiliation of leaving to my heirs an estate burdened with a rent that they will have to pay for all time to come. Still, one really must pay one's debts, however foolishly the money may have been spent. So much for one tun. But what about the other five?

C.: One is required to pay for government services, the civil list, the judges who see to it that you get back the bit of land your neighbor tries to appropriate for himself, the policemen who drive away robbers while you are asleep, the road mender who maintains the highway leading to the city, the parish priest who baptizes your children, the teacher who educates them, and your humble servant, who does not work for nothing either.

J.G.: That's fair enough. Service for service. I have nothing to say against that. I'd just as soon make my own arrangements directly with my parish priest and my schoolmaster; but I do not insist on it. So much for the second tun. That's still a long way from six.

C.: Do you feel that two tuns are too much for your contribution toward the expenses of the army and the navy?

J.G.: Alas, that's very little, considering what they have cost me already; for they have taken from me two sons, whom I loved dearly.

C.: It is absolutely essential to maintain the balance of power in Europe.

J.G.: Good heavens! The balance of power would be quite as well maintained if the armed forces of every country were reduced by one-half or three-fourths. We should then be able to keep our children and the fruits of our labor. It would take no more than mutual understanding.

C.: Yes; but that is precisely what is lacking.

J.G.: That is what astonishes me. After all, everybody suffers from it.

C.: You have only yourself to blame, James Goodfellow.

J.G.: You are joking, Mr. Tax Collector. Do I have any voice in the matter?

C.: Whom did you support for deputy?

J.G.: A gallant army general who will soon be a marshal if God spares him.

C.: And what does this gallant general live on?

J.G.: My tuns, I presume.

C.: And what would happen to him if he voted for a reduction in the army and in your share of the tax?

J.G.: Instead of being made a marshal, he would be obliged to retire.

C.: So you understand now why you have only yourself . . . .

J.G.: Let's go on to the fifth tun, if you please.

C.: That one goes off to Algeria.

J.G.: To Algeria? And yet we are assured that all Moslems are averse to wine-drinking, the savages! I have often wondered whether they know nothing of Médoc because they are infidels, or whether, as is more likely, they are infidels because they know nothing of Médoc. Besides, what services do they perform for me in exchange for this nectar that has cost me so much labor?

C.: None; but, then, it is not intended for Moslems, but for some good Christians who spend all their time in Barbary.

J.G.: And what do they do there that could be useful to me?

C.: They carry out raids, and are attacked in their turn by raiders; they kill and are killed; they catch dysentery, and come home to be cured; they dredge harbors, open up roads, build villages and people them with Maltese, Italians, Spaniards, and Swiss, who will live off your tun and many another that I'll come back to ask you for.

J.G.: Heaven help me! This is too much. I flatly refuse to give you my tun. Any vineyardist who would be guilty of such folly would be sent to Bicêtre.* Open up roads through the Atlas Mountains—good God! When I cannot leave my own farm for lack of a road! Dredge harbors in Barbary, when the Garonne is silting up all the time! Deprive me of my beloved children and send them to harass the Kabyles!† Make me pay for houses, seed, and horses to

* [Village near Paris containing the best-known insane asylum in France.—TRANSLATOR.]
† [A Berber people of Algeria and Tunisia.—TRANSLATOR.]

be handed over to the Greeks and the Maltese, when there are so many poor people right here at home!

C.: The poor! That's just it; we are relieving the country of this *surplus population!*

J.G.: To be sure, by sending after them to Algeria the funds that would support them here!

C.: And then you are laying the foundations of a *great empire;* you are bringing *civilization* to Africa; you are crowning your fatherland with immortal glory.

J.G.: You are a poet, Mr. Tax Collector; but I am just a vineyardist, and I refuse.

C.: Just think that in a few thousand years you will get back your investment a hundredfold. That is what those who have charge of the enterprise are saying.

J.G.: Meanwhile, they first asked for only a puncheon of wine to defray the expenses, then two, then three, and here I am being taxed a whole tun!* I persist in my refusal.

C.: It is too late for that. Your *legislative representative* has agreed that your share of the tax shall be one tun or four full puncheons.

J.G.: That is but too true. What confounded weakness on my part! It seemed foolish to me, too, to choose him to represent me, for what can there be in common between an army general and a poor vineyardist?

C.: You see very well that you do have something in common, were it only the wine that you are laying in and that he is voting himself in your name.

J.G.: You may well laugh at me, Mr. Tax Collector; I deserve it. But be reasonable. Leave me at least the sixth tun. The interest on the national debt has been paid, the civil list provided for, the government services assured, and the war in Africa extended into perpetuity. What more do you want?

C.: You won't get anywhere haggling with me. You should have told the general your desires. Now he has disposed of your vintage.

J.G.: Damned Bonapartist relic! But what do you expect to do

---

* [The puncheon was a varying measure, but it might take four to make a tun of 252 gallons.—TRANSLATOR.]

with this poor tun, the best of my stock? Come, just taste this wine. How mellow it is, how rich, how full-bodied, how smooth, how choice!

C.: Excellent! Delicious! It will be just to the taste of M. D. . . . , the textile manufacturer.

J.G.: Of M. D. . . . , the manufacturer? What do you mean?

C.: That he'll make good use of it.

J.G.: In what way? What are you talking about? Devil take me if I understand you!

C.: Don't you know that M. D. . . . has started a splendid establishment which, though highly useful to the country, still incurs a considerable financial loss every year?

J.G.: My heart bleeds for him. But what can I do about it?

C.: The Chamber has come to the conclusion that if things go on like this, M. D. . . . will either have to operate more efficiently or close his mill.

J.G.: But what do the ill-advised and unprofitable business ventures of M. D. . . . have to do with my tun of wine?

C.: The Chamber thought that if it turned over to M. D. . . . a little wine from your cellar, a few hectoliters of wheat from your neighbors, and one or two sous cut from the workers' wages, his losses might be converted into profits.

J.G.: The recipe is as infallible as it is ingenious. But confound it! It is terribly unfair. What! Is M. D. . . . to recoup his losses by taking my wine from me?

C.: Not exactly the wine, but its price. This is what we call an *incentive subsidy,* or bounty. But you look so amazed! Do you not see what a great service you are rendering to your fatherland?

J.G.: You mean to M. D. . . . ?

C.: To the fatherland. M. D. . . . assures us that, thanks to this arrangement, his business is flourishing; and this, he says, is how the country is enriched. That is what he has been saying recently in the Chamber, of which he is a member.

J.G.: It's an outright fraud! What! Some incompetent goes into a foolish enterprise and dissipates his capital; and if he can extort enough wine or wheat from me to make good his losses and even to leave him a profit besides, this is regarded as a gain for the whole country!

C.: Since your *representative* has come to that conclusion, you have no choice but to hand over to me the six tuns of wine and sell the fourteen tuns that I leave you for as good a price as you can get.

J.G.: That is my business.

C.: The thing is, you see, that it would be most regrettable if you did not get a high price for them.

J.G.: I shall see to that.

C.: For there are many things that this price must take care of.

J.G.: I know, sir. I am aware of that.

C.: In the first place, if you buy iron to make new spades and plows, a law decrees that you shall pay the ironmaster twice what it is worth.

J.G.: But is not this precisely what happens in the Black Forest?*

C.: Then, if you need oil, meat, cloth, coal, wool or sugar, each by law will cost you twice what it is worth.

J.G.: But this is horrible, frightful, abominable!

C.: What good are these complaints? You yourself, through your *legally authorized representative.* . . .

J.G.: Leave my representative out of this. I have made a strange choice, it is true. But I will not be imposed upon again, and I shall be represented by some good, honest peasant.

C.: Bah! You'll re-elect the gallant general.

J.G.: I re-elect the general, to have my wine distributed among Africans and manufacturers?

C.: You will re-elect him, I tell you.

J.G.: That's going a little too far. I will not re-elect him if I do not want to.

C.: But you will want to, and you will re-elect him.

J.G.: Just let him come here and try for election. He will soon see whom he has to deal with.

C.: Well, we shall see. Farewell. I am taking your six tuns and am going to distribute them as the general has decided.[1]

* [There tribute was often exacted from the unwary traveler.—TRANSLATOR.]

11

The Utopian[1]

"If only I were His Majesty's prime minister . . . . !"

"Well, what would you do?"

"I would begin by . . . . by . . . . really, by being very much embarrassed. For after all, I should not be prime minister if I did not have a majority; I should not have a majority if I did not win it for myself; I should not have won it for myself, at least by honorable means, if I did not govern according to its ideas. . . . . Thus, if I undertook to make my ideas prevail by opposing those of the majority, I should no longer have a majority; and if I did not have a majority, I should no longer be His Majesty's prime minister."

"I shall assume that you are and that consequently the majority do not stand in your way. What would you do?"

"I should first seek for ways of attaining *justice.*"

"And then?"

"I should seek for ways of improving *well-being.*"

"And next?"

"I should seek to determine whether they are mutually compatible or antagonistic."

"And if you found that they are incompatible?"

"I should say to King Philip:

"'Take back your cabinet post.'

"The rhyme is not rich, and the style is old-fashioned,

"But do you not see that this is much better

204

"Than these *transactions* against which good sense protests
"And that honesty speaks out there quite pure?"*

"But suppose you discover that both *justice* and *well-being* are attained by one and the same means?"

"Then I shall proceed straight on."

"Very well. But in order to attain well-being by way of justice a third element is required."

"And what is that?"

"The opportunity."

"You granted me that."

"When?"

"Just now."

"How?"

"By conceding me a majority."

"This seems a risky concession to have made, after all, for it implies that the majority clearly sees what is just and what is useful, and sees no less clearly that they are in perfect harmony."

"And if the majority saw all this so clearly, good would result, so to speak, all by itself."

"This is the point to which you are constantly directing my attention: that reform is possible only by way of progress in general enlightenment."

"And that such progress renders every necessary reform inevitable."

"Admirably put. But this prerequisite progress is itself a little slow and long-drawn-out. Let us assume it to have been accomplished. What would you do? For I am most eager to see you set to work, getting things done and putting your ideas into practice."

"First, I should reduce the postage on letters to ten centimes."

"I understood you to say five centimes."[2]

"Yes; but since I have other reforms in mind, I must proceed cautiously if I am to avoid a deficit."

* [Bastiat again offers a parody of Molière, this time the words of Alceste in the dialogue about the poor sonnet, from *The Misanthrope*, Act I, scene ii.—TRANSLATOR.]

"Gracious! What discretion! Your proposal already involves a deficit of thirty millions."

"Next, I should reduce the tax on salt to ten francs."

"Fine! That will give you another deficit of thirty millions. You have doubtless invented a new tax?"

"Heaven preserve me from that! Besides, I do not pretend to have so inventive a mind."

"Nevertheless, it takes a great deal. . . . Ah! I have it. Why did I not think of it before? You are simply going to reduce expenditures. It never occurred to me."

"You are not the only one who has overlooked that possibility. I do plan on resorting to such measures, but for the moment, they are not what I am counting on."

"Yes, very likely. You reduce revenue without reducing expenditures, and you avoid a deficit?"

"Yes, by reducing other taxes at the same time."

(Here, the interlocutor, touching his brow with the index finger of his right hand, sadly shakes his head, which may be translated as: "He's out of his mind.")

"To be sure, this scheme of yours is most ingenious. I now pay one hundred francs into the treasury; you reduce my salt tax by five francs and my postal rate by five francs; and, in order for the treasury to receive no less than one hundred francs, you are going to reduce some other tax of mine by ten francs."

"Exactly! You have quite caught my meaning."

"Devil take me if I have! I am not even sure that I heard you aright."

"I repeat that I recoup one tax reduction by another."

"The deuce you do! I have a few moments to spare; I might as well use them to hear you expound this paradox."

"The whole mystery is easily explained: I know a tax that costs you twenty francs, of which not a centime reaches the treasury; I have half of it refunded to you and the other half sent to the tax collector."

"Really, you are a peerless financier! There is only one problem. In what way, if you please, do I pay a tax that does not go to the treasury?"

"How much did that suit cost you?"

"One hundred francs."

"And if you had had the cloth brought from Verviers,* how much would it have cost you?"

"Eighty francs."

"Then why did you not order it from Verviers?"

"Because that is interdicted."

"And why is it interdicted?"

"So that the suit would cost me one hundred francs instead of eighty."

"That interdiction thus costs you twenty francs."

"Without a doubt."

"And where do these twenty francs go?"

"Where would they go? To the textile manufacturer."

"Very well. Give me twenty francs for the treasury, I shall have the interdiction removed, and you will still be ten francs ahead."

"Oh, I am beginning to see it all clearly now. This is what the balance sheet of the treasury would look like: five francs lost on the postal service, and five francs on salt; and ten francs gained on the cloth. Hence, everything comes out even."

"And here is what your own balance sheet would show: five francs gained on salt, and five francs on the postal service; and ten francs on the cloth."

"Total, twenty francs. This proposal is very agreeable to me. But what will happen to the unfortunate textile manufacturer?"

"Oh, I have not forgotten him. I manage to find some way of compensating him, always by means of tax reductions that will be profitable for the treasury; and what I have done for you in regard to cloth, I shall do for him with respect to wool, coal, machinery, etc.; so that he will be in a position to lower his price without suffering any loss."

"But are you sure that everything will balance?"

"The tendency will be all in that direction. The twenty francs that I have you gain on the cloth will be increased by those I shall save you on meat, fuel, wheat, etc. That will amount to a good deal; and a like saving will be realized by each of the thirty-five

* [A textile-manufacturing city in Belgium.—TRANSLATOR.]

million of your fellow citizens. There is enough there to buy all
the cloth in Verviers and Elbeuf* too. The nation will be better
clothed, that is all."

"I shall have to think about it; for it is all a little confused in my
mind."

"After all, as far as clothing is concerned, the essential thing is to
be clothed. Your limbs are your property, and not that of the manufacturer. Protecting them from the cold is your business, and not
his. If the law takes his side against you, the law is unjust, and you
have authorized me to reason according to the hypothesis that
what is unjust is harmful."

"Perhaps I have gone too far, but continue the description of
your financial plan."

"Then I shall make a tariff law."

"In two folio volumes?"

"No, in two articles."

"Then, for once, people will no longer say that the famous
axiom, 'Ignorance of the law is no defense,' is a fiction. Let us see
your tariff, then."

"Here it is:

" 'Art. 1. All imported goods shall pay a duty of five per cent
ad valorem.' "

"Even *raw materials?*"

"Unless they have no *value.*"

"But they all have some, more or less."

"In that case, they shall pay more or less."

"How do you expect our factories to compete with foreign factories that get their *raw materials* duty-free?"

"Assuming that government expenditures remain the same, if
we shut off this source of revenue, we shall have to open up another; that will not lessen the relative inferiority of our factories,
and there will be one more government bureau to establish and
pay for."

"True; I was reasoning as if it were a question of abolishing the
tax and not of redistributing it. I shall have to think about that.
Let us see your second article."

* [A textile-manufacturing city in France, near Paris.—TRANSLATOR.]

" 'Art. 2. All exported goods shall pay a tax of five per cent ad valorem.' "

"Mercy on us, Mr. Utopian! You are going to get yourself stoned, and, if need be, I shall cast the first stone."

"We have supposed that the majority is already enlightened."

"Enlightened! Do you maintain that an *export tax* is not burdensome?"

"Every tax is burdensome, but this one is less so than any other."

"I suppose a certain amount of eccentric behavior must be expected at carnival time. Please be so kind as to make this new paradox plausible, if you can."

"How much did you pay for this wine?"

"One franc a liter."

"How much would you have paid outside the customs gate?"

"Fifty centimes."

"Why this difference?"

"Ask at the octroi, where they took ten sous extra."

"And who created the octroi?"*

"The commune of Paris, in order to pave and light the streets."

"Then it is an import duty, is it not? But suppose it were the adjacent communes that had erected the octroi for their benefit, what then?"

"I should nonetheless pay one franc for my fifty-centime wine, and the additional fifty centimes would go for the paving and lighting of the streets of Montmartre and Les Batignolles."†

"So that it is ultimately the consumer who pays the tax?"

"That is beyond doubt."

"Then, by imposing a duty on exports, you make foreigners contribute toward the payment of your expenses."

"Here I must find fault with you, for what you are proposing is no longer *justice*."

---

* [A local tax on certain commodities (foodstuffs, liquids, fuels, fodder, building materials, etc.) imposed as a condition of their being brought into a town or district. The term is also used, by extension, as here, to refer to the place where the octroi is payable or the official body empowered to collect it.—TRANSLATOR.]

† [Two suburban communes that became parts of the city of Paris in 1860.—TRANSLATOR.]

"Why not? In order to make a product, a country must have a school system, police, roads—all things that cost money. Why should not foreigners, if they are the ultimate consumers, bear all the costs involved in making the product?"

"But that is contrary to received opinion."

"Not in the least. The ultimate consumer should defray all the direct or indirect costs of production."

"Whatever you may say, it is as clear as can be that such a measure would paralyze trade and cut us off from our foreign markets."

"That is an illusion. If you had to pay this tax over and above all the others, you would be right. But if the one hundred millions levied in this way reduce other taxes by the same amount, your products now appear on foreign markets with all your advantages, and even with greater advantages if this tax proves less burdensome and costly."

"I shall give the matter some thought. And so, that takes care of salt, the postal service, and the customhouse. Are you all finished?"

"I have hardly begun."

"Please, acquaint me with your other utopian ideas."

"I lost sixty millions on salt and the postal service. The customs duty allows me to recoup them; but it gives me something still more valuable."

"And what in the world is that, if you please?"

"International relations founded on justice, and a probability of peace that is equivalent to a certainty. I shall demobilize the army."

"The whole army?"

"Except for the special branches, which will be recruited voluntarily, like all other professions. You see what I mean; conscription is abolished."

"I beg your pardon, sir. You must use the term *recruitment*."

"Ah! I forgot. It is amazing how easy it is, in certain countries, to perpetuate the most unpopular policies by giving them another name."

"The same is true of *combined duties,* which have become *in-direct taxes."**

"And the *police*† have taken the name of *municipal guards."*

"In brief, you are disarming the country in expectation of a utopia."

"I said that I would disband the army, not that I would disarm the country. On the contrary, I expect to give it an invincible armed force."

"How do you extricate yourself from such a tangle of contradictions?"

"I propose to summon all the citizens into service."

"It was hardly worth your trouble to discharge a few soldiers only to call everybody back into the service."

"You did not make me prime minister simply to leave things just as they are. Therefore, on attaining power, I shall say, like Richelieu:‡ 'The maxims of the state have changed.' And my principal maxim, which shall serve as the fundamental principle of my administration, is this: Every citizen must know how to do two things: to provide for his own existence and to defend his country."

"That does seem to me, at first sight, to show at least some glimmerings of good sense."

"Consequently, I propose to base the national defense on a law containing two articles:

" 'Art. 1. Every able-bodied citizen, without exception, shall remain in service for four years, between the ages of twenty-one and twenty-five, to receive military training.' "

"A big saving, indeed! You discharge four hundred thousand soldiers and create ten million."

"Wait for my second article.

" 'Art. 2. Unless he proves, at the age of twenty-one, that he has completely mastered platoon drill.' "

* [The French word for "tax" here, and in many other places in the book, is *con-tribution.* This word also means in French a voluntary and nongovernmental act. —TRANSLATOR.]

† [French *gendarmes,* a word with no exact English equivalent.—TRANSLATOR.]

‡ [Armand Jean du Plessis, Cardinal de Richelieu (1585–1642), brilliant chief minister of France, 1624–1642.—TRANSLATOR.]

"I did not expect that ending. In order to avoid four years of service, our young men would surely vie with one another in learning 'squads-right!' and 'forward march, double time!' The idea is fantastic."

"It is better than that. For, after all, without bringing sorrow to any family or violating the principle of equality, does it not assure the country, in a simple and inexpensive manner, ten million defenders capable of defying a coalition of all the standing armies in the world?"

"I must say that, if I were not a cautious man, I should end by giving support to these fantastic ideas of yours."

The utopian, warming to his subject: "Thank heaven, I have found a means of reducing my budget by two millions! I shall abolish the octroi, reform the system of indirect taxation. . . ."

"Just a moment, Mr. Utopian!"

The utopian, warming more and more to his subject: "I shall establish freedom of religion and freedom of education.* New projects: I shall buy the railroads,† repay the national debt, and halt speculation."

"Mr. Utopian!"

"Freed from excessive responsibilities, I shall concentrate all the powers of the government on suppressing fraud, on administering prompt and equal justice to all, ..."

"Mr. Utopian, you are undertaking too many things; the nation will not follow you!"

"You gave me a majority."

"I take it away from you."

"Very well! In that case I am no longer prime minister, and my plans remain what they are, utopian."

---

* ["Freedom of education" for Bastiat involved lessening or removing the strict controls on the schools imposed by both the Roman Catholic Church and certain government officials.—TRANSLATOR.]

† [The first French railroads were constructed partly by private British capital, and partly by co-operation between the French government and private French capital.—TRANSLATOR.]

12

Salt, the Postal Service, and the Tariff [1]

A few days ago, people expected to see the mechanism of representative government create an utterly novel product that its wheels had not yet succeeded in grinding out: *the relief of the taxpayer.*

Everyone anxiously awaited the outcome; the experiment affected men's pocketbooks as much as it aroused their curiosity. No one, then, doubted that the machine had sufficient impulsion, because when self-interest and novelty turn the wheels, it runs admirably at all times, in all places, during all seasons, and under all circumstances.

But as for reforms tending to simplify and equalize the costs of government and to render them less burdensome, no one yet knows what it can do.

People said: "You will soon see. Now is the time. This is a job for the *fourth session,* when public approval is worth something. In 1842, we got the railroads; in 1846, we are to get a lowering of the salt tax and postal rates; we shall have to wait until 1850 for the reform of the tariff and a change in our system of indirect taxation. The fourth session is the jubilee year for the taxpayer."*

Hence, everyone was full of hope, and everything seemed to favor the experiment. The *Moniteur* had announced that from one quarter to the next, government revenue kept increasing; and

* [These were simply the meetings of the Chambers in election years. The same principle is well known in the United States.—TRANSLATOR.]

what better use could be made of these unanticipated funds than to permit the villager an extra grain of salt for his warm water* and an extra letter from the battlefield where his son is risking his life?

But what happened? Just as two sweet substances, it is said, prevent each other from crystallizing, or like the two dogs that fought so fiercely that nothing was left but their tails, the two reforms nullified each other. All that we have left are the tails, that is to say, a number of proposed laws, arguments for and against them, reports, statistics, and addenda, in which we have the consolation of seeing our sufferings appreciated in humanitarian terms and diagnosed for homeopathic therapy. As for the reforms themselves, they did not crystallize. Nothing came from the crucible, and the experiment failed.

Soon the chemists will present themselves before the members of the jury in order to explain this failure, and will address them in the following terms:

One: "I *proposed* postal reform; but the Chamber wanted to lower the tax on salt, and I had to withdraw my proposal."

Another: "I *voted* for the reduction of the salt tax; but the ministry proposed postal reform, and the vote did not carry."

And the jury, finding this logic excellent, will start the experiment all over again with the same data and will send the same chemists back to work on it.

This shows us that there could very well be something sensible, despite the source, in the practice, introduced half a century ago on the other side of the Channel, which consists, so far as the public is concerned, in undertaking just one reform at a time.† It is time-consuming and tedious, but it does result in something.

We have about a dozen reforms in progress at the same time; they press on one another like the souls of the departed before the gate to oblivion, and not one enters.

---

* [This is a reference to the common practice of drinking hot water for therapeutic purposes.—TRANSLATOR.]

† [In Bastiat's own time he might have referred to British parliamentary reform in 1832, postal reform in 1839, and fiscal reform piecemeal from 1842 on.—TRANSLATOR.]

> Alas! how weary I am!
> One at a time, for mercy's sake!*

That is what Jacques Bonhomme† was saying in a debate with John Bull over postal reform. It is worth repeating.

JACQUES BONHOMME

JOHN BULL

JACQUES BONHOMME: Oh, who will deliver me from this whirlwind of reforms! My head is splitting. People seem to be inventing them every day: educational reform, financial reform, sanitary reform, parliamentary reform, electoral reform, commercial reform, social reform, and now here comes *postal* reform!

JOHN BULL: The last is so easy to carry out, and so useful, as we have discovered here, that I may venture to recommend it to you.

JACQUES: Still, they say that it turned out badly in England, and that it cost your Exchequer ten million.

JOHN: Which brought the public a hundred million.

JACQUES: Is that quite certain?

JOHN: Look at all the signs of public satisfaction. Observe how the whole nation, under the ministries of Peel and Russell, has given Mr. Rowland Hill,‡ in British fashion, tangible evidence of its gratitude. Look at the poor, mailing their letters only after showing their sentiments by an imprint of a seal bearing the device: *The people grateful for postal reform.* Note the declaration made by the heads of the League§ on the floor of Par-

---

* [Quoted from the "Largo al factotum" aria in the first act of *The Barber of Seville.*—TRANSLATOR.]

† [I.e., James Goodfellow, the French counterpart of John Bull.—TRANSLATOR.]

‡ [Sir Robert Peel (1788–1850), English statesman, member of the Conservative Party, Prime Minister in the 1840's; Lord John Russell (1792–1878), English statesman, member of the Whig Party, Peel's successor as Prime Minister; later, Sir Rowland Hill (1795–1879), British educator and administrator chiefly responsible for the introduction of the "penny post" in England in 1840. The reference in the text is to the sum of £13,360 presented to Mr. Hill by public subscription in 1846. —TRANSLATOR.]

§ [The Anti-Corn-Law League, organized in England to publicize the desirability of repealing the import duties on grains, and to bring pressure on Parliament to enact this repeal. It soon broadened its efforts into a general free-trade movement. —TRANSLATOR.]

liament that without it they would have needed thirty years to complete their great work of freeing the food of the poor from all customs restrictions. Look at the statement made by the officials of the Board of Trade deploring the fact that the English monetary system does not lend itself to an even greater reduction in the postal rate on letters. What more proof do you need?

JACQUES: Yes, but the treasury?

JOHN: Are not the treasury and the public in the same boat?

JACQUES: Not exactly. And besides, is it quite certain that our postal system needs reforming?

JOHN: That is precisely the question. Let us take a look at the way things are done. What happens to letters that are put in the mail?

JACQUES: Oh, the whole mechanism is wonderfully simple. The postmaster opens the mailbox at a certain hour and takes out, let us assume, a hundred letters.

JOHN: And then?

JACQUES: Then he examines them one after another. With the aid of a geographic table and a scale, he assigns each to its appropriate category on the basis of both its destination and weight. There are only eleven zones and a like number of weight classifications.

JOHN: That makes a good one hundred and twenty-one combinations for each letter.

JACQUES: Yes, and we must double this number, for the letter may or may not be posted for *rural delivery*.

JOHN: This means, then, that the hundred letters will have to be scrutinized 24,200 times. Then what does the postmaster do?

JACQUES: He writes the weight in one corner and the amount of the postage due in the very middle of the address, in the form of a conventional symbol in use in the postal service.

JOHN: And then?

JACQUES: He postmarks them; he divides the letters into ten packets, according to the post offices to which they are to be sent; and he adds up the total postage for the ten packets.

JOHN: And then?

JACQUES: Next, he writes the ten sums down a column in one account book, and across the columns of another.

JOHN: And then?

JACQUES: Then he writes a letter to the postmaster at each of the ten points of destination in order to inform him of the accounting item that concerns him.

JOHN: Suppose the letters are prepaid?

JACQUES: Oh, then, I must admit, the service becomes a little complicated. The postmaster must receive the letter, weigh it and determine the distance it is to travel, as before, collect the postage due, and make change; choose from among thirty postmarks the one that applies; note on the letter its zone number, its weight, and the postage; transcribe the entire address first into one account book, then into a second, then into a third, then onto a separate slip; wrap the letter in the slip, send the whole well tied with string to the postmaster at the point of destination, and record each of these circumstances in a dozen columns of the fifty that line his ledger.

JOHN: And all that for just forty centimes!

JACQUES: Yes, on the average.

JOHN: I see that the *departure* is really rather simple. Let us see how things go on the *arrival* of the letter at its destination.*

JACQUES: The postmaster opens the mailbag.

JOHN: And after that?

JACQUES: He examines the ten bills from the postmasters at the points of origin.

JOHN: And after that?

JACQUES: He compares the total indicated on each bill with the total he gets by adding up the amounts in each packet of letters.

JOHN: And after that?

JACQUES: He computes the grand total to determine how much in all he will hold the postmen responsible for.

JOHN: And after that?

JACQUES: After that, with the aid of a table of distances and a scale, he verifies and corrects the postage on each letter.

JOHN: And after that?

* [Bastiat here reverts to the case of the letter that is not prepaid.—TRANSLATOR.]

JACQUES: He writes in one account book after another, in one column after another, depending upon innumerable circumstances, the *overcharges* and the *undercharges*.

JOHN: And after that?

JACQUES: He enters into correspondence with the ten postmasters to call their attention to errors amounting to ten or twenty centimes.

JOHN: And after that?

JACQUES: He sorts all the letters he has received in order to give them to the postmen.

JOHN: And after that?

JACQUES: He computes the total postage that each postman is charged with.

JOHN: And after that?

JACQUES: The postman verifies the charges; he and the postmaster discuss the meaning of the symbols. The postman pays the sum in advance, and leaves.

JOHN: Go on.*

JACQUES: The postman goes to the home of the addressee; he knocks at the door; a servant comes down and opens it. There are six letters for that address. The servant and the mailman add up the postage due, first independently, then together. They find it comes to two francs seventy centimes.

JOHN: Go on.

JACQUES: The servant goes to find his master; the latter proceeds to verify the symbols. He takes threes for twos, and nines for fours; he has doubts about the weights and the distances; in brief, the postman has to be summoned upstairs, and, while waiting for him, the master tries to guess who sent the letters, thinking it might be wise to refuse them.

JOHN: Go on.

JACQUES: The postman gets there and pleads the case for the postal administration. He and the master of the house discuss, examine, and weigh the letters, and calculate the distances; at last, the addressee accepts five letters and refuses to accept one.

* [This "Go on" and the six that follow are in English in the original.—TRANSLATOR.]

JOHN: Go on.

JACQUES: Now the only question is that of payment. The servant runs to the grocer's to get small change. Finally, after twenty minutes, the postman is free to leave, and he runs downstairs to begin anew the same ritual from one door to the next.

JOHN: Go on.

JACQUES: He returns to the post office. He and the postmaster go over his figures twice. He returns the letters refused and gets a refund of the money he has advanced. He recounts the objections of the addressees in regard to weights and distances.

JOHN: Go on.

JACQUES: The postmaster looks for the account books, the ledgers, and the special forms needed to make his accounting of the *letters refused*.

JOHN: Go on, if you please.

JACQUES: Good heavens, I am not a postmaster. We might go on from here to the statements of the tenth, the twentieth, and the end of the month; to the methods devised, not only to set up, but also to audit, such detailed accounts for 50 million francs resulting from postal charges averaging 43 centimes and from 116 million letters, each one of which might belong to any of 242 categories.

JOHN: That certainly looks like a rather complicated kind of simplicity. Surely the man who resolved this problem must have had a hundred times the genius of your M. Piron* or of our Rowland Hill.

JACQUES: You seem to be laughing at our system; suppose you explain yours.

JOHN: In England, the government has arranged for the sale of envelopes and paper wrappers at a penny apiece, at all places it deems appropriate.†

JACQUES: And after that?

JOHN: You write your letter, fold it in four, put it into one of these envelopes, and mail it.

* [Alexis Piron (1689–1773), a minor poet and dramatist, but a legendary figure because of his brilliant and devastating wit, which often bested even the redoubtable Voltaire.—TRANSLATOR.]

† [For some reason there is no mention of stamps, although the first ones appeared in 1840, and this essay was written in 1846.—TRANSLATOR.]

JACQUES: And after that?

JOHN: And after that, there is nothing more to be said. That is all there is to it. There are no considerations of weight or distance, no *overcharges* or *undercharges*, no *letters refused,* no forms to fill out, no account books or ledgers or columns to total, no book-keeping or auditing to be done, no change to give or receive, no symbols to interpret, no compulsion, etc., etc.

JACQUES: I must say that does appear simple. But is it not too simple? A child could understand it. It is reforms like this that stifle the genius of great administrators. For my part, I prefer the French method. And then, your *uniform postal rate* has the greatest of all defects. It is unjust.

JOHN: Why in the world do you say that?

JACQUES: Because it it unjust to make people pay as much for a letter carried to a neighbor as for one carried a hundred leagues away.

JOHN: In any case, you will admit that the extent of the injustice is limited to a penny.

JACQUES: What difference does that make? It is still an injustice.

JOHN: In fact, it is limited to just a halfpenny, for the other half goes to defray costs that are the same for all letters, regardless of the distance they are carried.

JACQUES: Penny or halfpenny, it is still unjust in principle.

JOHN: Finally, the injustice, which, *at most,* is only a halfpenny in a particular case, is completely wiped out in the total correspondence of each citizen, since everyone writes sometimes to distant points and at other times to points in the neighborhood.

JACQUES: I still do not accept it. The injustice may, if you like, be infinitely attenuated and mitigated; it may be imperceptible, infinitesimal, innocuous, but it exists.

JOHN: Does the government make you pay more for the gram of tobacco you buy on the rue de Clichy than for that sold you on the Quai d'Orsay?*

JACQUES: What connection is there between the two objects being compared?

* [Tobacco was and is a government monopoly in France.—TRANSLATOR.]

JOHN: The fact that, in one case as in the other, someone must pay the costs of transportation. It would be just; mathematically, if each pinch of tobacco cost a millionth of a centime more on the rue de Clichy than on the Quai d'Orsay.

JACQUES: True enough. After all, one should not demand the impossible.

JOHN: To say nothing of the fact that your postal system is just only in appearance. Two houses are situated side by side, but one is outside the zone and the other is inside. The first will have to pay ten centimes more than the second, which is as much as the entire cost of posting the letter in England. You can see quite readily that, in spite of appearances, injustice occurs in your country on a far greater scale.

JACQUES: That seems quite true. My objection is of no great importance, but there is still the revenue loss.

Here I stopped listening to the two interlocutors. It seems, however, that Jacques Bonhomme was entirely converted; for, a few days later, after the report of M. de Vuitry* had appeared, he wrote the distinguished legislator the following letter:

Jacques Bonhomme to M. de Vuitry, Deputy,
Chairman of the Committee in Charge of
the Bill Relating to Postal Rates

"Sir:

"Although I am not unaware of the extreme disapprobation that one runs the risk of incurring when one takes one's stand on the basis of an *absolute theory,* I do not believe I ought to abandon the cause of a *uniform postal rate no higher than the amount needed merely to reimburse the government for the service rendered.*

"I am well aware that in writing to you I am putting myself at a disadvantage, for I do nothing more than underline the contrast between us. On the one hand, a hothead, a doctrinaire reformer, who talks of suddenly overthrowing a whole system without providing for any period of transition; a dreamer who perhaps has never set eyes on that mountain of laws, administrative decrees, tables, addenda, and statistics that accompany your report; in a

---

* [Adolphe Vuitry (1813–1885), French economist and legislator.—TRANSLATOR.]

word, a *theorist!* On the other, a sober, judicious, and temperate legislator, who weighs everything carefully and compares one proposal with another, who gives due consideration to all the different interests that may be affected, and who rejects all *systems*, or, what amounts to the same thing, forms one of his own out of what he borrows from all the others. Surely there can be no doubt concerning the outcome of a struggle so unequal.

"Nevertheless, while the question is pending, a person has the right to state his convictions. I know that mine are sufficiently plain to evoke a smile of derision on the lips of the reader. All that I dare expect from him is that he bestow it on me, if there be occasion for it, after, and not before, hearing my reasons.

"For after all, I too can invoke *experience.* A great nation has put it to the test. What is their opinion of it? No one denies that they are expert in these matters, and their opinion should carry some weight.

"Well, there is not a single voice in England that does not bless the *postal reform.* Witness the subscription fund raised in honor of Mr. Rowland Hill; witness the original way in which the people, according to what John Bull tells me, are expressing their gratitude; witness this oft-repeated acknowledgement by the League: 'Never, without *penny postage,* would we have developed the public opinion that is turning against the protectionist system.' Witness the following statement, which I find in a work emanating from an official source:

"The postal rate on letters ought to be set, not in consideration of a fiscal goal, but with the sole purpose of covering the costs.

"To which Mr. MacGregor* adds:

"It is true that since the postal rate has been reduced to the level of our coins of lowest denomination, it is not possible to lower it further,

* [John MacGregor (1797–1857), statistician, historian, diplomat, and freetrader. In 1840 he became one of the joint secretaries of the British Board of Trade. He published between 1841 and 1850 voluminous reports on tariff regulations in various countries.—TRANSLATOR.]

although it still produces some net revenue. But this net revenue, which will go on increasing, should be devoted to improving the service and to extending our system of packet boats on every ocean.*

"This leads me to examine the fundamental idea on which the committee bases its reasoning, namely, that, on the contrary, the postage on letters ought to be a source of revenue for the government.

"This idea dominates your whole report, and I have to admit that, as long as such a preconception had any influence, you could not accomplish anything great or produce anything finished; you would be fortunate if, in trying to reconcile all systems, you did not combine their various disadvantages.

"The fundamental question that confronts us, then, is this: Is correspondence between private individuals a fit *subject for taxation?*

"I shall not revert to abstract principles. I shall refrain from mentioning that, since society exists only by virtue of the communication of ideas, the object of all government should be to encourage and not to hamper that communication.

"I shall simply examine the facts of the situation.

"The total length of the national, departmental, and connecting roads is about 1,000,000 kilometers. Assuming that each kilometer cost 100,000 francs, that makes a capital expenditure of 100 billions by the state in order to facilitate the movement of men and things.

"Now, I ask you, if one of your distinguished colleagues were to propose in the Chamber a law phrased in this manner:

"On and after January 1, 1847, the state shall levy on all travelers a tax calculated not only to cover the costs of the roads but also to secure the return, into its general funds, of four or five times the total of these costs. . . . .

* [What Mr. MacGregor actually wrote on this subject in his *The Commercial and Financial Legislation of Europe and America* (London: Henry Hooper, 1841) was: "The tax imposed upon the public by the late post-office reform is so very moderate, that while it still yields a considerable revenue, which we believe confidently will increase, no one can desire any alteration in the rate of postage" (p. 264).—TRANSLATOR.]

would you not find such a proposal socially destructive and intrinsically abominable?

"How does it happen that this notion of *profit*—what am I saying?—of simple *remuneration,* is never entertained when the circulation of things is in question, yet appears so natural to you when it is a question of the movement of ideas?

"I dare say that this is the result of habit. If what was in question were the *creation* of the postal service, certainly it would appear abominable to base it on the *fiscal principle.*

"And please observe that in this case the compulsion is more clearly marked.

"When the state opens a road, it does not force anyone to use it. (It would no doubt do so if the use of the road were taxed.) But when once a national postal service is established, nobody can send a letter, even to his mother, by any other means.

"Thus, in principle, the postal rate on letters should be no more than what is required to render it *remunerative,* and, for that reason, *uniform.*

"Now, if one begins with this idea, how can one fail to be struck by the beauty and simplicity of the reform and by the ease with which it can be carried out?

"Here it is in its entirety, and, save for editing, drafted in the form of a bill:

"Art. 1. On and after January 1, 1847, there shall be placed on sale, wherever the government deems it useful, *stamped envelopes and stamped wrappers* at the price of five (or ten) centimes.

"Art. 2. Every letter placed in one of these envelopes and not exceeding fifteen grams in weight, every *newspaper* or piece of *printed matter* enclosed in one of these wrappers and not exceeding . . . . grams, shall be carried and delivered, without charge, to its address.

"Art. 3. The accounting division of the postal service is entirely abolished.

"Art. 4. All criminal and penal laws on the subject of the postage are repealed.

"This is very simple, I admit—much too simple—and I anticipate a storm of objections.

"But, granting that this system has its disadvantages, these are not in question; the question is whether your system does not have still greater ones.

"And in all honesty, can it in any respect whatsoever (except for revenue) stand a moment's comparison with the system I am proposing?

"Examine the two of them; compare them in terms of ease, convenience, speed, simplicity, orderliness, economy, justice, equality, the promotion of business, emotional satisfactions, intellectual and moral development, and cultural impact; and tell me, in all good conscience, whether it is possible to hesitate for one moment.

"I shall refrain from expatiating on any of these considerations. I content myself merely with mentioning the headings of a dozen chapters, and I leave the rest blank, convinced that no one is more competent than you to fill them in.

"But, since there is only one objection, the *revenue,* I really must say a word about that.

"You have made a chart showing that a uniform postal rate, even at twenty centimes, would involve a loss of twenty-two millions for the treasury.

"At ten centimes, the loss would be twenty-eight millions; at five centimes, thirty-three millions—hypotheses so terrifying that you did not even formulate them.

"But permit me to call your attention to the fact that these figures in your report are a little too much subject to variation to be allowed to pass unchallenged. In all your charts, in all your calculations, you tacitly presuppose the words *'other things being equal.'* You assume that a simple administrative system will cost the same as a complicated one, and that the same number of letters will be mailed when the average rate is forty-three centimes as when there is a uniform rate of twenty centimes. You limit yourself to the rule of three, thus: Eighty-seven million letters at forty-two and one-half centimes yield so much. Hence, at twenty centimes they would yield so much; conceding, however, some variations—when they are adverse to the cause of reform.

"In order to compute the real sacrifice that the treasury would have to make, it would be necessary to know, first, what would be saved in the operation of the postal service; and then, to what extent the volume of mail would increase. Let us take into account only the latter datum, because we can assume that the savings realized in the costs of operation would amount to no more than the economies effected by having the existing personnel handle an increased volume of mail.

"No doubt it is impossible to anticipate in precise numerical terms the amount of this increase in the volume of mail. But, in these matters, a reasonable basis of approximation has always been considered acceptable.

"You yourself say that in England a reduction of seven-eighths in the postal rate led to an increase of 360% in the total volume of mail.

"In our country, lowering the postal rate, which presently averages forty-three centimes, to five centimes would likewise constitute a reduction of seven-eighths. It is therefore reasonable to expect the same result, that is to say, 417 million letters instead of 116 million.

"But let us calculate on the basis of 300 million.

"After the postal reform in England, the per capita number of letters increased to thirteen. Are we going too far, then, in assuming that, if our postal rate is reduced to one-half that of the English, our per capita volume of mail will increase to eight?

300 million letters at 5 centimes	15 million fr.
100 million newspapers and pieces of printed matter at 5 centimes	5 million fr.
Travelers using mail coaches	4 million fr.
Shipments of money	4 million fr.
Total receipts	28 million fr.
Present expenditures (which may be reduced)	31 million fr.
Minus that of packet boats	5 million fr.
Remainder on mailbags, travelers, and shipments of money	26 million fr.
Net yield	2 million fr.
Net yield today	19 million fr.
Loss, or rather, *reduction of profit*	17 million fr.

"Now, should not the state, which makes a *positive sacrifice* of 800 millions each year in order to facilitate the *free* movement of persons, make a *negative sacrifice* of seventeen millions in order *not to profit* on the movement of ideas?

"But, after all, the Treasury has, I know, become used to taking certain things for granted; and just as it easily falls into the habit of seeing receipts increase, so it accustoms itself only with difficulty to seeing them diminished by a centime. It is as if it were equipped with those wonderful valves which allow our blood to flow in one direction but prevent it from flowing in the other. So be it. The treasury is a little too old for us to be able to change its ways. Therefore, let us not entertain any hopes of persuading it to give up any of its accustomed revenue. But what would it say if I, Jacques Bonhomme, were to call its attention to a simple, easy, convenient, essentially practical way of conferring a great boon upon the country that would not cost it a centime?

Gross revenue from the postal system .... 50 million fr.
Gross revenue from the salt tax .... 70 million fr.
Gross revenue from the tariff .... 160 million fr.

Total from these three sources .... 280 millions

"Well, set the postage on letters at the uniform rate of five centimes.

"Lower the tax on salt to ten francs per quintal, as the Chamber has voted.

"Give me authority to modify tariff rates by *formally prohibiting me to raise any duty, but permitting me to lower duties as I see fit.*

"And I, Jacques Bonhomme, guarantee you, not 280, but 300 millions. Two hundred French bankers will be my security. All I ask for myself is what the three taxes will produce above and beyond 300 millions.

"Now, do I need to enumerate the advantages of my proposal?

"1. The nation will reap all the benefits of *cheapness* in the price of an article of prime necessity, viz., salt.

"2. Fathers will be able to write to their sons, and mothers to their daughters. Feelings of affection, demonstrations of love and friendship will not, as today, be suppressed within the depths of men's hearts by the hand of the treasury.

"3. Carrying a letter from one friend to another will not be proscribed in our laws as a criminal act.

"4. Commerce will flourish anew, along with free trade; our merchant marine will recover from its humiliating condition.

"5. The treasury will gain, at first, *twenty millions;* and after that, all that will flow into other channels of taxation through the savings realized by each citizen on salt, on letters, and on the commodities on which the customs duties have been lowered.

"If my proposal is not accepted, what conclusion should I draw? Assuming that the group of bankers whom I find to sponsor it offer sufficient guarantees, under what pretext could my offer be rejected? Certainly not the need for a *balanced budget.* It will indeed be unbalanced, but unbalanced in such a way that receipts will exceed expenditures. What is at issue here is not a theory, a system, a set of statistics, a probability, a conjecture; you are being made an offer, an offer like that of a company seeking the concession for a railroad. The treasury lets me know what it receives from the postal system, from the salt tax, and from the tariff. I offer to give it *more.* Hence, the objection cannot come from the treasury. I offer to reduce the salt tax, postal rates, and customs duties; I give my pledge not to raise them; hence, the objection cannot come from the taxpayers. Where, then, could it come from? The monopolists? It remains to be seen whether their voice is to drown out that of the French government and the French people. To protect us from that, I urge you to transmit my proposal to the Council of Ministers.

"JACQUES BONHOMME

"P.S. Here is the text of my offer:

"I, Jacques Bonhomme, representing a group of bankers and businessmen, prepared to give all assurances and to post all the necessary bonds;

"Having learned that the state obtains only 280 millions from the tariff, the postal system, and the salt tax, at the rates presently fixed;

"Offer to give it 300 millions of gross revenue from these three sources;

"Even after it has reduced the salt tax from thirty francs to ten francs;

"Even after it has reduced the postal rate on letters from an average of forty-two and one-half centimes to a single, uniform rate of from five to ten centimes;

"On the sole condition that I be permitted, not to *raise* customs duties (which I shall be expressly forbidden to do), but to *lower* them as much as I choose.

"JACQUES BONHOMME"

"But you are mad," I told Jacques Bonhomme, when he showed his letter to me; "you never have been able to do anything in moderation. Only the other day you yourself were protesting against the *whirlwind of reforms,* and here you are, demanding three of them, making one the condition of the other two. You will ruin yourself."

"Set your mind at ease," he said. "I have taken everything into account. Would to heaven my proposal were accepted! But it will not be."

Thereupon we parted company, his head full of figures, and mine filled with reflections that I spare the reader.

13

Protectionism, or the
Three Aldermen

A DEMONSTRATION IN FOUR SCENES

SCENE 1.

The scene takes place in the mansion of Peter, an alderman. The window looks out upon a beautiful grove of trees; three gentlemen are seated at a table near a blazing fire.

PETER: I must say, there is nothing like a good fire after a satisfying meal. You have to admit that it is very agreeable indeed. But, alas, how many good people, like the Roi d'Yvetot

> Are blowing on their fingers
> From lack of firewood!*

Unfortunate creatures! A charitable idea that must be an inspiration from Heaven has just occurred to me. You see those fine trees? I want them cut down and the wood distributed among the poor.

PAUL AND JOHN: What! Free of charge?

PETER: Not exactly. My good deeds would soon be at an end if I dissipated my estate that way. I estimate my grove of trees to be

* [Reference to the most famous of all the popular songs of Pierre-Jean de Béranger (1780–1857).—TRANSLATOR.]

worth a thousand livres;* by chopping them down, I shall get a good deal more for them.

PAUL: Not so. Your wood as it stands is worth more than that of the neighboring forests, because it performs services that the latter cannot perform. Once your trees are chopped down, they will be good only for firewood, like the rest, and not be worth a denier† more per load.

PETER: Ho, ho! Mr. Theorist, you are forgetting that I am a practical man. I should think my reputation as a speculator well enough established to prevent me from being taken for a fool. Do you think I am going to amuse myself by selling my wood at the same price as floated wood?‡

PAUL: You will simply have to.

PETER: How naive you are! And suppose I stop floated wood from reaching Paris?

PAUL: That would change matters. But how would you go about it?

PETER: Here is the whole secret. You know that floated wood pays ten sous a load on entering the city. Tomorrow I persuade the aldermen to raise the duty to 100, 200, 300 livres—in short, high enough to keep even a single log from getting in. Now do you understand? If the good people do not want to die of cold, they will have no alternative but to come to my woodyard. They will scramble for my wood, I shall sell it for its weight in gold, and this well-organized charitable undertaking will put me in a position to conduct others.

PAUL: What a wonderful project! It gives me the idea for another just as efficacious.

JOHN: Tell us what it is. Does it also involve philanthropy?

PAUL: What do you think of this butter from Normandy?

JOHN: Excellent.

PAUL: Well, maybe! It seemed tolerable to me a moment ago. But do you not find that it burns your throat? I intend to produce

* [An old French monetary unit, originally equal to the value of a pound of silver, but gradually reduced and finally replaced by the franc.—TRANSLATOR.]

† [A coin of minor denomination, worth about three-fifths of a sou, deriving from the Roman denarius, in use up to the French Revolution.—TRANSLATOR.]

‡ [Wood for fuel used to be floated down the Seine into Paris.—TRANSLATOR.]

a better quality in Paris. I shall have four or five hundred cows and arrange to distribute milk, butter, and cheese among the poor.

PETER AND JOHN: What! As charity?

PAUL: Nonsense! Let us always maintain an appearance of charity. It has so fair a face that even its mask is an excellent passport. I shall give my butter to the people, and the people will give me their money. Do you call that selling?

JOHN: Not according to *Le Bourgeois gentilhomme;** but whatever you may choose to call it, you will ruin yourself. Can Paris compete with Normandy in the raising of cows?

PAUL: I shall gain the advantage by saving the costs of transportation.

JOHN: All right. But even after paying these costs, the Normans can still beat the Parisians.†

PAUL: Do you call it *beating* someone to let him have things at low prices?

JOHN: That is the customary term. The fact remains that *you* will be the one who is beaten.

PAUL: Yes, like Don Quixote. The blows will fall on Sancho. John, my friend, you forget the octroi.

JOHN: The octroi! What connection does it have with your butter?

PAUL: From tomorrow on, I shall demand *protection;* I shall persuade the commune to keep butter from Normandy and Brittany from entering Paris. Then the people will either have to get along without it or buy mine, and at my price, too.

JOHN: I must say, gentlemen, I feel myself quite caught up in the wave of your humanitarianism.

"One learns to howl," says the proverb, "by living with the wolves."

My mind is made up. No one shall say that I am an unworthy alderman. Peter, this crackling fire has set your soul aflame; Paul, this butter has activated your intellectual faculties; and now I feel

---

* [In Molière's *The Would-Be Gentleman,* a flatterer assures M. Jourdain that his father did not "sell" dry goods; he merely "gave them away for money," thus "proving" that he was a noble and not a bourgeois.—TRANSLATOR.]

† [There is a pun here almost impossible to render into English. The French word *battre,* which means "beat," also means "churn."—TRANSLATOR.]

that this piece of salt pork is likewise sharpening my wits. To-morrow I shall vote, and have others vote, for the exclusion of pigs, living or dead; that done, I shall build superb pens in the heart of Paris

For the unclean animal forbidden to the Hebrews.

I shall become a swineherd and pork butcher. Let us see how the good people of Paris will avoid coming to provision themselves at my shop.

PETER: Not so fast, gentlemen. If you increase the price of butter and salt pork in this way, you will cut beforehand the profit I was expecting from my wood.

PAUL: Well, my project will no longer be so wonderful either, if you levy tribute on me for your logs and your hams.

JOHN: And what shall I gain by overcharging you for my sausages, if you overcharge me for faggots and for the butter on my bread?

PETER: Well, there is no reason why we should quarrel about this. Let us rather co-operate with one another and make reciprocal concessions. Besides, it is not good to consult only one's own self-interest; one should consider mankind as well. Must we not make sure the people are warm?

PAUL: Quite true. And the people must have butter to spread on their bread.

JOHN: Undoubtedly. And a bit of bacon for their stew.

ALL: Hurrah for charity! Long live humanitarianism! Tomorrow we shall take the City Hall by storm.

PETER: Ah! I forgot. One more word; it is essential. My friends, in this age of selfishness, the world is distrustful; and the purest intentions are often misinterpreted. Paul, you plead the case for *local* wood; John, you defend *local* butter; and I, for my part, shall devote myself to the protection of the *local* hog. It is well to forestall evil-minded suspicions.

PAUL AND JOHN (leaving): Upon my word, there's a clever man!

Scene 2.

Meeting of the Board of Aldermen

PAUL: My dear colleagues, every day large quantities of wood enter Paris, and as a result large sums of money leave the city. At this rate we shall all be ruined in three years, and then what will become of the poor? [*Cheers.*] Let us ban all foreign wood. It is not on my behalf that I am speaking, because all the wood I own would not make one toothpick. Hence, I am completely free from any personal interest in regard to this question. [*Hear! Hear!*] But Peter here has a grove of trees and will guarantee to supply fuel for our fellow citizens, who will no longer be dependent upon the charcoal sellers of the Yonne.* Has it ever occurred to you that we run the danger of dying of cold if the owners of foreign forests took it into their heads not to deliver wood to Paris any longer? Therefore, let us ban their wood. By this means we shall prevent the draining away of our money, create a domestic woodcutting industry, and open to our workers a new source of employment and income. [*Applause.*]

JOHN: I support this proposal by the distinguished previous speaker, who is so humanitarian, and, as he himself said, so completely disinterested. It is high time we put a stop to this brazen *laissez passer,* which has brought unbridled competition into our market, so that there is not one province whose situation is at all advantageous for the production of any commodity whatsoever that does not *flood* us with it, undersell us, and destroy Parisian industry. It is the duty of the government to equalize the conditions of production by the imposition of judiciously selected duties, to admit only goods that cost more outside Paris than they do within the city, and in this way to extricate us from an unequal contest. How, for instance, can we be expected to produce milk and butter in Paris in competition with Brittany and Normandy? Just remember, gentlemen, that it costs the Bretons less for their land, their fodder, and their labor. Is it not only common sense to

* [A French department southeast of Paris, situated on the Yonne River, a tributary of the Seine.—TRANSLATOR.]

equalize opportunities by a protective town tariff? I demand that the duty on milk and butter be raised to 1000%, and higher if need be. Breakfast may cost the people a little more on that account, but how their wages will go up as well! We shall see barns and dairies rising, creameries multiply, new industries established. It is not that I stand to profit in the least from the adoption of my proposal. I am not a cowherd, nor do I wish to be one. My only desire is to be helpful to the toiling masses. [*Cheers and applause.*]

PETER: I am delighted to find that this assembly includes statesmen so pure in heart, so enlightened, so dedicated to the best interests of the people. [*Cheers.*] I admire their disinterestedness, and I can do no better than imitate their noble example. I second their motion, and I add to it a motion of my own to prohibit the entry of pigs from Poitou.* It is not that I have any desire to become a swineherd or a pork butcher; in that case, my conscience would make it my duty to remain silent. But is it not disgraceful, gentlemen, that we should be forced to pay *tribute* to these Poitou peasants, who have the audacity to come right into our own market and seize possession of an industry that we ourselves could carry on; and who, after flooding us with their sausages and hams, take perhaps nothing from us in return? In any case, who will tell us that the balance of trade is not in their favor and that we are not obliged to pay them the balance due in hard cash? Is it not clear that if this industry were transplanted from Poitou to Paris, it would create jobs for Parisian workingmen? And then, gentlemen, is it not quite possible, as M. Lestiboudois[1] so well observed, that we may be buying salt pork from Poitou, not with what we sell them in return, but with our capital? How long can we go on doing that? Let us not, then, allow a pack of greedy, grasping, false-hearted competitors to come here and undersell us and make it impossible for us to produce the same commodities ourselves. Aldermen, Paris has put her trust in us; it is for us to justify that trust. The people are without jobs; it is for us to create jobs for them; and if salt pork costs them a little more, we shall at least have the consciousness of having sacrificed our personal interests

---

* [A province of France, southwest of Paris.—TRANSLATOR.]

to those of the masses, as every right-thinking alderman should do. [*Thunderous applause.*]

A VOICE: I hear a great deal of talk about the poor; but, under the pretext of giving them jobs, you begin by depriving them of what is worth more than the job itself—wood, butter, and soup.

PETER, PAUL, AND JOHN: Put our motions to a vote! Put them to a vote! Away with utopians, theorists, abstract thinkers! Put them to a vote! Put them to a vote! [*The three motions are carried.*]

SCENE 3.

Twenty Years Later: Jacques Bonhomme and His Son.

THE SON: Father, make up your mind to it; we must leave Paris. We cannot live here any longer. There is no work to be had, and everything is frightfully expensive.

THE FATHER: My son, you do not know what a wrench it is for one to leave the place where one was born.

THE SON: It is even worse to starve to death.

THE FATHER: Go, my son, seek a more hospitable land. As for myself, I shall not leave this place, where your mother, your brothers, and your sisters are buried. I long to find at last by their side the rest that has been denied me in this city of desolation.

THE SON: Take heart, dear father; we shall find work somewhere else—in Poitou, in Normandy, or in Brittany. It is said that all the industries of Paris are gradually moving to these distant provinces.

THE FATHER: That is quite understandable. Being unable any longer to sell us wood and provisions, the people of these provinces have ceased to produce beyond their own needs; whatever time and capital they have available they devote to making for themselves what we once used to furnish them with.

THE SON: Just as at Paris they have stopped making fine furniture and beautiful clothing, and have turned to planting trees and raising pigs and cows. Although still young, I have lived to see great stores, elegant neighborhoods, and busy docks along the banks of the Seine overgrown with weeds and underbrush.

THE FATHER: While the hinterland is being covered with cities,

Paris is becoming a bare field. What an appalling reversal! And it took just three misguided aldermen, helped by public ignorance, to bring this frightful calamity upon us.

THE SON: Tell me its history, Father.

THE FATHER: It is really quite simple. Under the pretext of establishing three new branches of industry in Paris and of thereby increasing job opportunities for the working classes, these men had the importation of wood, butter, and meat prohibited. They arrogated to themselves the right to provide their fellow citizens with these commodities. First, their prices rose to exorbitant heights. No one was earning enough to afford them, and the small number of those who could obtain some, by spending all their earnings on them, were no longer able to buy anything else. This at once spelled the doom of all the industries in Paris, and the end came all the more quickly as the provinces no longer provided our city with a market for its products. Poverty, death, and emigration began to depopulate Paris.

THE SON: And when is this going to stop?

THE FATHER: When Paris has become a forest and a prairie.

THE SON: The three aldermen must have made a great deal of money.

THE FATHER: At first they realized enormous profits; but in the long run they were engulfed in the general misery.

THE SON: How is that possible?

THE FATHER: This ruin you are looking at was once a splendid mansion encircled by a beautiful grove of trees. If Paris had continued to expand, Squire Peter would get more in rent from it than he could sell it for today.

THE SON: How can that be, since he no longer has any competition?

THE FATHER: Competition among sellers has disappeared, but competition among buyers is disappearing every day and will continue to disappear until Paris has become open country and the brushwood of Squire Peter has no more value than an equal area of brushwood in the forest of Bondy.* It is thus that monopoly,

* [A forest just north of Paris, notorious as a resort of thieves.—TRANSLATOR.]

like every injustice, carries within it the seeds of its own destruction.

THE SON: That does not seem altogether clear to me, but what is incontestable is the decadence of Paris. Is there, then, no way of repealing this iniquitous law that Peter and his colleagues had the town council adopt twenty years ago?

THE FATHER: I am going to tell you a secret. I am staying in Paris to do just that. I shall call the people to my assistance. It depends upon them to restore the town tariff duties to their former basis, to rid them of the deadly principle that was grafted onto them and that has continued to vegetate there like a parasitical fungus.

THE SON: You are sure to succeed in this from the very first.

THE FATHER: Oh, on the contrary, the task is difficult and toilsome. Peter, Paul, and John understand one another wonderfully well. They are ready to do anything rather than permit wood, butter, and meat to enter Paris. They have on their side the people themselves, who see clearly the jobs that these three protected industries give them, who know how many woodcutters and cowherds they give employment to, but who cannot have as clear an idea of how much employment would develop in the spacious atmosphere of free trade.

THE SON: If that is all they need, you will enlighten them.

THE FATHER: My child, at your age one never lacks confidence. If I write, the people will not read what I have to say; for with all the hours they must work to eke out their miserable existence, they have no time left for reading. If I speak, the aldermen will shut my mouth. Thus, the people will long continue in their disastrously mistaken ways, and the political parties that place their trust in arousing popular passions will concern themselves far less with dispelling error than with exploiting the prevailing prejudices. Therefore, I shall have on my hands at one and the same time the two most powerful forces of our age—the people and the political parties. Oh! I see a frightful storm ready to burst over the head of anyone bold enough to venture a protest against an iniquity so deeply rooted in this country.

THE SON: You will have justice and truth on your side.

THE FATHER: And they will have force and calumny on theirs. If only I were young again! But age and suffering have exhausted my strength.

THE SON: Well, father, dedicate what strength you still have to the service of your country. Begin this work of liberation and leave me as my legacy the task of completing it.

SCENE 4.

Popular Uprising

JACQUES BONHOMME: Parisians, let us demand the reform of the town tariff duties; let us insist that they be restored to their original purpose. Let every citizen be *free* to buy wood, butter, and meat wherever he sees fit.

THE PEOPLE: Long live *freedom!*

PETER: Parisians, do not let yourselves be misled by that word. What difference does the freedom to buy make to you, if you do not have the means? And how can you have the means, if you do not have a job? Can Paris produce wood as cheaply as the forest of Bondy, meat as inexpensively as Poitou, butter as easily as Normandy? If you open your gates freely to these competitive products, what will become of the cowherds, the woodcutters, and the pork butchers? They cannot do without protection.

THE PEOPLE: Long live *protection!*

JACQUES BONHOMME: Protection! But is it you, the workers, who are being protected? Do you not compete with one another? Then let the wood dealers experience competition in their turn. They have no right to raise the price of their wood by law unless they also raise wage rates by law. Are you no longer in love with equality?

THE PEOPLE: Long live *equality!*

PETER: Do not listen to this agitator. We have, it is true, raised the price of wood, of meat, and of butter; but we have done so in order to be able to give good wages to the workers. We are prompted by motives of charity.

THE PEOPLE: Long live *charity!*

JACQUES BONHOMME: Use the town tariff duties, if you can, to raise wages, or else do not use them to raise commodity prices. What the people of Paris demand is not charity, but justice.

THE PEOPLE: Long live *justice!*

PETER: It is precisely high commodity prices that make for high wages.

THE PEOPLE: Long live *high prices!*

JACQUES BONHOMME: If butter is dear, it is not because you are paying high wages to the workers; it is not even because you are making big profits; it is solely because Paris is ill-situated for that industry, because you insisted that people produce in the city what they should be producing in the country, and in the country what used to be produced in the city. It is not that there are more jobs for the people, but only jobs of a different kind. It is not that their wages are higher, but that the prices at which they buy things are no longer as low.

THE PEOPLE: Long live *low prices!*

PETER: This man is seducing you with his honeyed words. Let us put the question in all its simplicity. Is it not true that if we grant entry to butter, wood, and meat, we shall be flooded with them? Shall we not perish of the surfeit? There is, thus, no other way of saving ourselves from this new species of invasion than by slamming the gates in its face, and no other way of maintaining commodity prices than by producing an artificial scarcity.

SOME FEW SCATTERED VOICES: Long live *scarcity!*

JACQUES BONHOMME: Let us put the question to the test of truth. One can divide among all the people in Paris only what there is in Paris; if there is less meat, less wood, less butter, each person's share will be smaller. Now, there will be less of these commodities if we ban them than if we admit them. Parisians, there can be abundance for everyone only in so far as there is general abundance.

THE PEOPLE: Long live *abundance!*

PETER: This man can talk all he wants; he will never be able to show you that it is in your interest to be subjected to unbridled competition.

THE PEOPLE: Down with *competition!*

JACQUES BONHOMME: This man can declaim all he wants; he cannot make it possible for you to taste the sweets of restriction.

THE PEOPLE: Down with *restriction!*

PETER: And I, for my part, declare that if the poor cowherds and swineherds are to be deprived of their daily bread, if they are to be sacrificed to theories, I can no longer be answerable for public order. Workingmen, put no faith in that man. He is an agent of perfidious Normandy; he goes there to get his orders. He is a traitor; he must be hanged. (*The people remain silent.*)

JACQUES BONHOMME: Parisians, everything I am saying today, I was saying twenty years ago, when Peter took it into his head to exploit the town tariff duties for his own advantage and to your disadvantage. I am not, then, an agent of the Normans. Hang me if you will, but that will not make oppression any the less oppressive. Friends, it is neither Jacques Bonhomme nor Peter who must be killed, but free trade if it frightens you, or restriction if it does you harm.

THE PEOPLE: Let us hang no one, and set everybody free.

14

Something Else[1]

"What is restriction?"

"It is a partial interdiction."

"What is interdiction?"

"It is an absolute restriction."

"So that what is true of the one is true of the other?"

"Yes; the difference is only one of degree. The relation between them is the same as that between the arc of a circle and the circle itself."

"Therefore, if interdiction is bad, restriction cannot be good?"

"No more than the arc of a circle can be anything but circular."

"What is the generic name for both restriction and interdiction?"

"Protectionism."

"What is the ultimate effect of protectionism?"

"To require that men expend *more labor for the same result.*"

"Why are men so attached to the protectionist system?"

"Because, as free trade enables them to attain the same result *with less labor,* this apparent diminution of labor terrifies them."

"Why do you say *apparent?*"

"Because all the labor that has been saved can be devoted to *something else.*"

"What else?"

"That is what cannot be specified and does not need to be."

"Why?"

"Because, if the total quantity of consumers' goods enjoyed by the French people could be obtained with one-tenth less labor, no one can predict what new satisfactions they would try to obtain for themselves with the remaining available labor. One person would want to be better clothed; another, better fed; this one, better educated; that one, better entertained."

"Explain to me the functioning and the effects of protectionism."

"That is not so easy. Before considering the more complicated cases, one should study the simpler ones."

"Take the simplest case you wish."

"You remember how Robinson Crusoe managed to make a board when he had no saw?"*

"Yes. He cut down a tree; then, by trimming the trunk, first on one side and then on the other, with his axe, he reduced it to the thickness of a plank."

"And that cost him a great deal of labor?"

"Two full weeks."

"And what did he live on during that time?"

"On his provisions."

"And what happened to the axe?"

"It became very dull as a result."

"Quite right. But perhaps you do not know this: just as he was about to strike the first blow with his axe, Robinson Crusoe noticed a plank cast up on the beach by the waves."

"Oh, what a lucky accident! He ran to pick it up?"

"That was his first impulse; but then he stopped and reasoned as follows:

" 'If I go to get that plank, it will cost me only the exertion of carrying it, and the time needed to go down to the beach and climb back up the cliff.

" 'But if I make a plank with my axe, first of all, I shall be assuring myself two weeks' labor; then, my axe will become dull, which will provide me with the job of sharpening it; and I shall consume my provisions, making a third source of employment, since I shall have to replace them. Now, *labor is wealth*. It is clear

* [What follows is based on *Robinson Crusoe*, the famous novel by the English author, Daniel Defoe (1659–1731). A number of students of economics, including Bastiat, have used what has been called the "Crusoist" approach to economic problems by starting with the simplest possible economic organization.—TRANSLATOR.]

that I shall only be hurting my own interests if I go down to the beach to pick up that piece of driftwood. It is vital for me to protect my *personal labor,* and, now that I think of it, I can even create additional labor for myself by going down and kicking that plank right back into the sea!' "

"What an absurd line of reasoning!"

"That may be. It is nonetheless the same line of reasoning that is adopted by every nation that *protects* itself by interdicting the entry of foreign goods. It kicks back the plank that is offered it in exchange for a little labor, in order to give itself more labor. There is no labor, even including that of the customs official, in which it does not see some profit. It is represented by the pains Robinson Crusoe took to return to the sea the present it was offering him. Consider the nation as a collective entity, and you will not find an iota of difference between its line of reasoning and that of Robinson Crusoe."

"Did he not see that he could devote the time he could have saved to making *something else?*"

"What *else?*"

"As long as a person has wants to satisfy and time at his disposal, he always has *something* to do. I am not obliged to specify the kind of work he could undertake to do."

"I can certainly specify precisely the kind that probably escaped his attention."

"And I maintain, for my part, that, with incredible blindness, he confused labor with its result, the end with the means, and I am going to prove it to you. . . . ."

"You do not have to. The fact still remains that this is an illustration of the system of restriction or interdiction in its simplest form. If it seems absurd to you in this form, it is because the two functions of producer and consumer are here combined in the same individual."

"Let us therefore proceed to a more complicated case."

"Gladly. Some time later, after Robinson had met Friday, they pooled their resources and began to co-operate in common enterprises. In the morning, they hunted for six hours and brought back four baskets of game. In the evening, they worked in the garden for six hours and obtained four baskets of vegetables.

"One day a longboat landed on the Isle of Despair. A handsome foreigner* disembarked and was admitted to the table of our two recluses. He tasted and highly praised the products of the garden, and, before taking leave of his hosts, he addressed them in these words:

" 'Generous islanders, I dwell in a land where game is much more plentiful than it is here, but where horticulture is unknown. It will be easy for me to bring you four baskets of game every evening, if you will give me in exchange only two baskets of vegetables.'

"At these words, Robinson and Friday withdrew to confer, and the debate they had is too interesting for me not to report it here in full.

"Friday: Friend, what do you think of it?

"Robinson: If we accept, we are ruined.

"F.: Are you quite sure of that? Let us reckon up what it comes to.

"R.: It has all been reckoned up, and there can be no doubt about the outcome. This competition will simply mean the end of our hunting industry.

"F.: What difference does that make if we have the game?

"R.: You are just theorizing! It will no longer be the product of our labor.

"F.: No matter, since in order to get it we shall have to part with some vegetables!

"R.: Then what shall we gain?

"F.: The four baskets of game cost us six hours of labor. The foreigner gives them to us in exchange for two baskets of vegetables, which take us only three hours to produce. Therefore, this puts three hours at our disposal.

"R.: You ought rather to say that they are subtracted from our

* [There is a nuance of meaning here in the French that cannot be reproduced in English. The French word *étranger* means both "foreigner" and "stranger." Bastiat's point, as is evident in what follows, is, not that the visitor was just a stranger, but that he was a foreigner in the sense of being external to Robinson's and Friday's economic system.—TRANSLATOR.]

productive activity. That is the exact amount of our loss. *Labor is wealth,* and if we lose one-fourth of our working time, we shall be one-fourth less wealthy.

"F.: Friend, you are making an enormous mistake. We shall have the same amount of game, the same quantity of vegetables, and—into the bargain—three more hours at our disposal. That is what I call progress, or there is no such thing in this world.

"R.: You are talking in generalities! What shall we do with these three hours?

"F.: We shall do *something else.*

"R.: Ah! I have you there. You are unable to mention anything in particular. *Something else, something else*—that is very easy to say.

"F.: We can fish; we can decorate our cabin; we can read the Bible.

"R.: Utopia! Who knows which of these things we shall do, or whether we shall do any of them?

"F.: Well, if we have no wants to satisfy, we shall take a rest. Is not rest good for something?

"R.: But when people lie around doing nothing, they die of hunger.

"F.: My friend, you are caught in a vicious circle. I am talking about a kind of rest that will subtract nothing from our supply of game and vegetables. You keep forgetting that by means of our foreign trade, nine hours of labor will provide us with as much food as twelve do today.

"R.: It is very clear that you were not brought up in Europe. Had you ever read the *Moniteur industriel,* it would have taught you this: 'All time saved is a dead loss. What counts is not consumption, but production. All that we consume, if it is not the direct product of our labor, counts for nothing. Do you want to know whether you are rich? Do not measure the extent of your satisfactions, but of your exertion.' This is what the *Moniteur industriel* would have taught you. As for myself, being no theorist, all I see is the loss of our hunting.

"F.: What an extraordinary inversion of ideas! But. . . .

"R.: But me no buts. Moreover, there are political reasons for rejecting the selfish offers of the perfidious foreigner.

"F.: Political reasons!

"R.: Yes. First, he is making us these offers only because they are advantageous to him.

"F.: So much the better, since they are so for us too.

"R.: Then, by this traffic, we shall make ourselves dependent upon him.

"F.: And he will make himself dependent on us. We shall have need of his game; and he, of our vegetables; and we shall all live in great friendship.

"R.: You are just following some abstract system! Do you want me to shut you up for good?

"F.: Go on and try. I am still waiting for a good reason.

"R.: Suppose the foreigner learns to cultivate a garden, and that his island is more fertile than ours. Do you see the consequence?

"F.: Yes. Our relations with the foreigner will be severed. He will no longer take our vegetables, since he will have them at home with less labor. He will no longer bring us game, since we shall have nothing to give him in exchange, and we shall then be in precisely the same situation that you want us to be in today.

"R.: Improvident savage! You do not see that after destroying our hunting industry by flooding us with game, he will destroy our gardening industry by flooding us with vegetables.

"F.: But this will happen only so long as we shall be in a position to give him *something else,* that is to say, so long as we shall be able to find *something else* to produce with a saving in labor for ourselves.

"R.: *Something else, something else!* You always come back to that. You are up in the clouds, my friend; there is nothing practical in your ideas.

"The dispute went on for a long time and left each one, as often happens, unchanged in his convictions. However, since Robinson had great influence over Friday, he made his view prevail; and when the foreigner came to learn how his offer had been received, Robinson said to him:

" 'Foreigner, in order for us to accept your proposal, we must be very sure about two things:

" 'First, that game is not more plentiful on your island than on ours; for we want to fight only *on equal terms.*

" 'Second, that you will lose by this bargain. For, as in every exchange there is necessarily a gainer and a loser, we should be victimized if you were not the loser. What do you say?'

" 'Nothing,' said the foreigner. And, bursting into laughter, he re-embarked in his longboat."

"The story would not be so bad if Robinson were not so absurd."

"He is no more so than the committee of the rue Hauteville."*

"Oh, their case is very different. In the hypothetical cases you cited, first, one man was living by himself, and then (what amounts to the same thing), two men were living in a state of common ownership. That is far from being the picture presented by the world in which we are living today; the division of labor and the intervention of tradesmen and money change the picture considerably."

"These conditions do, in fact, make transactions more complicated, but they do not change their essential nature."

"What! You want to compare modern commerce to simple barter?"

"Commerce is nothing but barter on a grand scale; barter and commerce are essentially identical in nature, just as labor on a small scale is of essentially the same nature as labor on a large scale, or as the force of gravitation that moves an atom is of essentially the same nature as the force of gravitation that moves a planet."

"Then, as you see it, these arguments, which are so clearly untenable when advanced by Robinson Crusoe, are no less so when advanced by our protectionists?"

"No less; the only reason the error is less evident is that the circumstances are more complicated."

"In that case, why not give us an example taken from conditions as they are at present?"

"Very well. In France, owing to custom and the demands of the climate, cloth is a useful item. Is the essential thing to *make it* or to *have it?*"

"A fine question! In order to have it, you must first make it."

* [The reference is to the Odier Committee. See *supra,* p. 167.—TRANSLATOR.]

"Not necessarily. In order to have it, someone must make it, no doubt; but it is not necessary that the person or the country that consumes it should also produce it. You did not make the fabric that clothes you so well, nor did France produce the coffee on which her inhabitants breakfast."

"But I bought my cloth, and France its coffee."

"Precisely, and with what?"

"With money."

"But you did not produce the metal for your money, nor did France either."

"We bought it."

"With what?"

"With the products we sent to Peru."

"Thus, in reality, it is your labor that is exchanged for cloth, and French labor that is exchanged for coffee."

"Undoubtedly."

"Hence, it is not absolutely necessary that you produce what you consume?"

"Not if we produce *something else* that we give in exchange."

"In other words, France has two ways of providing itself with a given quantity of cloth. The first is to manufacture it herself; the second is to make *something else,* and to exchange *that something else* with foreigners for cloth. Of these two ways, which is the better?"

"I hardly know."

"Is it not that which, *for a given amount of labor, yields a larger amount of cloth?*"

"It would seem so."

"And which is better for a nation, to be free to choose between these two ways of getting cloth, or to have a law interdicting one of them, on the chance of stumbling on the better of the two?"

"It seems to me that it is better for a nation to be free to choose, all the more so since in such matters it always chooses wisely."

"The law that bans foreign cloth thus determines that if France wants to have cloth, she must make it herself, and prohibits her from making that *something else* with which she could buy foreign cloth."

"True."

"And since the law compels the making of cloth and forbids the making of *something else,* precisely because that something else would require less labor (for otherwise there would be no need for the law to interfere), it thus virtually decrees that for a given quantity of labor France shall have but one meter of cloth by making it herself, whereas for the same amount of labor she would have had two meters by making *something else.*"

"But what else, for goodness' sake?"

"For goodness' sake, what difference does it make? Once given freedom of choice, she will make *something else* only in so far as there is *something else* to be made."

"That is possible; but I keep being haunted by the idea that foreigners may send us cloth and not take the *something else* from us in return, in which case we should be thoroughly victimized. In any case, this is the objection, even from your point of view. You do agree, do you not, that France will make this *something else* to exchange for cloth with less labor than if she had made the cloth itself?"

"Without a doubt."

"Therefore, there will be a certain quantity of her available labor supply that will be disemployed."

"Yes, but without her being any the less well clothed—a little circumstance that makes all the difference in the world. It was this that Robinson lost sight of, and that our protectionists either do not see or pretend not to see. The piece of driftwood also disemployed Robinson's labor for two weeks, at least in so far as it might have been applied to making a plank, but it did not deprive him of its use. We must, therefore, distinguish between two senses in which labor may be disemployed: that in which the effect is *privation,* and that in which the cause is *satisfaction.* They are worlds apart, and if you regard them as alike, your reasoning is no better than Robinson's. In the most complicated cases, as well as in the simplest, the sophism consists in *judging the utility of labor by its duration and intensity, and not by its results;* which leads to the economic policy of *reducing the results of labor with the aim of increasing its duration and intensity.*"[2]

15

The Little Arsenal of
the Freetrader[1]

Suppose someone tells you: "There are no absolute principles. Interdiction can be bad, and restriction good."

Answer: "Restriction *interdicts* the importation of everything it prevents from entering."

Suppose someone tells you: "Agriculture is the nutricial mother that furnishes the whole country with food."

Answer: "What furnishes the country with nutriment is not strictly agriculture, but *wheat*."

Suppose someone tells you: "The sustenance of the nation is dependent on agriculture."

Answer: "The sustenance of the nation is dependent on *wheat*. That is why a law compelling the nation to obtain *two* hectoliters of wheat by agricultural labor instead of the *four* hectoliters it might have obtained, in the absence of the law, by applying the same amount of labor to industrial production, far from being a law for the people's sustenance, is a law for their starvation."

Suppose someone tells you: "Restricting the importation of foreign wheat is conducive to an increase in domestic agriculture and, therefore, to an increase in domestic production."

Answer: "It is conducive to the extension of agriculture to the rocky slopes of mountains and the barren sands of the seashore. If you milk a cow and keep on milking, you will get more milk; for who can say just when you will no longer be able to squeeze out another drop? But that drop will cost you dear."

251

Suppose someone tells you: "Let the price of bread be high, for the farmer who becomes rich will enrich the industrialist."

Answer: "The price of bread is high when it is scarce; but scarcity makes only for poor people, or, if you like, *starving* rich people."

Suppose someone presses the point and says: "When the price of bread goes up, wages go up."

Answer by showing that in April, 1847, five-sixths of the workers were living on charity.

Suppose someone tells you: "A rise in wages must necessarily follow a rise in the cost of living."

Answer: "That is tantamount to saying that in a ship with no provisions everyone has as much to eat as if it were well stocked."

Suppose someone tells you: "The man who sells wheat must be assured a good price."

Answer: "Very well. But in that case the man who buys it must be assured a good wage."

Suppose someone tells you: "The landowners, who make the law, raised the price of bread without concerning themselves about wages because they know that, when the price of bread goes up, wages go up *quite naturally*."

Answer: "By the same token, then, when workers make the law, do not blame them if they fix a high wage rate without concerning themselves about protecting wheat, for they know that, when wages are raised, the cost of living rises *quite naturally*."

Suppose someone asks you: "What must we do, then?"

Answer: "Be just to everyone."

Suppose someone tells you: "It is essential for a great country to have an iron industry."

Answer: "What is more essential is that this great country *have iron*."

Suppose someone tells you: "It is indispensable for a great country to have a clothing industry."

Answer: "What is more indispensable is that the citizens of this great country *have clothes*."

Suppose someone tells you: "Labor is wealth."

Answer: "That is not true."

And, by way of explanation, add: "Bloodletting is not health; and the proof is that its object is to restore health."

Suppose someone tells you: "To compel men to dig a mine and to extract an ounce of iron from a quintal of iron ore is to increase their labor and consequently their wealth."*

Answer: "To compel men to dig wells by forbidding them to take water from the river is to increase their *useless* labor, but not their wealth."

Suppose someone tells you: "The sun gives its light and heat without remuneration."

Answer: "So much the better for me; it costs me nothing to see clearly."

And suppose someone replies: "Industry in general loses what you might have spent for artificial illumination."

Parry with: "No; for what I save by paying nothing to the sun, I use for buying clothing, furniture, and candles."

Similarly, suppose someone tells you: "These English scoundrels have *amortized* their investments."

Answer: "So much the better for us; they will not oblige us to make interest payments."

Suppose someone tells you: "These perfidious Englishmen find iron and coal in the same pit."

Answer: "So much the better for us; they will not charge us anything for bringing them together."

Suppose someone tells you: "The Swiss have lush pastures that cost little."

Answer: "The advantage is on our side, for this means that less labor will be demanded on our part to promote our domestic agriculture and provide ourselves with food."

Suppose someone tells you: "The fields of the Crimea have no value and pay no taxes."

Answer: "The profit is on our side, since the wheat we buy is exempt from these charges."

Suppose someone tells you: "The serfs of Poland work without wages."

Answer: "The misfortune is theirs, and the profit is ours; since

* [It would be uneconomic to work ore of such low grade.—TRANSLATOR.]

their labor does not enter into the price of the wheat that their masters sell us."

Finally, suppose someone tells you: "Other nations have many advantages over us."

Answer: "Through exchange, they are, in fact, compelled to let us share in these advantages."

Suppose someone tells you: "With free trade, we are going to be flooded with bread, beef à la mode, coal, and overcoats."

Answer: "Then we shall be neither hungry nor cold."

Suppose someone asks you: "What shall we use for money?"

Answer: "Don't let that worry you. If we are flooded, it will be because we are able to pay; and if we are not able to pay, we shall not be flooded."

Suppose someone tells you: "I should be in favor of free trade if foreigners, in bringing us their products, took ours in exchange; but they will take away our money."

Answer: "Money does not grow in the fields of the Beauce* any more than coffee does, nor is it turned out by the workshops of Elbeuf.† For us, paying foreigners with cash is like paying them with coffee."

Suppose someone tells you: "Eat meat."

Answer: "Permit it to be imported."

Suppose someone tells you, like *La Presse:* "When one does not have the means to buy bread, one must buy beef."

Answer: "This is advice just as wise as that of Mr. Vulture to his tenant:

> When one does not have the means to pay his rent,
> One has to get a house of one's own."‡

Suppose someone tells you, like *La Presse:* "The government should teach people why and how they ought to eat beef."

Answer: "The government has only to permit the importation

---

* [Flourishing grain region of north-central France.—TRANSLATOR.]

† [Industrial town in the vicinity of Rouen.—TRANSLATOR.]

‡ [From the play, *Mr. Vulture (Monsieur Vautour)*, by the French dramatist Marc Antoine Madeleine Désaugiers (1772–1827). The name became a common slang expression used to typify the heartless usurer, creditor, and landlord.—TRANSLATOR.]

of beef; the most civilized people in the world are sufficiently grown up to learn how to eat it without being taught."

Suppose someone tells you: "The government should know everything and foresee everything in order to manage the lives of the people, and the people need only let themselves be taken care of."

Answer: "Is there a government apart from the people? Is there any human foresight apart from humanity? Archimedes could have gone on repeating every day of his life, 'Give me a fulcrum and a lever, and I will move the earth'; he would never, for all that, have been able to move it, for want of a fulcrum and lever. The fulcrum of the state is the nation, and nothing is more senseless than to base so many expectations on the state, that is, to assume the existence of collective wisdom and foresight after taking for granted the existence of individual imbecility and improvidence."

Suppose someone tells you: "Good heavens! I am not asking for favors, but just enough of an import duty on wheat and meat to compensate for the heavy taxes to which France is subjected; only a small duty equal to what these taxes add to the sales price of my wheat."

Answer: "A thousand pardons, but I too pay taxes. If, then, the protection that you are voting yourself has the effect of adding to the price I pay for wheat an amount exactly equal to your share of the taxes, what your honeyed words really come to is nothing less than a demand to establish between us an arrangement that, as formulated by you, could be expressed in the following terms: 'Considering that the public charges are heavy, I, as a seller of wheat, am to pay nothing at all, and you, my neighbor who buys it, are to pay double, viz., your own share and mine as well.' Wheat merchant, you may, my neighbor, have might on your side; but you surely do not have right."

Suppose someone tells you: "It is, however, very hard for me, who pay taxes, to compete in my own market with a foreigner who pays none."

Answer:

"1. In the first place, it is not *your* market, but *our* market. I, who live on wheat and pay for it, ought to count for something too.

"2. Few foreigners nowadays are exempt from taxes.

"3. If the tax that you are voting repays you, in the form of roads, canals, security, etc., more than it costs you, you are not justified in barring, at my expense, the competition of foreigners who do not pay the tax, but who, by the same token, do not enjoy the advantages of the security, roads, and canals that you have. It would make just as much sense to say: 'I demand a compensatory duty, because I have finer clothes, stronger horses, and better plows than the Russian peasant.'

"4. If the tax does not repay you what it costs, do not vote it.

"5. And finally, after voting the tax, do you desire to exempt yourself from it? Then contrive some scheme that will shift it onto foreigners. But the tariff makes your share of the tax fall upon me, who already have quite enough of my own to bear."

Suppose someone tells you: "For the Russians free trade is necessary *to enable them to exchange their products to advantage.*" [Opinion expressed by M. Thiers in committee, April, 1847.]

Answer: "Free trade is necessary everywhere and for the same reason."

Suppose someone tells you: "Each country has its wants and *it must act* accordingly." [M. Thiers.]

Answer: "*It does so of its own accord* when it is not hindered from doing so."

Suppose someone tells you: "Since we have no sheet iron, we must permit its importation." [M. Thiers.]

Answer: "Much obliged!"

Suppose someone tells you: "Our merchant marine needs freight. The lack of cargoes on return voyages prevents our ships from competing with foreign vessels." [M. Thiers.]

Answer: "When a country wants to produce everything at home, it cannot have cargoes either to export or to import. It is just as absurd to want a merchant marine when foreign products are barred as it would be to want carts where all shipments have been prohibited."

Suppose someone tells you: "Even granting that the protectionist system is unjust, everything has been organized on the basis of it: capital has been invested; rights have been acquired; the system cannot be changed without suffering."

Answer: "Every injustice is profitable for someone (except, perhaps, restriction, which in the long run benefits nobody); to express alarm over the dislocation that ending an injustice occasions the person who is profiting from it is as much as to say that an injustice, solely because it has existed for a moment, ought to endure forever."

16

The Right Hand and the Left[1]

(A REPORT TO THE KING)

Sire,

When we see the advocates of free trade boldly disseminating their doctrine, and maintaining that the right to buy and to sell is included in the right to own property (a piece of insolence that has found its true champion in M. Billault),* we may quite properly feel serious concern about the fate of our *domestic industry;* for to what use will the French people put their hands and their minds when they live under a system of free trade?

The government that you have honored with your confidence has been obliged to concern itself with so grave a situation, and has sought in its wisdom to discover a means of *protection* that might be substituted for the present one, which seems endangered. They propose *that you forbid your loyal subjects to use their right hands.*

Sire, do not do us the injustice of thinking that we have lightly adopted a measure that at first sight may seem bizarre. Deep study of the *protectionist system* has revealed to us this syllogism, upon which the whole of it is based:

The more one works, the richer one is.

The more difficulties one has to overcome, the more one works.

Ergo, the more difficulties one has to overcome, the richer one is.

What, in fact, is *protection,* if not an ingenious application of this line of reasoning, so cogent and conclusive that it must resist even the subtlety of M. Billault himself?

Let us personify the country and view it as a collective being

---

* [Auguste Adolphe Marie Billault (1805–1863), an economist and member of the Chamber of Deputies.—TRANSLATOR.]

with thirty million mouths and, as a natural consequence, sixty million hands. It makes a clock that it intends to exchange in Belgium for ten quintals of iron.

But we tell it: "Make the iron yourself."

"I cannot," it replies; "it would take too long. I could not make more than five quintals in the time that I can make one clock."

"Utopian dreamer!" we reply; "that is precisely the reason why we are forbidding you to make the clock and ordering you to make the iron. Do you not see that we are providing employment for you?"

Sire, it could not have escaped your discernment that this is exactly the same as if we were to say to the country: *Work with your left hand, and not with your right.*

The old system of *restriction* was based on the idea of creating obstacles in order to multiply job opportunities. The new system of *restriction* that we are proposing to take its place is based on exactly the same idea. Sire, to make laws in this fashion is not to innovate; it is to carry on in the traditional way.

As for the efficacy of the measure, it is incontestable. It is difficult, much more difficult than people think, to do with the left hand what one is accustomed to doing with the right. You will be convinced of this, Sire, if you will deign to put our system to the test in performing some act that is familiar to you, such as, for instance, that of shuffling cards. We can, therefore, flatter ourselves on opening to labor an unlimited number of job opportunities.

Once the workers in every branch of industry are restricted to the use of their left hands alone, imagine, Sire, the immense number of people that will be needed to meet the present demand for consumers' goods, assuming that it remains constant, as we always do when we compare different systems of production. So prodigious a demand for manual labor cannot fail to bring about a considerable rise in wages, and pauperism will disappear from the country as if by magic.

Sire, your paternal heart will rejoice at the thought that this law will extend its benefits also to the more interesting part of the large family whose destiny engages all your solicitude. What future is there now for women in France? The bolder and hardier sex is imperceptibly driving them from every branch of industry.

There was a time when they could always get a job in the lottery offices. These have been closed by a pitiless humanitarianism, and on what pretext? "To save," it was said, "the pennies of the poor." Alas! Have the poor ever enjoyed, for the price of a single coin, entertainment as mild and as innocent as that provided by the mysterious urn of Fortune? Deprived as they were of all the sweets of life, when they used to put, fortnight after fortnight, the price of a day's labor on a *quaterne sec,** think how many hours of delightful anticipation they gave their families! There was always a place for hope at the domestic hearth. The garret the family occupied was peopled with illusions: the wife hoped to eclipse her neighbors by the splendor of her wardrobe; the son would see himself as a drum major; and the daughter imagined herself led to the altar on the arm of her betrothed.

> There is something to be said, after all, for dreaming
> beautiful dreams!†

Oh, the lottery was the poetic vision of the poor, and we have let it slip away!

Now that the lottery is gone, what other means do we have for taking care of the ladies we are seeking to protect? The tobacco industry and the postal service.

Let it be the sale of tobacco, by all means; its use is spreading, thank heaven, and thanks also to the genteel habits that our elegant young men have been most skillfully taught by the example of certain august personages.

But the postal service! . . . . We shall say nothing about it; it will constitute the subject of a special report.

Thus, apart from the sale of tobacco, what employment remains for your female subjects? Nothing but embroidering, knitting, and sewing—sorry makeshifts that the barbarous science of mechanics is limiting more and more.

---

* [A ticket at odds of 75,000 to one.—TRANSLATOR.]

† [This is quoted from Collin d'Harleville (1785–1806), minor dramatist and writer of light verse.—TRANSLATOR.]

But as soon as your new law is promulgated, as soon as all right hands are either cut off or tied down, things will change. Twenty times, thirty times as many embroiderers, pressers and ironers, seamstresses, dressmakers and shirtmakers, will not suffice to meet the national demand (shame to him who thinks ill of it), always assuming, as before, that it remains constant.

It is true that this assumption may be disputed by dispassionate theorists; for dresses will cost more, and so will shirts. The same could be said of the iron that we extract from our mines, as compared with what we could obtain *in exchange for the produce of our vineyards.* Hence, this argument is no more acceptable against *left-handedness** than against *protectionism;* for this high cost is itself at once the result and the sign of the superabundance of effort and labor that is precisely the basis on which, in the one case as in the other, we maintain that the prosperity of the working class is founded.

Yes, we may picture a touching scene of prosperity in the dressmaking business. Such bustling about! Such activity! Such animation! Each dress will busy a hundred fingers instead of ten. No young woman will any longer be idle, and we have no need, Sire, to indicate to your perspicacity the moral consequences of this great revolution. Not only will more young women be employed, but each of them will earn more, for all of them together will be unable to satisfy the demand; and if competition reappears, it will no longer be among the workers who make the dresses but among the fine ladies who wear them.

You see, Sire, our proposal is not only in accord with the economic traditions of the government, but is essentially moral and democratic as well.

In order to appreciate its consequences, let us assume that it has been put into effect, and, transporting ourselves in imagination into the future, let us imagine that the system has been in operation for twenty years. Idleness has been banished from the country; steady employment has brought affluence, harmony, content-

---

* [There is a pun here that cannot be rendered into English. The French word *gaucherie* means both "left-handedness" and "clumsiness," and Bastiat clearly intended this double sense.—TRANSLATOR.]

ment, and morality to every household; poverty and prostitution are things of the past. The left hand being very clumsy to work with,* jobs are superabundant, and the pay is satisfactory. Everything has been organized on this basis; consequently, the workshops are thronged. Is it not true, Sire, that if at such a time utopian dreamers were suddenly to appear, demanding freedom for the right hand, they would throw the country into a panic? Is it not true that this supposed reform would upset everyone's life? Hence, our system must be good, since it cannot be destroyed without causing suffering.

And yet we have a gloomy foreboding that one day there will be formed (so great is human perversity!) an association for the freedom of right hands.

We have the feeling that we can already hear the advocates of freedom for the right hand, at Montesquieu Hall,† speaking in this manner:

"My friends, you think yourselves richer because you have been deprived of the use of one hand; you take account only of the additional employment which that brings you. But, I beg you, consider also the high prices that result from it, and the forced diminution in the supply of consumers' goods of all kinds. This measure has not made capital more abundant, and capital is the fund from which wages are paid. The waters that flow from this great reservoir are directed into other channels, but their volume has not been increased; and the ultimate consequence for the nation as a whole is a loss of wealth equal to all that the millions of right hands could produce over and above what the same number of left hands can turn out. Therefore, let us form an association, and, at the price of a few inevitable dislocations, let us win the right to work with both hands."

Happily, Sire, there will be formed an *association in defense of labor with the left hand,* and the advocates of *left-hand labor* will have no trouble in demolishing all these generalities, speculations,

* [Another pun in French: *La main gauche étant fort gauche à la besogne,* . . . .—TRANSLATOR.]

† [It was at Montesquieu Hall that the first public meeting of the French freetraders was held, on August 28, 1846.—TRANSLATOR.]

assumptions, abstractions, reveries, and utopian fantasies. They will need only to exhume the *Moniteur industriel* of 1846; and they will find ready-made arguments against *freedom of trade* that will do quite as well against *freedom for the right hand* if they will merely substitute one expression for the other.

The Parisian league for *free trade* did not doubt that it would receive the support of the workers. But the workers are no longer men to be led about by the nose. They have their eyes open, and they are better informed about political economy than our Ph.D. professors. . . . . "Free trade," they replied, "would deprive us of our jobs, and our jobs are all that we really possess. Employment is the great sovereign that rules over our destinies. *With employment, with jobs abundant, the price of commodities is never beyond our reach.* But without a job, even if bread costs only one sou per pound, the workingman is forced to die of hunger. Now, your doctrines, instead of increasing the present number of jobs in France, will lessen it, which means that you will reduce us to poverty." [Issue of October 13, 1846.]

When there are too many commodities in the market, it is true that their price falls; but as wages fall when commodity prices drop, the result is that, instead of being in a position to buy more, we are no longer able to buy anything. Therefore, it is when commodities are at their lowest price that the workingman is in the worst situation. [Gauthier de Rumilly, *Moniteur industriel,* November 17.]

It will not be inappropriate for the proponents of *left-hand labor* to intermingle a few threats among their fine theories. Here is a model for them:

"What! You wish to substitute the labor of the right hand for that of the left, and thus force down, if not entirely abolish, wages, the sole resource of almost the entire nation!

"And this at a time when poor harvests are already imposing painful sacrifices upon the worker, causing him to worry about his future, and making him more readily disposed to listen to bad advice and to abandon the wise course of conduct to which he has hitherto adhered!"

We are confident, Sire, that, armed with such cogent reasoning, if it comes to a battle, the left hand will emerge the victor.

Perhaps there will also be formed an association with the aim of inquiring whether the right hand and the left hand are not both wrong, and whether a third hand can be found to mediate between them.

After depicting the advocates of freedom for the right hand as misled by the *apparent latitude of a principle whose correctness has not yet been tested by experience,* and the proponents of left-handed labor as entrenching themselves in the positions they have gained, the association may argue as follows:

Can it be denied that there is a third position that can be taken in the midst of the conflict? Is it not evident that the workers have to defend themselves at one and the same time against those who want nothing changed in the present situation, because they find it advantageous, and those who dream of an economic revolution of which they have calculated neither the extent nor the implications? [*National* of October 16.]

Nevertheless, we do not intend to conceal from Your Majesty that there is one respect in which our project is vulnerable. We may be told that in twenty years all left hands will be as skillful as right hands are now, and it will then no longer be possible to count on *left-handedness* to increase the number of jobs in the country.

Our reply to this is that, according to learned doctors, the left side of the human body has a natural weakness that is completely reassuring for the future of labor.

If, then, Your Majesty consents to sign the decree, a great principle will be established: *All wealth stems from the intensity of labor.* It will be easy for us to extend and vary its applications. We shall ordain, for example, that it shall no longer be permissible to work except with the foot. This is no more impossible (as we have seen) than to extract iron from the mud of the Seine. Men have even been known to write without using either hands or feet. You see, Sire, that we shall not be lacking in means of increasing the number of job opportunities in your realm. As a last resort, we should take recourse to the limitless possibilities of amputation.

Finally, Sire, if this report were not intended for publication, we should call your attention to the great influence that all measures of the kind we are proposing to you are likely to confer upon men in power. But this is a matter that we prefer to reserve for a private audience.

17

Domination through Industrial Superiority[1]

"Just as, in time of war, a nation attains ascendancy over its enemies by virtue of its superiority in weapons, can a nation, in time of peace, attain ascendancy over its competitors by virtue of its industrial superiority?"

This is a question of the highest interest in an age when no one seems to doubt that in the field of industry, as on the field of battle, *the stronger crushes the weaker*.

For this to be so, someone must have discovered, between the labor that is exerted upon things and the violence that is exerted upon men, a melancholy and discouraging analogy; for how could these two kinds of operations be identical in their effects if they are opposite in nature?

And if it is true that in industry, as in war, ascendancy is the necessary result of superiority, why do we concern ourselves with progress or with political economy, since we live in a world in which everything has been so arranged by Providence that one and the same effect—oppression—inevitably follows from principles that are directly opposed to each other?

In regard to the entirely new policy into which free trade is leading England, many people are making the following objection, which, I must admit, carries weight even with the most open-minded among us: Is England doing anything else than pursuing the same end by different means? Has she not always aspired to world supremacy? Assured of superiority in capital and labor, is she not inviting free competition in order to stifle Continental industry, reign supreme, and win for herself the privilege of feeding and clothing the nations she has ruined?

It would be easy for me to demonstrate that these alarms have no basis in fact; that our supposed inferiority is greatly exaggerated; that every one of our major industries is not only holding its ground, but is actually expanding under the impact of foreign competition, and that its inevitable effect is to bring about a general increase in consumption that is capable of absorbing both domestic and foreign products.

Today I propose, rather, to make a frontal attack upon this objection, allowing it all the strength and the advantage of the ground it has chosen. Disregarding for the moment the special case of the English and the French, I shall seek to discover, in general terms, whether a country that, by its superiority in one branch of industry, succeeds in eliminating foreign competition in that industry, has thereby taken a step toward domination over the other country, and the latter a step toward dependence on it; whether, in other words, both do not profit from the operation, and whether it is not the nation that has been bested in this commercial rivalry that profits the most.

If a product is viewed only as *an opportunity for expending labor,* the alarms of the protectionists are certainly well founded. If we consider iron, for example, only in connection with ironmasters, we might well fear that the competition of a country in which iron is a gratuitous gift of Nature could extinguish the fires in the blast furnaces of another country in which there is a scarcity of ore and fuel.

But is this a complete view of the subject? Is iron connected only with those who make it? Does it have no connection with those who use it? Is its sole and ultimate end simply to be produced? And if it is useful, not on account of the labor for which it provides employment, but by reason of the qualities it possesses, the numerous services for which its hardness and its malleability render it fit, does it not follow that a foreigner cannot reduce its price, even to the point of rendering its production in our country completely unprofitable, without doing us more good in the latter respect than harm in the former?

It should be kept in mind that there are many things that foreigners, on account of the natural advantages by which they are surrounded, prevent us from producing directly, and with relation to which we are situated, *in fact,* in the hypothetical position we have been considering with regard to iron. We produce at home neither tea, coffee, gold, nor silver. Does this mean that our industry as a whole thereby suffers some diminution? No; it means only that, in order to create the equivalent value needed to acquire these commodities by way of exchange, we employ *less* labor than would be required to produce them ourselves. We thus have more labor left over to devote to satisfying other wants. We are that much richer and stronger. All that foreign competition has been able to do, even in cases in which it has absolutely eliminated us from a particular branch of industry, is to save labor and increase our productive capacity. Is this the way for the foreigner to attain *mastery* over us?

If someone found a gold mine in France, it does not follow that it would be to our interest to work it. In fact, it is certain that the enterprise should not be undertaken if each ounce of gold absorbed more of our labor than would an ounce of gold bought from Mexico with cloth. In that case it would be better to continue to regard our looms as gold mines. And what is true of gold is no less true of iron.

The illusion has its source in our failure to see that foreign superiority eliminates the need for but one particular kind of labor in the domestic market and renders that particular kind of labor superfluous only by putting at our disposal the result of the very labor so eliminated. If men lived in diving bells under water and had to provide themselves with air by means of a pump, this would be an immense source of employment for them. To do anything that might interfere with their employing their labor in this way, *while leaving their conditions unchanged,* would be to inflict frightful harm on them. But if their labor ceases only because there is no longer a need for it, because the men are placed in another environment in which air is introduced into their lungs without effort, then the loss of this labor is in no way regrettable, except in the eyes of those who persist in seeing the sole value of labor in the labor itself.

It is precisely this type of labor that machinery, free trade, and progress of every kind are gradually eliminating; not productive labor, but labor that has become superfluous, surplus labor devoid of purpose or result. Protectionism, on the contrary, puts it back to work; it places us once again under water, in order to furnish us with the opportunity of using the air pump; it compels us to seek for gold in the inaccessible domestic mine rather than in our domestic looms. Its whole effect is expressed in the phrase: *waste of energy.*

It will be understood that I am speaking here of general effects, and not of the temporary inconveniences occasioned by the transition from a bad system to a good one. A momentary disturbance necessarily accompanies every advance. This may be a reason for easing the transition as much as possible; it is not a reason for systematically prohibiting all progress, still less for failing to recognize it.

Industrial competition is generally represented as a conflict; but this is not a true picture of it, or it is true only if we confine ourselves to the consideration of each industry in terms of its effects upon another, similar industry, isolating both of them, in thought, from the rest of mankind. But there is something else to be considered: their effects upon consumption and upon general well-being.

That is why it is not permissible to compare commercial relations, as is often done, to war and to treat the two of them as analogous.

In war, *the stronger overcomes the weaker.*

In business, *the stronger imparts strength to the weaker.* This utterly destroys the analogy.

The English may be strong and skillful; they may have enormous *amortized* investments; they may have at their disposal the two great forces of production: iron and fuel; all this means that the products of their labor are *cheap.* And who profits from the low cost of a product? The person who buys it.

It is not within the power of the English to annihilate absolutely any part whatsoever of our labor. All they can do is to render it superfluous with respect to a given result that has already been achieved, to furnish us the air and at the same time dispense with the pump, to increase thereby the productive capacities at our disposal, and—what is especially noteworthy—to render their alleged ascendancy over us the less possible the more their industrial superiority becomes incontestable.

Thus, by a rigorous yet reassuring demonstration, we reach the conclusion that *labor* and *violence,* which are so opposite in nature, are none the less so in their effects, whatever protectionists and socialists may say of them.

In order to reach this conclusion all that we have to do is to distinguish between labor that has been *abolished* and labor that has been *saved*.

To have less iron *because* one works less, and to have more iron *although* one works less, are things that are more than just different; they are opposite. The protectionists confuse them; we do not. That is all.

We should realize that if the English undertake enterprises that involve a great deal of activity, labor, capital, and intelligence, and a great number of natural resources, it is not just for show, but to procure for themselves a great number of satisfactions in exchange for their products. They certainly expect to receive at least as much as they give, and *what they produce in their own country pays for what they buy elsewhere.* If, therefore, they flood us with their products, it is because they expect to be flooded with ours. In that case, the best way to acquire for ourselves as many of their products as possible is to be free to choose between these two means of obtaining them: direct production or indirect production. All the arts of British Machiavellism cannot force us to make a poor choice.

Let us, then, cease this childish practice of comparing industrial competition to war; whatever element of plausibility this faulty analogy has comes of isolating two competing industries in order to determine the effects of their competition. As soon as one introduces into this calculation the effect produced upon the general well-being, the analogy breaks down.

In a battle, he who is killed is utterly destroyed, and the army is so much the weaker. In industry, a factory closes only when what it produced is replaced, *with a surplus besides,* by the whole of domestic industry. Imagine a state of affairs in which, for each man killed in action, two spring from the ground full of strength and energy. If there is a planet where such things happen, war, it must be admitted, is conducted there under conditions so different from those we see down here that it no longer deserves even to be called by the same name.

Now, this is the distinguishing characteristic of what has been so inappropriately called *industrial warfare.*

Let the English and the Belgians lower the price of their iron, if they can; let them keep on lowering it until they send it to us for nothing. They may quite possibly, by this means, extinguish the fire in one of our blast furnaces, i.e., in military parlance, kill one of our soldiers; but I defy them to prevent a thousand other branches of industry from springing up at once, as a *necessary* consequence of this very cheapness, and becoming more profitable than the one that has been killed.

Our conclusion must be, then, that domination through industrial superiority is impossible and self-contradictory, since every superiority that manifests itself in a nation is transformed into low-cost goods and in the end only imparts strength to all other nations. Let us banish from political economy all expressions borrowed from the military vocabulary: *to fight on equal terms, conquer, crush, choke off, be defeated, invasion, tribute.* What do these terms signify? Squeeze them, and nothing comes out. Or rather, what comes out is absurd errors and harmful preconceptions. Such expressions are inimical to international co-operation, hinder the formation of a peaceful, ecumenical, and indissoluble union of the peoples of the world, and retard the progress of mankind.[2]

Notes

FIRST SERIES

NOTES TO INTRODUCTORY COMMENTS

1. [The brief volume containing the first series of the *Economic Sophisms* appeared at the end of 1845. Several chapters in it had been published in the *Journal des économistes,* in the April, July, and October, 1845, issues.—EDITOR.]
2. [This concept was afterward the basis for the pamphlet, "What Is Seen and What Is Not Seen" (*Selected Essays on Political Economy,* chap. 1).—EDITOR.]

NOTES TO CHAPTER 1

1. [The author modified the terms of this proposition in a later work. Cf. *Economic Harmonies,* chap. 11.—EDITOR.]
2. We have no noun in French to express the idea that is opposite to *high price* ("cheapness" in English). It is quite noteworthy that the people instinctively express this idea by this paraphrase: advantageous market, good market [*bon marché*]. The protectionists really ought to do something about changing this expression. It implies a whole economic system that is the converse of theirs.
3. [The author has treated this subject at greater length in *Economic Harmonies,* chap. 11, and, in another form, in the article "Abundance" written for the *Dictionnaire de l'économie politique.*—EDITOR.]

NOTE TO CHAPTER 2

1. [Cf. on this same subject *infra,* Second Series, chap. 14, and *Economic Harmonies,* chaps. 3 and 11.—EDITOR.]

NOTES TO CHAPTER 3

1. For this reason, and for the sake of conciseness, we ask the reader to pardon us if we henceforth designate this system by the term *Sisyphism.*
2. It is only fair to state that M. d'Argout put this strange language into the mouths of the opponents of the sugar beet. But he expressly appropriated it and sanctioned it besides by virtue of the very law for which it served as justification.
3. Assuming that from 48,000 to 50,000 hectares are enough to provide for the present per capita consumption, it would require 150,000 if per capita consumption were tripled, as M. d'Argout admits is possible. Furthermore, if the sugar-beet crop were rotated every six years, it would occupy successively 900,000 hectares, or 1/38 of the arable land.

4. [Cf. on the same subject *infra*, Second Series, chap. 16, and *Economic Harmonies*, chap 6.—Editor.]

NOTES TO CHAPTER 4

1. The Vicomte de Romanet.
2. Mathieu de Dombasle.
3. It is true that labor does not receive a uniform remuneration. It varies according to whether it is more or less exhausting, dangerous, skilled, etc. Competition establishes for each category a current price, and it is this variable price that I am discussing.
4. [The theory sketched in this chapter is the same as the one that, four years later, was expanded in *Economic Harmonies*. Remuneration paid exclusively for human labor; the gratuitous utility of natural resources; the progressive harnessing of these resources for the benefit of mankind, whose common patrimony they thus become; the raising of the general standard of living and the tendency toward relative equalization of conditions: these can be recognized as all the essential elements in the most important of Bastiat's works.—Editor.]

NOTES TO CHAPTER 5

1. [Cf. *Economic Harmonies*, chap. 18.—Editor.]
2. [Cf., in Vol. V (of the French edition), the pamphlet "Peace and Liberty." —Editor.]

NOTE TO CHAPTER 6

1. [In March, 1850, the author was again forced to combat the same sophism, which he heard expressed in the Chambers. He amended the preceding demonstration by excluding from his calculations the costs of transportation, etc. Cf. *Selected Essays on Political Economy*, chap. 13.—Editor.]

NOTES TO CHAPTER 11

1. [This thought often recurs in the author's writings. In his eyes it was of capital importance, and it led him, four days before his death, to make this recommendation: "Tell M. de F.* to treat economic questions always from the consumer's point of view, for the interest of the consumer is identical with that of mankind."—Editor.]
2. [Cf. *infra*, Second Series, chap. 5, and *Economic Harmonies*, chap. 4. —Editor.]

NOTE TO CHAPTER 12

1. [Cf. *Economic Harmonies*, chap. 14.—Editor.]

NOTES TO CHAPTER 13

1. [*De l'administration commerciale opposée a l'économie politique*, page 5. —Editor.]†

* [Fontenay, the French editor.—Translator.]
† [F. L. A. Ferrier (1777–1861), French tariff administrator and author of books on tariffs and finance.—Translator.]

2. Could we not say: In what a frightfully prejudicial light Messrs. Ferrier and Saint-Chamans are put by the fact that economists of *every school,* that is, all the men who have studied the question, have reached the conclusion that, after all, freedom is better than coercion, and the laws of God are wiser than those of Colbert?

3. *Du système de l'impôt, etc.,* by the Vicomte de Saint-Chamans, p. 11.

4. [Cf. chap. 15.—EDITOR.]

NOTE TO CHAPTER 14

1. [Cf., *infra,* chaps. 18 and 20, and the letter to M. Thiers entitled "Protectionism and Communism," *Selected Essays on Political Economy,* chap. 7.—EDITOR.]

NOTE TO CHAPTER 18

1. [Cf., in Vol. V (of the French edition), the first letter to M. de Larmartine, and *Economic Harmonies,* chap. 1.—EDITOR.]*

NOTE TO CHAPTER 19

1. [Cf. the pamphlet entitled "Justice and Fraternity," *Selected Essays on Political Economy,* chap. 4. Cf. also the Introduction to "Cobden and the English League," and the "Second Campaign of the League," in Vol. II (of the French edition).—EDITOR.]

NOTE TO CHAPTER 20

1. *Du système de l'impôt, etc.,* p. 438.

NOTE TO CHAPTER 21

1. I do not mention explicitly here that portion of the remuneration which reverts to the entrepreneur, the capitalist, etc., for several reasons: first, if one looks at the matter closely, one will see that this always involves the reimbursement of money paid in advance or the payment for *labor* already performed; secondly, because under the general term *labor* I include not only the wages of the workingman but also the legitimate recompense of all factors co-operating in the work of production; and thirdly, and above all, because the production of manufactured goods is, like that of raw materials, burdened with interest charges and costs other than those for *manual labor,* so that the objection, in itself absurd, would apply to the most complicated spinning operation just as well as, and even better than, to the most primitive kind of agriculture.

2. [Cf., in Vol. I (of the French edition), the brief work dated 1834, entitled: "Reflections on the Petitions from Bordeaux, from Le Havre, etc."—EDITOR.]

* [Alphonse Marie Louis de Prat de Lamartine (1790–1869), leading French poet, a less important historian, a member of the Chamber of Deputies, and a major political figure just after the fall of King Louis Philippe in 1848.—TRANSLATOR.]

NOTES TO CONCLUSION OF FIRST SERIES

1. [We noted, at the end of chapter 4, that it obviously contained the germ of the doctrines expanded in *Economic Harmonies*. Here again we find, on the author's part, a desire to undertake the writing of this last work at the first suitable opportunity.—EDITOR.]

2. [This thought, which ends the first series of *Economic Sophisms*, was to be taken up again and expanded by the author at the beginning of the second series. The impact of plunder upon the fate of man concerned him deeply. Having touched on this subject several times in *Economic Sophisms* and *Selected Essays on Political Economy* (cf., in particular, "Property and Plunder," chap. 6, and "Plunder and Law," chap. 8), he reserved a place for a lengthy discussion of it in the second part of *Economic Harmonies*, among the "Disturbing Factors," chap. 18. Final testimony of the importance that he attached to it was his statement on the eve of his death: "An important task for political economy is to write the history of plunder. It is a long history involving, from the very beginning, conquests, migrations of peoples, invasions, and all the disastrous excesses of violence at grips with justice. All this has left an aftermath that still continues to plague us and that renders it more difficult to solve the problems of the present day. We shall not solve them so long as we are unaware of the way, and of the extent to which, injustice, present in our very midst, has gained a foothold in our customs and laws."—EDITOR.]

SECOND SERIES

NOTE TO SECOND SERIES

1. [The second series of *Economic Sophisms*, several chapters of which had been published in the *Journal des économistes* and the newspaper, *Le Libre échange*, appeared at the end of January, 1848.—EDITOR.]

NOTES TO CHAPTER 1

1. [Cf., in Vol. VI (of the French edition), chaps. 18, 19, 22, and 24, for the further remarks planned and begun by the author on "Disturbing Factors" (*Economic Harmonies*, chap. 18) affecting the harmony of natural laws. —EDITOR.]

2. [Cf., in Vol. I (of the French edition), the letter addressed to the President of the Peace Congress at Frankfort.—EDITOR.]

3. [Cf., in Vol. I (of the French edition), the letter addressed to M. Larnac; and in Vol. V (of the French edition), "Parliamentary Inconsistencies." —EDITOR.]

4. [Cf. *Selected Essays on Political Economy*, chap. 5, "The State," and chap. 2, "The Law," and *Economic Harmonies*, chap. 17, "Private and Public Services."—EDITOR.]

5. [For the distinction between true monopolies and what have been called natural monopolies, cf., in *Economic Harmonies*, chap. 5, note 2, accompanying the analysis of Adam Smith's theory of value.—EDITOR.]

6. [The author was soon to witness an increase in this source of disruption and to wage energetic war against it. Cf. *Selected Essays on Political Economy*, chap. 5, "The State"; Vol. II (of the French edition), "Disastrous Illusions," and Vol. VI (of the French edition), the final pages of chap. 4. —EDITOR.]

NOTES TO CHAPTER 5

1. [This chapter first appeared as an article in *Le Libre échange*, issue of July 25, 1847.—EDITOR.]
2. Recently M. Duchâtel,* who had formerly advocated free trade, with a view to low prices, stated in the Chamber, "It would not be difficult for me to prove that protectionism results in low prices."
3. [The author, in the speech he gave on September 29, 1846, at Montesquieu Hall, provided a striking illustration demonstrating this very principle. Cf. this speech in Vol. II (of the French edition).—EDITOR.]
4. [In *Le Libre échange* of August 1, 1847, the author presented an exposition of this topic that we deem worthy of reprinting here.—EDITOR.]

NOTES TO CHAPTER 6

1. [This chapter first appeared in the *Courier français* (September 18, 1846), whose columns were opened to the author so that he could reply to the attacks which had appeared in *L'Atelier*. It was only two months later that the newspaper *Le Libre échange* appeared.—EDITOR.]
2. [Cf., in Vol. II (of the French edition), the point-blank polemic against various newspapers.—EDITOR.]

NOTE TO CHAPTER 8

1. [Taken from *Le Libre échange*, December 6, 1846.—EDITOR.]

NOTES TO CHAPTER 9

1. [Taken from the *Journal des économistes*, January, 1846.—EDITOR.]
2. Possessing a farm that provides him with his living, he belongs to the *protected* class. This circumstance should disarm criticism. It shows that, if he does use harsh words, they are directed against the thing itself, and not against anyone's motives.
3. Here is the text: "May I cite again the tariff laws of the 9th and 11th of last June, whose object is in large part to encourage overseas shipping by increasing on several articles the *surtaxes* on goods entering under foreign flags. Our tariff laws, as you know, are generally directed toward this end, and, little by little, the surtax of ten francs, established by the law of April 28, 1816, being often insufficient, is disappearing, to give place to

---

* [Charles Jacques Marie Tanneguy, Comte de Duchâtel (1803–1867), author of *Considérations d'économie politique sur la bienfaisance* (1836). He collaborated with Pierre Leroux and others in editing *Le Globe*, a political and literary review, served as a cabinet minister under the July monarchy, and was one of the promoters of the tariff reform of 1834.—TRANSLATOR.]

. . . . a form of protection that is more efficacious and more consonant with the relatively *high cost* of our shipping." (M. Cunin-Gridaine, meeting of December 15, 1845, opening statement.) The expression ". . . . is disappearing" is really precious!

4. [Cf. *supra,* First Series, chap. 5.—EDITOR.]

NOTE TO CHAPTER 10

1. [Cf., in Vol. I (of the French edition), the "Letter to M. Larnac," and, in Vol. V (of the French edition), "Parliamentary Inconsistencies."—EDITOR.]

NOTES TO CHAPTER 11

1. [First published in *Le Libre échange,* January 17, 1847.—EDITOR.]
2. [In fact, the author had said five centimes, in May, 1846, in an article in the *Journal des économistes,* which became chapter 12 in the second series of *Economic Sophisms.*—EDITOR.]

NOTE TO CHAPTER 12

1. [First published in the *Journal des économistes* of May, 1846.—EDITOR.]

NOTE TO CHAPTER 13

1. [Cf. *supra,* First Series, chap. 6.—EDITOR.]

NOTES TO CHAPTER 14

1. [First published in *Le Libre échange,* March 21, 1847.—EDITOR.]
2. [Cf. *supra,* First Series, chaps. 2 and 3, and *Economic Harmonies,* chap. 6. —EDITOR.]

NOTE TO CHAPTER 15

1. [First published in *Le Libre échange,* April 26, 1847.—EDITOR.]

NOTE TO CHAPTER 16

1. [First published in *Le Libre échange,* December 13, 1846.—EDITOR.]

NOTES TO CHAPTER 17

1. [First published in *Le Libre échange,* February 14, 1847.—EDITOR.]
2. [If the author had lived longer, he probably would have published a third series of *Economic Sophisms.* The chief contents of such a book would appear to have already been published in the columns of *Le Libre échange.* —EDITOR.]

Index of Names

Prepared by Vernelia A. Crawford

NOTE: This index includes titles of chapters listed under the appropriate subject classification. With the exception of these specific page references, which are hyphenated, the numbers in each instance refer to the *first* page of a discussion. A page number followed by a figure or letter in parentheses indicates a footnote reference. Translator's notes are at the bottom of the page; all other notes are at the end of the text. Explanation of a name or term is given in its initial entry.

Index of Subjects

283

Protectionism (*Cont.*)
  fallacies, vii
  foreign policy, 232
  industrial, 159, 258
  introduced, 180
  isolation, 91
  labor, 102
  national independence, 99
  plunder, 70
  policy, 67, 70, 258
  prices, 164
  production and consumption, 28, 86
  purpose, 28
  raw materials, 107
  rivers obstructed, 92–93
  sophisms, 3
  taxation, 192
  transportation, 94
  wage rates, 74–79, 82
  see also Tariff
Providence, 33, 100, 148, 187, 266
Public opinion
  corrected, 121
  dominance, 136
  enlightened, 139, 143
  free trade, 107
  influence, 125
  misled, 146
  observations, 107, 133
Publications, 5, 8, 38
Punishment, 134
Purchase and purchaser, 118

Quintal, 24, 113

Railroad, negative, xiv, 94–95
Raw materials, 107–15, 208
Reals, 194
Reciprocity, 67–69, 90–91, 99, 195
Reductio ad absurdum, xiii, xiv
Reformers, 148, 205, 213, 239
Religion, 49, 133, 138, 148, 151
Remuneration, 273(3), 274(1)
Restriction
  advantages, 169
  buying and selling, 157
  government, 141, 156

Restriction (*Cont.*)
  industrial, 169
  interdiction and, 242, 251
  labor, 259
  law, 14, 23, 33
  prices, 163
  purpose, 179
  supply and demand, 71
  tariff, 108, 179
Result and effort, 20–27
Right and left hand, 258–65
Rivers, obstructed, as advocates for protectionists, 92–93
Robbery, 132, 189–97

Sacrifices, 67, 227
Salt, postal service, and tariff, 213–29
Savings, 10, 52, 74; *see also* Wealth
Scarcity and abundance, 7–15, 108, 124, 168, 240, 252
Sciences, 121, 122; *see also* Economics; Political economy
Security, 74, 140
Self-interest
  aspects, 9
  consumer, 123
  manufacturing, 12
  motives, 45, 116, 147, 179
  national, 100
  production and consumption, 11, 58
  slavery, 130, 135
  transportation, 94
Selling. *See* Buying and selling
Services
  exchanged, 132, 140
  exercised, 130
  government, 140, 199
  judged, 140
  postal, 213–29
Sisyphism, 20, 23, 27, 272(1)
Slavery, 130, 135, 148
Socialism, xiii
Society, 9, 116, 140, 148, 181; *see also* Self-interest
Sophistry, vii, 125
Speculation, 74
Standard of living, 184, 236, 273(4)

About the Publisher

The Foundation for Economic Education, Inc., was established in 1946 by Leonard E. Read to study and advance the moral and intellectual rationale for a free society.

The Foundation publishes *The Freeman*, an award-winning monthly journal of ideas in the fields of economics, history, and moral philosophy. FEE also publishes books, conducts seminars, and sponsors a network of discussion clubs to improve understanding of the principles of a free and prosperous society.

FEE is a non-political, non-profit 501 (c)(3) tax-exempt organization, supported solely by private contributions and the sales of its literature.

For further information, please contact The Foundation for Economic Education, 30 South Broadway, Irvington-on-Hudson, New York 10533; telephone (914) 591-7230; fax (914) 591-8910; e-mail freeman@westnet.com.

Additional Books by Frederic Bastiat

Economic Harmonies
An inspiring exposition of the natural harmony that results when people are free to pursue their own individual interests.

The Law
A powerful summary of Bastiat's critique of socialism.

Selected Essays on Political Economy
Economic principles stated simply and eloquently.

Additional Books by Henry Hazlitt

Economics in One Lesson
This primer on economic principles brilliantly analyzes the seen and unseen consequences of economic and political actions.

From Bretton Woods to World Inflation
The current world monetary crisis is a direct result of the decisions made at Bretton Woods in 1944.

The Inflation Crisis and How to Resolve It
Hazlitt lays bare the facts about the New Inflation and analyzes problems the media scarcely skim.

The Failure of the "New Economics"
A brilliant analysis of the Keynesian fallacies.

The Conquest of Poverty
Capitalist production, not government programs, has been the real conqueror of poverty.

The Foundations of Morality
The author presents a consistent moral philosophy based on the principles required for voluntary social interaction.

Available from
The Foundation for Economic Education, Inc.
30 South Broadway, Irvington-on-Hudson, NY 10533
Telephone (914) 591-7230; fax (914) 591-8910
E-mail freeman@westnet.com.